# Strategies for Artificial Intelligence in Healthcare

*Strategies for Artificial Intelligence in Healthcare* sheds light on the ever-changing world of Artificial Intelligence (AI) within the healthcare industry.

As AI technology rapidly advances, the healthcare industry is becoming its most significant and impactful beneficiary. From the authors' viewpoint, AI is revolutionizing healthcare with the promise of improving patient outcomes, lowering costs, and increasing access and efficiency. The use of AI in healthcare is not a new concept. In fact, it has been around for decades, but it is only in recent years that its potential has been fully realized. From the development of new surgical techniques to the use of telemedicine for remote patient care, technology has revolutionized the way healthcare is delivered. With the rise of big data and cloud computing, AI will be an essential toolkit for healthcare professionals, enabling them to harness the immense data power in ways that were previously unimaginable. With real-world case studies, practical applications, and purpose methods, *Strategies for Artificial Intelligence in Healthcare* is the ultimate guide to navigating the modern healthcare industry with AI. The second edition provides up-to-date material and refreshes and updates case studies.

Whether you're an experienced healthcare professional wanting to stay up to date or simply curious about the latest technology, this book offers unique and valuable insights for the future of healthcare with Artificial Intelligence by its side.

# Strategies for Artificial Intelligence in Healthcare

## Generative AI, Predictive Analytics, and the Future of Digital Medicine

Second Edition

Dr. Frank Papay and Dr. Piyush Mathur

Routledge
Taylor & Francis Group
A PRODUCTIVITY PRESS BOOK

Designed cover image: Shutterstock

Second edition published 2027
by Routledge
605 Third Avenue, New York, NY 10158

and by Routledge
4 Park Square, Milton Park, Abingdon, Oxon, OX14 4RN

First edition published in 2024 by independent publisher

*Routledge is an imprint of the Taylor & Francis Group, an informa business*



ISBN: 9781041117964 (hbk)
ISBN: 9781041117957 (pbk)
ISBN: 9781003661627 (ebk)

DOI: 10.4324/9781003661627

Typeset in Garamond
by Deanta Global Publishing Services, Chennai, India

# Contents

# Preface

We, Dr. Frank Papay and Dr. Piyush Mathur, are excited to present today our ideas about artificial intelligence in healthcare. We embarked on a journey in authoring this book, *Strategies for Artificial Intelligence in Healthcare*, to shed light on the ever-changing world of Artificial Intelligence (AI) within the healthcare industry. As AI technology rapidly advances, the healthcare industry is becoming its most significant and impactful beneficiary. From our viewpoint, AI is revolutionizing healthcare with the promise of improving patient outcomes, lowering costs, and increasing access and efficiency.

Using AI in healthcare is not a new concept. In fact, researchers have been using AI in healthcare for decades, but it is only in recent years that they have fully realized its potential. Technology has revolutionized the delivery of healthcare, from developing new surgical techniques to utilizing telemedicine for remote patient care. With the rise of big data and cloud computing, AI will be an essential toolkit for healthcare professionals, enabling them to harness immense data power in ways that were previously unimaginable.

Although we wrote this book as an open look into implementing AI in healthcare, we identified multiple challenges. One of the main lay concerns is the potential for AI to replace rather than augment human decision-making.

Comparative AI may be impressive in its quick calculus of analyzing correlatives within data points, but it cannot replace the critical thinking and compassion that healthcare professionals bring. Therefore, it is crucial to find the right balance between the use of AI and human input. The goal of this book is to provide guidance and bring forth a rational argument supporting advancing AI technology to better the medical industry.

*Strategies for Artificial Intelligence in Healthcare* is a comprehensive reference to applying AI, from the basics of AI technology to its specific applications in healthcare. As our readers, you will discover how AI is transforming the healthcare industry and learn about the latest developments in this field. The book explores different AI technologies and how they can improve patient outcomes and enhance healthcare delivery.

This book provides readers with an in-depth understanding of the challenges and opportunities associated with implementing AI in healthcare. It thoroughly discusses issues such as data privacy, security, regulation, and ethical considerations, enabling readers to gain a comprehensive understanding of the complexities of AI in healthcare. We explore and highlight real-world examples of how AI is currently being used, from personalized medicine to disease diagnosis and management; our book highlights the broad range of applications of AI in healthcare.

This book aims to provide an overview of AI technology, including machine learning, deep learning, and natural language processing, and how it can apply to the healthcare industry. Within this book, we explore how AI can utilize potential applications in medical imaging, drug discovery, and personalized medicine in healthcare. With the help of leading experts in healthcare and AI, extensive experience in research, development, and implementation of AI technology in healthcare, we present our expertise, providing readers with a comprehensive understanding of the potential of AI in healthcare.

We offer a unique perspective on applying AI in healthcare, drawing upon our diverse backgrounds in medicine, skill sets, and experience. Combining our knowledge and experience makes this book a must-read for anyone interested in the future of healthcare and AI's role in shaping it. *Strategies for Artificial Intelligence in Healthcare* is not only a useful resource for healthcare professionals and researchers but also for policymakers, investors, and entrepreneurs who are looking to invest in this rapidly growing field. The book provides valuable insights and guidance on how to navigate the complex regulatory and ethical landscape associated with AI in healthcare, as well as identifying key market opportunities for those looking to capitalize on the potential of AI in healthcare.

By balancing the benefits of AI with the need for human empathy and critical thinking, this book offers a holistic approach to applying AI in healthcare that recognizes prizing both technological innovation and human-centered care. As the healthcare industry continues to evolve, we hope that

*Strategies for Artificial Intelligence in Healthcare* will remain an indispensable resource for anyone interested in the intersection of technology and healthcare, offering a roadmap for navigating AI's exciting and complex world in healthcare.

Godspeed
Dr. Frank Papay and Dr. Piyush Mathur

# Acknowledgments

The authors wish to express their deepest gratitude to Jeffrey A. Mangus, whose contributions to the first edition of *Strategies for Artificial Intelligence in Healthcare* were nothing short of indispensable. Jeffrey lent not only his considerable skill as a writer and editor but also his patience, insight, and unwavering commitment to clarity throughout the long arc of this project. From the earliest drafts to the final manuscript, Jeffrey helped shape ideas into prose, sharpened arguments that had grown unwieldy, and brought a discerning eye to every chapter. His editorial judgment elevated the work at every turn, transforming complex and often technical material into a narrative that is both rigorous and readable. Beyond his craft, Jeffrey brought a spirit of genuine collaboration and good humor to the endeavor—qualities that made the demanding process of penning and editing this book not merely bearable but, at times, a pleasure. For his tireless effort, his generosity with time and talent, and his steadfast belief in this project, we are profoundly thankful.

# About the Author: Dr. Frank A. Papay

**Dr. Frank A. Papay**, MD, MS, DSc(hon), FACS, FAAP, FNAI, is a physician–executive, surgeon–scientist, inventor, and healthcare systems innovator whose career spans more than three decades at Cleveland Clinic (Cleveland, Ohio, USA), one of the world's leading academic health systems. He currently serves as Chief Clinical Business Development Officer of Cleveland Clinic Enterprise and former Chairman of Dermatology and Plastic Surgery Institute, where he advises enterprise leadership on growth strategy, innovation portfolio governance, translational commercialization, and AI-enabled care delivery across a $16B+ global healthcare organization.

Dr. Papay is internationally recognized for pioneering work at the intersection of advanced surgery, medical technology, and artificial intelligence. As lead surgeon for America's first total face transplant, he helped establish the clinical, ethical, and regulatory framework for vascularized composite allotransplantation in the United States. His career includes numerous surgical "firsts," including novel neuromodulation approaches for chronic pain and migraine, robotic endoscopic nerve reconstruction, and minimally invasive skull-base procedures that replaced high-morbidity open operations.

A prolific innovator, Dr. Papay is an inventor on 40+ issued U.S. patents and 70+ provisional patents spanning surgical devices, digital platforms, neuromodulation technologies, and AI-assisted systems. He has founded and advised multiple venture-backed healthcare companies, guiding technologies from concept through first-in-human trials, regulatory pathways, and institutional capital raises. His experience includes collaboration with venture capital, private equity, and sovereign-aligned investment platforms focused on scaling healthcare innovation globally.

A central focus of his recent work is the integration of artificial intelligence into clinical operations, surgical navigation, and healthcare system performance. Dr. Papay is Co-Founder of BrainX.AI, a global consortium developing machine learning systems for healthcare applications, including surgical intelligence, predictive analytics, and AI-driven decision support. His work emphasizes responsible AI adoption, clinical governance, and translating data science into measurable improvements in patient outcomes, operational efficiency, and system scalability.

Dr. Papay has authored or co-authored more than 260 peer-reviewed scientific publications and multiple foundational scholarly texts. His books include *Reconstructive Allotransplantation*, a landmark reference in composite tissue transplantation; *Virtual Surgical Planning in Surgery*, advancing digital precision surgery; *Voices of Innovation: Essays on Artificial Intelligence in Healthcare*; and *Artificial Intelligence Strategies in Healthcare*, where he contributes leadership perspectives on AI governance, clinical integration, and system transformation.

He is a Fellow of the National Academy of Inventors and recipient of the Cleveland Clinic's prestigious Sones Centennial Innovation Award, among many national and international honors. Across his clinical, academic, and executive roles, Dr. Papay's work bridges medicine, engineering, and AI, shaping how intelligent technologies are responsibly deployed to build the next generation of healthcare delivery systems worldwide.

# About the Author: Dr. Piyush Mathur

**Dr. Piyush Mathur**, MD, FCCM, FASA FAMIA, is a Staff Anesthesiologist and Critical Care Physician at Cleveland Clinic, Ohio, USA, with more than 20 years of experience as a clinician. He is the Innovation Lead for the Department of Anesthesiology, Cleveland Clinic.

He has also served in the role of the Quality Improvement Officer and Chair, Compliance Committee, Anesthesiology Institute for more than a decade. He completed his medical school training in India at the Armed Forces Medical College (AFMC, Pune), followed by residency in Anesthesiology and a fellowship in Critical Care at Cleveland Clinic.

He subsequently completed a one-year quality fellowship at Cleveland Clinic. He has completed training in computer programming, machine learning, and deep learning. He is the Past Program Director of the Anesthesiology Critical Care fellowship program at Cleveland Clinic. A recognized leader in critical care, quality, education, and artificial intelligence applications in healthcare, he has led many of the local and national programs, including serving as the chair of the post-graduate education and coding and documentation committees of the Society of Critical Care Medicine (SCCM).

He is currently a member of the CPT Editorial Advisory Committee, AMA (American Medical Association) and a primary advisor to SCCM. Trained in computer programming, machine learning, and deep learning, he is the founder of BrainX, an AI in healthcare application research and development company. He also founded one of the largest groups for machine learning in healthcare, BrainX Community. He has focused his research on applications of artificial intelligence (AI) in healthcare for many years. He is a leader in quality and patient safety who has innovated and successfully implemented many algorithms and tools in electronic health records such as difficult airway identification (EPIC), anesthesia awareness alert (DSS, Talis), and antibiotic alert (ACG, Talis).

Recipient of multiple innovation awards at Cleveland Clinic, he is leading innovation efforts in integrating machine learning and artificial intelligence in healthcare. Current projects include AIDE (Artificial Intelligence Diagnosis Engine), SALUS (robotic artificial intelligence patient safety system), and BRAINS (Biologically Relational Artificial Intelligence Networking System).

He is a recipient of numerous local and international awards including the Institute of Healthcare Improvement (IHI) Permanente Award and the prestigious Presidential Citation from the Society of Critical Care Medicine (SCCM). He has made numerous local, national, and international presentations and publications in the fields of anesthesiology, critical care, quality, education, and artificial intelligence applications in healthcare. For his work in the field of AI and healthcare, he was awarded the AI Clinician of the Year at the 2025 AIMed Conference.

# 1 THE WHY (OF AI IN HEALTHCARE)

# Chapter 1

# History and Evolution of AI in Healthcare

A generation which ignores history has no past and no future.

**—Robert Heinlein, American author (1907–1988)**[1]

Technical revolution. Throughout human history, historical events have differed in terms of methods, duration, and motivating ideology. Their results include significant changes in culture and philosophy. Still, revolution can also describe change, coming full circle, all in the pursuit of discovering answers and hoping to progress. Across countless industries, the AI revolution has transformed how people collect and process data in search of potential solutions to complex problems. But there is no going back now on big data, machine learning and implementing AI.

Every field has seen an explosion in data collection and machine learning capabilities. Everything from biological databases, such as those for genomes and proteins, is booming, and astronomy, with its petabytes of data (Figure 1.1). We can even recognize it in social science, analyzing hundreds of millions of posts and tweets circulating on the web every day. And yet, as the tsunami of data floods in, so does the need and ability to analyze it. But with the advances in computing that helped deliver it, we need new tools to make sense of it all.

Researchers are unleashing artificial intelligence (AI) on data torrents in a revolution that extends throughout science and exploration. Unlike earlier AI attempts, such "deep learning" systems do not require expert programming.

DOI: 10.4324/9781003661627-2

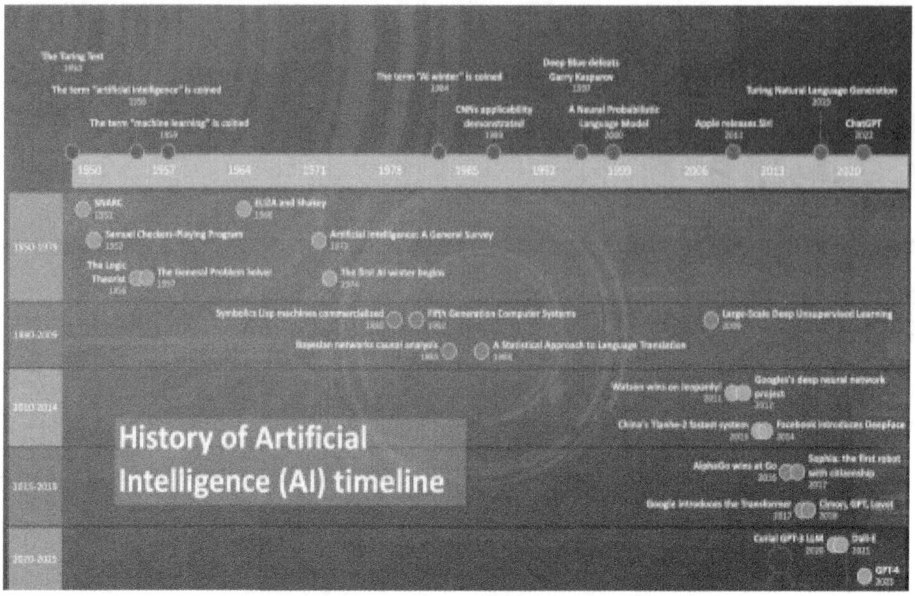


**Figure 1.1 Trends and growth of artificial intelligence**

***Source:*** **Image (https://www.officetimeline.com/blog/artificial-intelligence-ai-and-chatgpt-history-and-timelines).**

Instead, they learn independently, often through large-scale training data sets, until they can spot patterns in unmanageable data sets. The rise of artificial intelligence extends beyond science and industry; it includes emerging "deep learning" systems that do not rely on expert programming (Figure 1.2).

AI systems rely on domain knowledge, data generation, and machine learning for support. While domain knowledge is an understanding and expertise of the real-life scenario on why and how to engineer a task, data preparation refers to preparing the databases needed to feed the algorithms. Machine learning recognizes patterns in training data, predicts outcomes, and performs tasks automatically. In healthcare, no day goes by without a report or article depicting that machines can diagnose diseases better than human doctors, clinicians, caregivers, and even radiologists. Naturally, this has led to speculation about machines replacing human medical staff, especially pathologists, surgeons, and radiologists. They supported this idea when, in 2016, Geoffrey Hinton, British cognitive psychologist and "godfather" of artificial intelligence, predicted typesetters and bank tellers would replace radiologists.

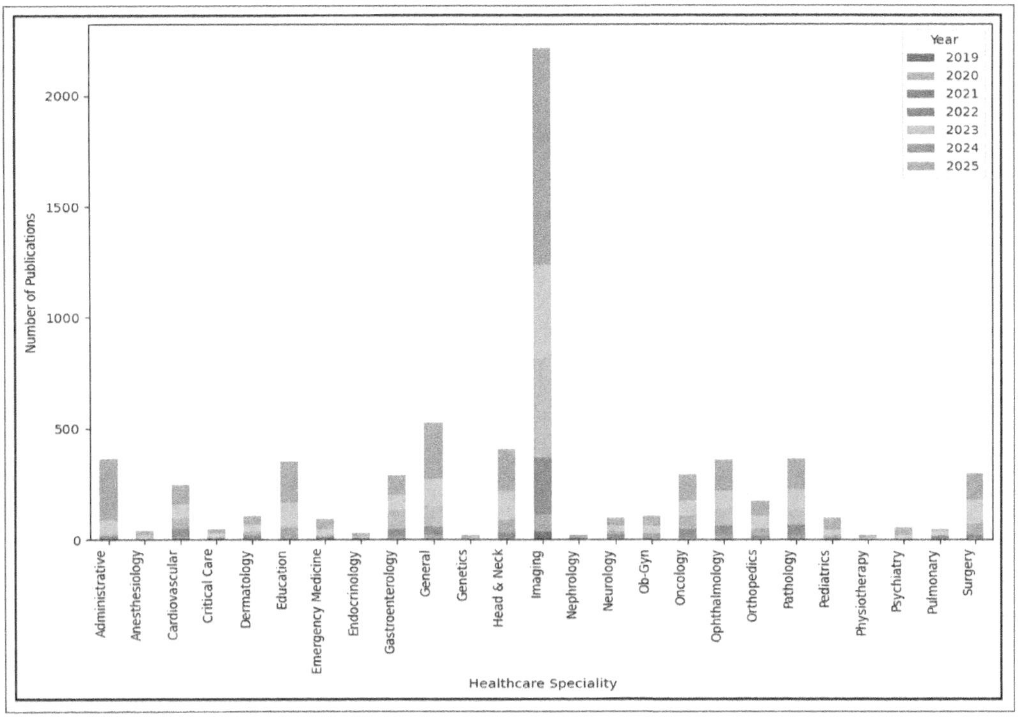


**Figure 1.2 A) Year-wise percentage of mature articles published from 2019 to 2022. B) Specialty-wise number of mature articles 2019–2022**

> If you work as a radiologist, you are like the coyote already over the cliff's edge but has not yet looked down, so it does not yet realize there is no ground underneath him. People should stop training radiologists now. It is just self-evident that within five years, deep learning is going to do better.

Contrary to the ongoing changes in AI, there are no governors on clinicians in fields that require a lot of pattern recognition, like pathology and radiology. And yet, AI does not challenge scientists and physicians in any significant way. Rather, AI is here to assist, not replace. And as Tim Appenzeller put it in *Science*, "AI is still an apprentice scientist."[2] Despite Hinton's forecast, radiologists are still training to read images.

Radiologists are still in short supply worldwide, even though there are more of them, and modern radiologists are responsible for much more than viewing X-rays. While the demand for trained radiologists remains high, even five years after Hinton's statement, AI is nowhere near displacing radiologists. Google has taken the torch of artificial intelligence and created its "deep learning system" to assist radiology and radiologists. Google researchers discovered their deep learning model detected abnormal X-rays as accurately as and sometimes better than human radiologists. However, they emphasized that the system's value is improving radiologists' productivity. Rather than replacing doctors, health system administrators now view AI as a tool clinicians can use to improve everything from diagnosis to billing. As technologists have predicted, AI is progressing at an astronomical rate, making it a game-changer in healthcare, but integrating AI into healthcare across many fields of study has not been easy.

But before we go further, at BrainX, we thought it would be beneficial to explore the origins and history of AI in honor of knowledge, exploration, and learning from those before us. Today, news of breakthroughs and capabilities of artificial intelligence that are moving from the lab and research centers into everyday use overwhelms us. As we look ahead at the possibilities and applications in our professional and personal lives, it is worth reflecting on how we stand on the shoulders of those who came before us to understand the road ahead.

On December 9th, 1944, at the Remiremont Command Post in France, in an inspiring address to his troops before the Allied forces launched the Battle of the Bulge during World War II, General George S. Patton, the renowned American army general, famously uttered the words, "Prepare for the unknown by studying how others have coped with the unforeseeable and the unpredictable."[3] We must learn from history, ensuring we understand and forego our mistakes toward a better future.

With artificial intelligence (AI), we could write 20 books about the industry's history and how far it has come. So, we believe the best way to begin the voyage is to explore AI's humble beginnings, explain its origins, shed much-needed light on its founders, and explore the expeditionary journey of developing AI in healthcare.

AI technology and the science behind it date back centuries. As we examine AI throughout history, we do not have to look far to find that robots were mythological creatures to the Greeks and Chinese, and Egyptian engineers created "automatons." Even ancient philosophers attempted to describe human thinking as a symbolic system, leading to modern artificial intelligence's beginnings. No matter how it arrived, it is here, and there is no escaping the fact that AI is emerging into every aspect of our lives. It is already pervasive in our daily experiences, ranging from auto-complete on our mobile devices to unsolicited product recommendations based on our

Google searches, even down to our music suggestions based on listening history.

Every day, we use AI through technology, such as Alexa® and Google Assistant®, and for home protection, all of whom answer questions, adjust our thermostats, and can turn off the lights. Even with the mobile device you hold in your hand, or the computer you use to work, AI is making itself known across many sectors within the marketplace, from self-driving automobiles to maps, travel, and operating room robots. With improved diagnosis, preventive care, and data and operating system management, AI has proven to be the most significant and prolific advance in modern healthcare history.

In terms of conceptual roots, we can trace AI back over 80 years. The idea of inanimate objects becoming intelligent beings is a topic that is not strange or unheard of. The concerns of contemporaries like Elon Musk and Stephen Hawking have their roots in speculations dating back to 1863 about intelligent computers surpassing humans and taking over the world.

During the early 20th century, English author Samuel Butler published *Garland Among Machines*, which raised the idea that machines might surpass humans as the dominant species. Scientists from a wide range of fields, including mathematics, psychology, engineering, economics, and political science, began exploring the possibility of imbuing machines with intelligence in the 1940s. And as World War II took a devastating toll on people and countries across the globe, such an idea for artificial intelligence became more valuable. During the war, the Allies intercepted and manually decoded encrypted German messages they encountered, or encoded messages using an entirely unique method that defied deciphering. As a result, the Allies developed a new machine capable of automating cryptanalyst work to interpret this vital intelligence as quickly as possible.

Many consider reaching a significant milestone to be the official birth of AI as a formal scientific discipline. The AI revolution got its humble beginnings through the discovery of a young British polymath, Alan Turing, who explored the mathematical possibility of artificial intelligence. Fortunately, to answer the call, Turing, being a cryptanalyst, worked at the Government Code and Cipher School at Bletchley Park, where he collaborated with other leading minds of the era to create Colossus, the first functional digital computer. Although an impressive achievement, the high-speed paper tapes broke, and the behemoth prototype required 1,600 vacuum tubes and was unreliable despite serving a valuable purpose. It was a promising beginning.

**Figure 1.3 Alan Turing's Colossus computer**

***Source:*** **Turing. Colossus (https://en.wikipedia.org/wiki/Colossus_computer#).**

Turing hypothesized that if humans solved problems and made decisions based on information and reasoning, why couldn't a machine? Using this logical framework, he discussed in his 1950 paper, "Computing Machinery and Intelligence," how to build and test intelligent machines (Figure 1.3). Turing concluded that the words "think" and "machine" could not have a clear definition and proposed a more thought-provoking question: Can a machine win at a game?

Afterward, Turing suggested that instead of proving a machine is thinking, we should put it to the test if it could win a game called "Imitation Game," where he modified a game involving three participants in isolated rooms: a computer (which was being tested), a human, and a human judge. The human judge could converse with the human and the computer by typing into a terminal, as the computer and human tried to convince the judge that they were human.[4] The computer wins the game if the judge tells which is which. Afterward, the question became, "Can machines do what we (as thinking entities) can do?" Turing no longer asked whether a machine could "think" but considered how a machine could act indistinguishably from how a thinker works (Figure 1.4).

**Figure 1.4 Alan Turing—the beginning of artificial intelligence**

However, why did progress slow to a crawl, stopping Turing from getting to work? The first step was the drastic need to change computers. Before 1949, computers could not store commands, only execute them, which made them incapable of being intelligent. The computer could be told what to do, but could not remember what it did. The second reason was the high cost of computing. Only prestigious universities and big technology companies could afford to swim in those uncharted waters.

Despite progressing slowly, people did not discover until the 1970s that "Colossus" and electronic computations played a significant role in the World War II victory. Additionally, historians from the British government found that the use of Colossus, which eventually became known as artificial intelligence (AI), played a significant role in shortening the war in Europe by at least two years. This breakthrough demonstrated the critical nature of intelligent machines and laid the foundation for NASA's data science and information technology fields.

However, American computer scientist John McCarthy coined the term "artificial intelligence" in 1955 at the organized conference, famously known to start it all. McCarthy and MIT cognitive scientist Marvin Minsky organized Dartmouth's Summer Research Project on Artificial Intelligence, where they presented it.

During this historic conference, McCarthy and Minsky brought together top researchers from various fields to discuss artificial intelligence, the term he coined. Unfortunately, McCarthy's expectations were not met by the conference, as people came and went as they pleased, and no standard methods were agreed upon. Despite this, everyone felt AI was a realistic possibility, a catalyst for the next 20 years of AI research.

After the conference, McCarthy, a strong advocate of AI study and implementation, predicted that creating an intelligent machine would require 1.8 Einsteins and 10% of the Manhattan Project's resources. Marvin Minsky and many conference attendees were optimistic about AI's future in 1956. *AI: The Tumultuous Search for Artificial Intelligence* (Basic Books, 1994) quotes Minsky as saying, "The problem of creating artificial intelligence will be solved within a generation." Minsky stated, "There would be a machine with an overall intelligence equivalent to an average human in three to eight years."

The pioneering McCarthy contributed other concepts that have become part of mainstream computer science today, eventually leading to artificial intelligence's development. This includes McCarthy's development of LISP in 1958, shortly after FORTRAN was developed. McCarthy developed LISP as a programming language, becoming the most popular programming language used in AI research.

While LISP has undergone changes since its early days, people still use it today. For example, Arthur Samuel, considered a pioneer in the gaming industry, wrote a journal article outlining how a computer could be programmed to play a better game of checkers and demonstrated that computers could master a process in 1959. And by 1961, early forms of artificial intelligence were making themselves known and being used commercially.

This same year, the first industrial robot, "Unimate," began working on an assembly line in a New Jersey General Motors plant. While the space race was taking off, universities and private labs received significant investments to expand the capabilities and reach of this new science. The designers created the IBM 704 for artificial intelligence programs due to its ability to process symbolic information.

Then, in 1959, McCarthy invented "garbage collection" as an automated method for managing computer memory based on LISP. He realized that the garbage collector could reclaim memory no longer referenced by a program and repurpose it. Today, LISP interpreters use garbage collection to simplify manual memory management. However, machine learning was low, even with LISt Processing (LISP), Formula Translation (FORTRAN), and computer programs advancing in the early days of artificial intelligence and commercial and market interest. And because of the lack of interest, many experts coined this initial lag time the "AI Winter," an analogy derived from the term Nuclear Winter, characterized by the apparent reduction of funding and general interest from the scientific community. Because of those roller coaster hype cycles, AI experienced disappointment, criticism, funding cuts, and slow-coming renewed interest years and even decades later.

Despite the known issues and lack of commercial interest during the AI Winter, from 1957 to 1974, interest in and implementation of AI grew and flourished. AI improved across commercial and private sectors despite being undetected by the mainstream as computers became faster, cheaper, and easier to use, allowing them to store more information. Machine learning and algorithms improved, and people became more adept at selecting suitable algorithms for their intended use.

In 1957, Allen Newell and Herbert A. Simon's computer program, General Problem Solver (GPS)—along with Joseph Weizenbaum's ELIZA, which offered early examples of AI and machine learning, problem-solving, and language interpretation—opened many doors. Because of those successes, varying government agencies, including the Defense Advanced Research Projects Agency, funded AI research at several institutions.

Since this became known, the U.S. government became interested in developing a machine that could transcribe and translate spoken languages and process detailed data. Though there was optimism and lofty expectations, the primary proof of principle was there. There was still a long way to go before natural language processing, abstract thinking, and self-recognition became a reality with machines. However, everything pointed to AI resurging in a wide range of fields.

Unfortunately, in the early 1970s, pessimism in the AI community and ambivalence in the press led to severe funding cuts, followed by the end of in-depth research, bringing forth the second AI Winter. Although when the fog of AI cleared, it revealed a mountain of obstacles. Computers could not store or process enough information because of a lack of computational power.

During the early 1970s, Hans Moravec, a doctoral student of McCarthy, stated that, "Computers are more than a million times too weak to exhibit intelligence." Then, one of the first AI applications in healthcare occurred when research produced MYCIN, a rule-based expert system program that identified blood infection treatments. Unfortunately, there was still a massive decline in government funding and interest in artificial intelligence between 1974 and 1980, making it difficult to pursue and develop viable and functional artificial intelligence. AI researchers continued to proliferate, and in 1979, they founded the American Association for Artificial Intelligence—currently known as the Association for the Advancement of Artificial Intelligence, AAAI.

As AI enthusiasm spiraled out of control, two leading AI researchers, Roger Schank, a computer scientist and cognitive psychologist, Director of the Institute for the Learning Sciences at Northwestern University, and Marvin Minsky, warned the business community that disappointment with AI would follow. These trends, as predicted, continued into the 1980s. After that, the billion-dollar AI industry collapsed once again in just three years. Although many emerging technologies were promoted, over-inflated promises, lofty expectations, and extensive media coverage led to the second AI Winter.

In the 1980s, the British government returned to funding AI in response to the AI Winter, following a resurgence in the field. Medical advances emerged because of the development of new AI systems during the 1980s and 1990s, including the following:

- Collecting and processing data more quickly.
- Enhancing surgical precision.
- Analyzing and mapping DBA data in-depth.
- Implementation of electronic health records on a more comprehensive basis.

Once the industry escaped the clutches of the AI Winter, we increased our intelligence in the broad term and progressed with smarter coding of artificial intelligence. But how did we advance so quickly from the slowest of starts, and how do we keep up the momentum? To answer that question, we must look back to 1965, when Gordon E. Moore, then co-founder of Intel (INTC), predicted transistors would double every two years. Moore's insight became a prolific prediction, which grew into Moore's Law.

While Gordon Moore did not intend to create a philosophical "law," his statement gained momentum based on his observations of developing trends in chip manufacturing at Fairchild Semiconductor. Through Moore's keen observation, we can see that growth and technology are ever-growing and ever-rising entities that allow us to extend our knowledge and understanding.

In 1982, an American scientist, Dr. John J. Hopfield, known for his invention of an associative neural network, and his partner invented the associative neural network, allowing computers to learn from real-world experience. In his work, the Hopfield Neural Network comprised a single layer containing one or more fully connected recurrent neurons for auto-association and optimization.

Unfortunately, between 1987 and 1993, the AI field experienced another major winter because of the collapse of the general-purpose computer market and reduced government funding.

In addition, David Rumelhart, an American psychologist, made numerous contributions to the formal analysis of human cognition. Rumelhart worked within the frameworks of mathematical psychology, symbolic artificial intelligence, and parallel distributed processing. He admired formal linguistic approaches to cognition and explored the possibility of formulating formal grammar to capture story structure.

However, ACM Turing Award-winning computer scientist Edward Feigenbaum, the "father of expert systems," who worked in artificial intelligence, introduced expert systems as part of artificial intelligence. Developing "expert systems" encoded knowledge in several fields and provided recommendations on next steps. One of these was Mycin, developed by Stanford University researchers to aid in diagnosing the treatment of bacterial infections.

By mimicking a human expert's decision-making process, Feigenbaum's system imitated human decision-making. In most situations, the program would ask an expert what to do in a situation. Once introduced, that discovery became a tool in every situation, allowing anyone to receive advice from the program and a machine. After that, many industries started using expert systems, which prompted the Japanese government to fund the project as part of their Fifth Generation Computer Project (FGCP). From 1982 to 1990, the Japanese invested 400 million dollars in revolutionizing computer processing, implementing logic programming, and improving artificial intelligence, but they did not achieve their ambitious goals. FGCP inspired a generation of talented engineers and scientists, but Japanese funding ceased, and AI faded into obscurity.

Two factors—expanding the algorithmic toolkit and an increase in funding—sparked this reinvigoration of AI, yet AI flourished without government funding and public hype, and landmark goals of artificial intelligence were being achieved. Then, in 1997, IBM introduced "Deep Blue," which defeated Russian grandmaster Garry Kasparov to become the first computer to defeat a world champion in chess. In the same year, Windows introduced speech recognition software developed by Dragon Systems. This was a significant step forward in interpreting spoken languages, making it appear that there was nothing a machine could not do.

Next, Cynthia Breazeal, a scientist and entrepreneur specializing in robotics, created KISMET, a robot capable of recognizing and displaying human emotions. This showed that AI technology could also manage human emotions. All the events were momentous on many technological fronts, bringing AI and IBM back into the spotlight. The renewed interest and scientific study of the implications of AI rose across many business and private sectors, bringing an end to AI winters.

In 2009, Google started a secret project and developed a driverless car. Understanding Moore's Law, merging with the synergy of AI, the fundamental limit of computer storage that held us back 30 years before, was no longer an obstacle. And using the current technological advancements of AI-enabled IBM's "Watson" to defeat two of Jeopardy's greatest champions in 2011, giving AI massive exposure, enlightenment, movement, and regeneration. The computer's win stunned the tech industry, becoming a landmine explosion in U.S. pop culture.

IBM pulled it off with their technological masterpiece, "Watson." It began as an exhibition match between past champions, Ken Jennings and Brad Rutter, who had won over $5 million over the show's decades-long history and were among its top players. With 74 winning appearances, Ken Jennings had the longest unbeaten streak, while Brad Rutter won $3.25 million, the largest prize pot. Rutter and Jennings were prominent Jeopardy champions extraordinaire. So, in early 2011, they agreed to an exhibition match against an opponent who had never been to the Jeopardy stage and never would.

However, Jennings and Rutter did not know that the Jeopardy unknown had played at least over one hundred games against previous winners to improve his chances of winning. During the competition, Watson did not smile, gave his answers in an emotionless tone, and was not even in the same room as his fellow competitors. To play it cool, the loud and noisy Watson remained backstage in a room, and his answers were piped into the studio.[5] A rack of ten Power 750 servers, which comprised Watson, had to be kept separate from Rutter and Jennings because of its roaring cooling system. Watson came out of the gate swinging, starting with a run of winning answers. The amount of information Watson knew impressed everyone, including Jennings and Rutter.

While Watson knew everything about Beatles® songs, cartoons, and criminals, the new topic of Harry Potter® tripped him up. Yet, he still took the lead, leaving Jennings and Rutter thousands of dollars behind. Then a major problem arose; Watson slipped up on the "Decades" category. Rutter recognized the opportunity and exploited the weakness, piling up enough cash to make anyone who bet on Watson nervous. But, as Double Jeopardy rolled around, Watson was on fire, winning answers even with guesses he was not sure about.

By the end of the second episode, Watson had $25,000 more than Rutter, his closest competitor, and it became apparent they would get a beating from the new contestant. Throughout the game, Rutter and Jennings bobbed in frustration as the opponent buzzed in. Watson kept coming, clawing back enough money to make it a close race after Jennings's late comeback in episode three. All three correctly answered the final Jeopardy question, but Jennings added, "I welcome our new computer overlords." Watson—a giant IBM machine named after IBM founder Thomas Watson—had won. Although Watson received the questions in text rather than listening to the quizmaster, he played against Jennings and Rutter. Watson was right most of the time, winning over $77,147, leaving the champions behind with $21,600 and $24,000, respectively. Watson's victory on Jeopardy captured public attention as it showed that a computer can be programmed to mimic and portray human interaction.

Behind the scenes, as Watson's victory over two human champions entertained millions, IBM used the newfound interest in the computer to introduce a new software called "Watson Health," which they wanted to bring to the healthcare market. The premise was simple; with Watson Health, oncologists would have insight into cancer treatment, pharmaceutical companies would gain further developed knowledge and understanding of drug development while giving patients access to clinical trials, and more. In doing so, IBM was burnishing its reputation and pushing the frontiers of science, drawing tremendous attention from IBM customers now wanting one of their own. However, as IBM's executives and business leaders around the globe saw the potential and clear market for Watson Health, there was one problem: IBM had little to offer, and despite sounding revolutionary, it unfortunately failed, only to be reborn again within the healthcare field.

Six years after IBM first hinted at plans for an artificial intelligence physician's assistant, IBM launched Watson for cancer and oncology in 2011. While making constant announcements and partnerships over the last few years, it has not been clear just how the cognitive computing program will affect healthcare. During a formal meeting of the American Society of Clinical Oncology, they reported ongoing and positive performance by IBM

Watson in treatment decision-making and clinical trial matching, providing some insight into the potential impact on healthcare. During its pilot trials in India, Thailand, South Korea, and Mexico, Watson for Oncology, trained by Memorial Sloan Kettering (MSKCC), showed high concordance rates in multiple types of cancer. In a positive upswing, Watson got concordance rates of 96 and 93 percent for lung and rectal cancer cases and 81 percent for lung cancer cases at Manipal Comprehensive Cancer Center in Bengaluru. Then, reported in Thailand, Watson had an 83 percent concordance rate for multiple cancers, and in South Korea, he had a 73 percent concordance rate for colon cancer. Based on the data, IBM's Watson performed in line with its expectations.

To accomplish those numbers was an astounding accomplishment, and IBM's Watson system gained fame through natural language-interpreted queries, advanced analytics, and a powerful array of processors. Watson searched millions of pages in seconds and returned evidence-based, statistically ranked responses.

This plan enabled MSKCC's world-renowned oncologists to assist IBM Watson in developing a specialized algorithm that uses a patient's medical data to synthesize a wide variety of updated and vetted treatment guidelines, published research, and insights gained from MSKCC clinicians to offer physicians individualized recommendations. The tool gave users a detailed record of the evidence and data used to arrive at the recommended action.

With Watson's newfound solutions in place, the system showed robust evidence that AI solutions were working, delivering the numbers that researchers and clinicians need. Despite its performance, Watson did not provide the best answer but ensured that it presented the most relevant and robust knowledge. The promise and potential were apparent.

In retrospect, oncology treatment is becoming complex, thus justifying the need for this type of advanced AI technology. Cancer, the second leading cause of death in the United States after heart disease, is expected to result in 1.6 million new diagnoses nationwide this year, with outcomes varying across the country. Most times, we can divide cancer into hundreds of subtypes, each with its own genetic fingerprint. Over the past two decades, significant discoveries in molecular biology and genetics have enabled new insights into cancer biology. We have developed recent strategies to target specific molecular changes in tumors, but diagnostic and treatment challenges have also become more complex. Keeping up with the rapid changes in information poses a significant challenge for oncologists and physicians who are not specialists in specific types of cancer, which further drives the use of AI and machine learning.

As part of Google's exploration of driverless cars, in 2014, Google's vehicle passed the first state-level self-driving test in the United States. Next, Google showed its AI prowess by introducing AlphaGo, a multifaceted training algorithm designed to beat the game called *Go*, known as the world's most complex game. In 2015, Google's AlphaGo algorithm defeated the European *Go* champion, then the Korean champion in 2016, and the world champion in 2017. Following a loss to Google's AlphaGo in 2019, then-world champion Lee Sedol retired from professional play after claiming, "Artificial intelligence is unbeatable."

While Google and others may make AI seem easy, pursuing AI and embracing the advancements has been an arduous task of massive proportions. One of the biggest problems with AI is that even in the early days, the 1960s and 1970s, we could build programs that looked promising and exciting. Plus, we could get a program to understand or translate a sentence. Still, many problems have advanced today, and we need to create something substantial, solving actual problems with formal properties of vision, building robotic systems, proving theorems, or doing logical things.

In this age of "big data," which can collect vast amounts of information that a person cannot process, we can see that artificial intelligence is everywhere. Several industries, including technology, banking, marketing, and entertainment, along with significant implications in the healthcare field, have already benefited from artificial intelligence. We now recognize that artificial intelligence can learn through brute force using big data and massive computing, even if the quality of some algorithms is not up to par. While Moore's Law and technology are slowing down, the increase in data has not, and is on the rise, with breakthroughs in computer science, mathematics, science, neuroscience, and healthcare.

***

## The Evolution and Future of AI in Healthcare

AI is not sparking excitement because it is a new concept. Instead, the excitement is because of recent advances in computing power and big data, which have become routine to compile and manage massive data sets because of a branch of science called "machine learning." Today, machine learning, algorithms, and instructions for how a program works have become sophisticated enough to learn as they go, improving performance without requiring human intervention. While artificial intelligence in healthcare is not a new concept, AI-powered applications have now expanded and transformed the healthcare industry by reducing spending, improving patient outcomes, and increasing efficiencies overall.

Since AI refers to computer models and programs that mimic human cognition to solve complex problems and gather experience, most people consider current AI tools as "Narrow," meaning they can outperform humans in narrowly defined tasks. In addition, machine learning algorithms enable computers to learn, power current approaches, perform tasks, and adapt without human intervention (Figure 1.5).

However, questions need to be addressed. One question is at the forefront: where are we with AI in healthcare today? The answer lies in how AI and machine learning impact healthcare delivery across various medical specialties, including the following:

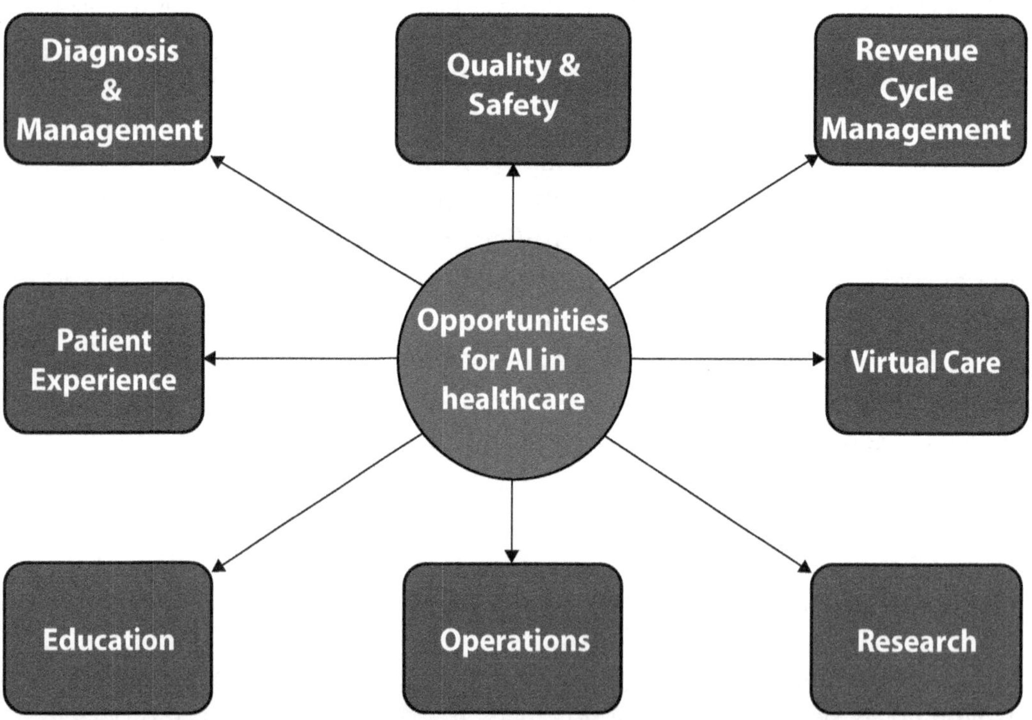


**Figure 1.5 Opportunities for application of AI in healthcare**

- Primary Care.
- Systems and Operations.
- Radiology.
- Psychiatry.
- Screening.
- Operating Rooms.
- Surgical Procedures.
- Virtual Health.
- Telemedicine.
- Disease Diagnosis.

Despite AI being prevalent in healthcare, the World Economic Forum predicts three significant changes in AI in healthcare between now and 2030:

- A connected approach to healthcare.
- Predictive care and decision-making powered by AI.
- Improved patient and staff satisfaction.

## A Connected Approach to Healthcare

With AI in healthcare, we can create a network of seamless data sharing, allowing patterns to be detected and different operating systems to be connected. Sharing data and information will create a global network of life-saving connections.

## Predictive Care and Decision-Making Powered by AI

Artificial intelligence (AI) has become an integral part of healthcare technology. At BrainX, we have seen how moving the delivery of data and patient care pushes the boundaries of science. Yet even though many of the utilizations and implementations remain a mystery, AI is changing case management, data retrieval, surgery, operations, and empowering critical care decision-making in hospitals nationwide. With this in mind, we at BrainX realize that better data and more robust AI algorithms will allow us to determine a person's future risk of contracting a disease and provide informative ways of treating each person on a case-by-case basis.

## Patient and Staff Satisfaction Improved

As AI develops, it will continue improving patient and provider experiences, including reducing patient wait times and improving overall efficiency in hospitals and health systems. We are harnessing and advancing AI to work suited to automation—allowing humans to focus on the work they can provide exceptional patient care.

At a surface level, artificial intelligence is the ability of a machine to learn from experience and produce behavior to perform specific tasks. Since we are far from the days of learning to play chess and beating humans at Jeopardy, AI in healthcare faces similar opportunities for data to be accessed and used in real-time, and it is astounding. Hospitals and organizations have vast data pools containing tens of millions of patient encounters, including hundreds of millions of orders, documents, and vitals.

Even though each health system has its own technological framework, administrators now recognize the need for specific algorithms because software from outside sources does not always integrate. As a result, hospitals are setting up engineering teams and developing internal artificial intelligence and other technology specific to their needs. Still, the purpose of this intelligence is not to replace the expertise of a health professional or clinician but to supplement and assist. The most promising uses of artificial intelligence in healthcare are diagnosis, clinical care decisions, assessing risk in real time, and aligning workflows with patient insight, which should enhance physicians' and nurses' expertise with AI. AI can analyze more data than the human brain can process.

In the past 25 years, we have learned at BrainX that implementing AI is a complex process, requiring much knowledge, vast amounts of communication, dataset interpretation, memory, and processing tremendous software engineering problems. AI is only a few years away from becoming an academic enterprise, so the rewards of exploration are just around the corner. Healthcare and the world must understand that the design of an artificial intelligence solution cannot contain "shortcuts." There is no magic bullet or pill that adds everything and makes it all fall into place. In the real world, computers are intelligent. As humans, we need to continue the painstaking journey of AI exploration, learning everything, testing, and sacrificing to accumulate much-needed vital information to better healthcare worldwide. Welcome to the expedition.

***

## Important Points

- At a surface level, artificial intelligence is the ability of a machine to learn from experience and produce behaviors to perform specific tasks.
- AI refers to computer models and programs that mimic human cognition to solve complex problems and gain experience. Most current AI tools are considered "Narrow," which means they can outperform humans in defined tasks.
- Researchers are unleashing artificial intelligence on data torrents in a revolution that extends throughout science and exploration.

## Notes

1. Heinlein Robert. Quote. Wikipedia.
2. Appenzeller T. The scientists' apprentice. *Science* 2017;357(6346):16–17. https://www.science.org/doi/10.1126/science.357.6346.16.
3. Patton S. George. Speech. Battle of the Bulge. France, December 1944. Quote.
4. Turing. Source Wikipedia. https://commons.wikimedia.org/wiki/File:Alan_Turing_by_Stephen_Kettle_2007.jpg.
5. Watson. IBM. Image (Source Wikipedia).

# Chapter 2

# Purpose to Impact

> The question is not whether intelligent machines can have any emotions, but whether machines can be intelligent with no emotions.
>
> **—Marvin Minsky, 1986**

In 2006, prominent and up-and-coming software developer Adam Bosworth had a "forthcoming" vision. Before joining Google® in 2004, Bosworth was BEA's chief architect and senior vice president of advanced development.

Bosworth played a crucial role in developing BEA's architecture and was renowned for his innovative approaches to software design. With Bosworth and his innovations leading the way, BEA acquired Crossgain®, which Bosworth co-founded in 2001. In addition, Bosworth created a system for aggregating health information from various sources, including electronic medical records, fitness trackers, and medical devices. With his vision and focus, he started Google Health as a project within Google that aimed to help people manage their health information online.

By creating a platform that collects, stores, and analyzes health data, individuals could track their health over time and make more informed healthcare decisions. As Google developed its new Google Health, in partnership with healthcare organizations globally, Google continued its research by drawing on diverse datasets, high-quality labels, and state-of-the-art deep learning techniques.

Google Health developed models that support medical specialists in diagnosing disease, paving the way toward new frontiers, showing that AI could enable transformative diagnostics across the health industry.


DOI: 10.4324/9781003661627-3

Unfortunately, despite high hopes, a substantial investment, and high-profile partnerships with major healthcare organizations, including the American Heart Association, Google Health's attempts to gain traction were thwarted.

Google said in 2011 that it was ending the project and reassigning the staff to other departments and initiatives due to worries about the feasibility of the business model and the difficulties of navigating the healthcare industry's complicated regulatory framework.

In 2018, Google announced that it would relaunch Google Health under Alphabet. The new initiative aims to improve patient outcomes and reduce healthcare costs with artificial intelligence and machine learning. However, a significant barrier to entry for Google was the unpredictable regulatory landscape of the healthcare industry, including compliance with HIPAA (Health Insurance Portability and Accountability Act) and other privacy laws. For Google, managing the complex relationships between patients, doctors, insurers, and other stakeholders in the healthcare system was a major challenge.

And much like Google, corporate healthcare companies are running into challenges with applying AI technology collaboratively. Everyone at BrainX, through a solid collaborative effort, aims to expound the purpose of artificial intelligence by addressing and easing barriers to improving patient care and the overall healthcare experience. Even though slower than expected, industry-wide, the value of AI is being embraced by early adopters, and its velocity and benefits are increasing as computer power and technology grow.

Today, it is challenging to find an industry that emerging AI has not touched. Read anything online, and we are hard pressed not to learn about advancements being made in artificial intelligence. That said, we cannot overstate the transformative power and purpose of AI to impact the healthcare industry—and we should not underestimate it either.

Over the last decade or so, AI has played a significant role in healthcare, powering software used by healthcare organizations and wearable gear and sensors used by patients. In the last few years, we have seen technology develop by orders of magnitude we could not have predicted, particularly in patient-centric healthcare.

One of the most significant effects of AI in healthcare is better access to care for individuals, particularly those who live in rural or underdeveloped areas with few medical practitioners or specialists nearby. Significant attention has accompanied emerging telemedicine. Although there has been a slight decrease in its popularity, virtual healthcare services could become a permanent solution for providing care to patients in rural areas who cannot attend appointments.

In a similar vein as a strong purpose to impact, virtual assistants powered by AI (e.g., chatbots) are being implemented to assist patients with appointment scheduling, guidance on the next course of action, and supplying fundamental healthcare information. By doing so, this reallocates time for physicians and personnel to attend to patient-centric obligations, providing great one-on-one care.

The ways in which assistive and autonomous AI technologies are implemented to expand patients' access to care extremely intrigued us at BrainX.

Assistive AI often involves the technology performing a task that provides additional information or analysis to the medical practitioner. The medical practitioner can then utilize this information to determine the course of treatment or diagnosis. Particularly helpful are tasks involving assistive AI, such as interpreting medical images, collecting measures, or evaluating massive datasets. Assistive AI can work as an additional pair of eyes for the clinician, aiding in the delegation of certain duties and mental burdens while enhancing back-office operations.

Autonomous AI refers to a technical system that conducts tasks and reaches a conclusion, such as providing a medical diagnosis, without necessitating human interpretation of the data. One example of the impact of AI is the ongoing study and diagnosis of diabetic retinopathy.

Varun Gulshan, a Google research scientist known for using AI in hand gestures, wanted to find a project that would meet a few criteria regarding its purpose of bringing health to the world through artificial intelligence. So, using Gulshan's background in developing AI algorithms, he emailed Phil Nelson, Director of Google Accelerated Science (GAS), asking if there was such a project in the works. To Nelson, Gulshan's experience with AI stood on its own merit and he had a project in mind, but first, he needed to know: could a model of artificial intelligence learn which images showed signs of diabetic retinopathy, a specific cause of blindness? Weeks later, Gulshan retrieved hundreds of anonymized retina scans from an Indian hospital. After seeing the impact of AI and deep learning in diabetic retinopathy, Gulshan knew it was the perfect skill set to diagnose and treat the ever-present problems of diabetic retinopathy.

The light-sensitive tissue in the back of the eye and the blood vessels in the retina are both impaired in diabetic retinopathy, brought on by elevated blood sugar levels. Among individuals of working age, diabetic retinopathy is the major cause of vision impairment and blindness among the thirty million Americans with diabetes. The disease is a global concern since 510 million diabetics are in danger of blindness worldwide (with the United States, China, and India having the highest incidence rates). The Jefferson School of Population Health projects that the number of individuals affected by diabetes will reach 53.1 million by 2025.

By employing AI and deep learning techniques, Gulshan and Google have identified novel patterns in diabetic retinopathy, which has a beneficial impact on investigating diabetes's ocular manifestations. Google has encountered scrutiny along the process as it awaited FDA permission. Yet, the wait ended in 2018 when the Food and Drug Administration of the United States granted approval for the sale of the first medical device that employed artificial intelligence to detect more severe forms of diabetic retinopathy in individuals diagnosed with diabetes in 2018.

With priorities including the diagnosis of conditions such as retinopathy and cancer, artificial intelligence is also assisting in expanding the patient load that medical practitioners can attend to simultaneously and, in some instances, can even improve healthcare's proactivity. Preventing permanent damage by detecting diseases in their early stages is a significant stride in the right direction.

Improving patient outcomes and lowering provider and patient expenses, as well as supporting clinicians in giving treatment early, allows the healthcare system to accommodate more people. Experts can create risk prediction models and early detection algorithms using artificial intelligence by using extensive data collection, including medical images, patient records, genetic information, and lifestyle data. However, dealing with massive amounts of data demands extensive validation and an ethical AI design and certification process.

At BrainX, we believe an initiative-taking approach to healthcare is not restricted to the doctor's office. Today, there are numerous ways for patients to take control of their own healthcare experience by using AI with wearable AI-powered gadgets, such as the Apple Watch or Fitbit. These devices can detect anomalies that may lead to the diagnosis of various health conditions and, at the least, provide warning signals that something is wrong with a patient's current health.

With purpose and value, AI in healthcare has made incredible progress with technology, but it is still far from perfect. Every day, there are news articles on bias in AI algorithms—and in healthcare, this can have a very real impact on patient outcomes and patients' lives.

In 2020, there was a documentary describing the problems we could face, focusing on facial recognition with AI. The documentary *Coded Bias* discussed faults in facial recognition technology that may lead to racial bias. We must be vigilant in addressing bias, as AI errors can have a harmful impact on this type of bias. As AI is trained on small data sets and shortcuts are implemented, care must be taken to ensure there is no ethical bias.

However, there are other groups dedicated to an ethical and fair solution. They focus on training on large data sets with a rigorous validation approach and on finding and reducing bias from conceptualization through design and implementation. We should emphasize evaluating the technology in real-world scenarios to ensure that it works well for everyone in all care settings; success and acceptance are contingent on this.

With a strong purpose to impact, healthcare and our industry will never be the same. AI is transforming how medical professionals care for patients and how we work within our organizations, addressing the reality that AI will not replace providers and caregivers. Rather, it will complement what they already do and provide them with added resources to care for more patients and reach those they would otherwise not have been able to treat.

As a purposeful and introduced impact, AI is reducing physician burnout, diagnosis and treatment times, and healthcare costs while increasing access and quality. This is just the beginning, and as we progress, we will see more changes with the growing role of AI in healthcare. Some say that AI will be "as big as creating the internet." While still in the early stages, it is hard to refute the immense impact AI could have on all our lives.

## Challenges Affecting AI

As we discuss the impact of AI, we need to examine the challenges set forth as technology advances. When implementing AI, we must focus on issues where designed systems can misdiagnose. Mistakes can occur, making properly developed AI algorithms crucial. In 2014, a U.S. study extrapolated the results from three studies to the U.S. adult population, showing a 5.08% diagnosis error rate in an outpatient setting, with 50% of these errors causing harm to patients. There is little doubt that researchers must adequately develop and test AI algorithms to reduce and ease these numbers, improving patient care.

### *Increased Costs*

Another impending difficulty is increasing costs rather than reducing them. As artificial intelligence develops, there are growing concerns that certain applications may increase costs rather than reduce them. Developing and maintaining complex algorithms might increase costs of training and research and development. A recent report said, "In industries such as financial services or healthcare, the use of AI could cause developing complex algorithms that require significant investment in both time and resources." Collaboratively, as an industry, we must look at the costs of ongoing maintenance, updates, development, and training.

### *Increased Need for Specialized Talent*

Another major barrier is the requirement for specialized personnel to design and implement AI solutions. According to research, "There is already a shortage of AI talent, and this might only worsen as demand develops." Hiring top-tier AI professionals is going to be expensive, and competition for such talent may cause increased pay. Training existing employees to use AI technologies can be an expensive task.

### *Generated Wrong Outcomes*

There are concerns that AI could create other costs by generating unexpected outcomes or errors. AI systems can amplify existing biases or generate new ones, and there is a risk that these biases could lead to unexpected or negative outcomes. For example, an AI-powered healthcare system that cannot consider the needs or preferences of certain groups of patients could lead to decreased patient satisfaction and increased costs.

### *Regulatory Challenges*

Implementation of AI may also incur costs because of regulatory obstacles.

According to a McKinsey report, regulatory obstacles could slow the adoption of artificial intelligence or increase compliance costs. Costs could increase if businesses must invest additional resources to ensure that their AI systems comply with regulations and standards.

Despite these potential obstacles, the report stresses that AI's benefits still outweigh its costs. The report states, "In many instances, the cost savings and other benefits that can be derived from AI will far outweigh the challenges."

AI has the potential to increase efficiency, improve decision-making, and generate new business opportunities.

However, it is important for companies to be aware of the potential costs and challenges associated with AI implementation to make informed decisions.

One solution to the potential cost challenges of AI is to adopt a strategic approach to implementation. Companies should take a strategic approach to adopting AI, focusing on use cases that offer the greatest potential for cost savings or revenue generation. By prioritizing AI applications that offer the highest return on investment, companies can minimize the potential costs associated with implementation.

## *Purpose-Filled Training*

Another possibility is investing in training and development programs that help existing employees acquire the skills necessary to work with AI technologies. Companies should make AI-friendly skill development a strategic priority. By investing in training and development, businesses can ensure that they have the talent and expertise needed to implement AI solutions and reduce the need for expensive external hires.

Additionally, companies can take steps to ensure their AI systems are designed with fairness and transparency in mind. The development and implementation of ethical AI standards should be a top priority for businesses. By addressing potential biases and ethical issues, businesses can reduce the risk of unanticipated or unfavorable outcomes that may lead to increased costs.

Despite the potential implementation costs connected with AI, the technology's benefits outweigh the risks. Businesses can reduce the potential costs of using AI while reaping major benefits by taking a strategic approach, investing in people's development, and considering ethical considerations. AI is a powerful technology that may help healthcare organizations generate considerable value and achieve significant commercial success if used intelligently.

Using AI in healthcare settings recalls the movie *Forrest Gump* and its pivotal scene, in which the protagonist visits the recently deceased grave of Jenny, the love of his life, and breaks down in an open plea, struggling to come to terms with her passing. It is at this moment that Forrest said something that stuck with him over thirty years ago: "I do not know if we each have a destiny, or if we are all just floating around accidentally, like on a breeze. Perhaps it is both." Thus, even though AI technology has been present for a while, technology and the healthcare sector are now coming together, developing and advancing serendipitously with the goal of affecting healthcare in ways that could never have been predicted.

***

## Important Points

- The value of AI is realized by early adopters, and its velocity is increasing as computer power grows.
- As the first device approved for marketing by the FDA, IDx-DR provides a screening decision without requiring clinicians to interpret images or results.

# 2

# THE WHO (OF AI IN HEALTHCARE)

# Chapter 3

# Team Building

> For over 250 years, the fundamental drivers of economic growth have been technological innovations. The most important of these are what economists call general-purpose technologies, including the steam engine, electricity, and the internal combustion engine. The most important general-purpose technology of our era is artificial intelligence, particularly machine learning.
>
> **—Erik Brynjolfsson and Andrew McAfee, 2018**

In April 2016, Uber partnered with *Circulation*, a digital transportation platform, to provide third-party, healthcare-related ride requests. Uber was the first company to use machine learning and AI to increase efficiency in this way. By collaborating with Uber for Circulation, the company showed the innovative uses of its technology. It showed how forming teams can bring together different disciplines and foster collaboration.

Uber's use of machine learning and AI was just the beginning and is a prime example of how technology is applied across a wide range of industries, from healthcare and education to transportation and logistics. AI and machine learning enable businesses to create more efficient, cost-effective, and customer-focused products and services. Skilled and knowledgeable teams are essential to conduct all of this.

To build a successful machine learning team, each team member's strengths and weaknesses, skills, talents, and ability to identify problematic areas had to be understood. We do not have to look far to find successful team-building examples. For instance, Google's Search Quality Team is a true exemplary example. They constantly refine and improve the search

DOI: 10.4324/9781003661627-5

engine by combining machine learning algorithms with extensive training of human evaluators. This cooperation with evaluators and AI teams worldwide is the main reason Google has maintained its position as the world's most popular search engine.

## Answering the WHY in Building a Team with AI

As we examine the Why, one of the first aspects is looking at the broader picture and recognizing the expected outcomes and results with an AI team.

Understanding the benefits of using a team with machine learning is essential for strategic planning, development, and implementation within the healthcare industry. Building teams with AI and machine learning can offer a wide range of benefits, including the following:

- Specialized Skill Sets.
- Improved Productivity.
- Enhanced Collaboration.
- Improved Problem-Solving.
- Increased Scalability.
- Enhanced Security.
- Competitive Advantage.
- Diversity of Perspectives.

### *Specialized Skill Sets*

AI and machine learning specialists can improve a team's performance by contributing to their distinct knowledge of data analysis, programming, and algorithm creation. Using the knowledge of AI/ML specialists can increase the team's skill and ability, leading to better problem-solving and more creative solutions.

### *Improved Productivity*

Teams using AI and machine learning capabilities can increase productivity by automating and analyzing data. Companies can decrease costs and improve project timelines. A group of AI/ML specialists can spot viable concerns before they become serious ones, enabling them to take preventive measures like corrective action.

## *Enhanced Collaboration*

Teams working together can use innovative technology to produce solutions more effectively. This can make the group more creative and productive in real time. AI and ML teams can offer improved insights into consumer patterns and demands, enabling more specialized solutions.

## *Improved Problem-Solving*

Teams can use AI and machine learning to solve complicated challenges more effectively and efficiently. AI techniques can help us find links and patterns in data that would be hard for humans to find. Teams that employ this technique can solve problems more rapidly and with less effort, arriving at an optimal answer.

AI/ML can facilitate better performance and decision-making to address outstanding problems.

## *Faster Innovation*

At BrainX, we understand that innovation and scalability require brilliant minds working together. Collaboratively, teams can prototype and test innovative ideas more quickly with AI and machine learning, which leads to faster innovation and iteration. It is crucial to recognize the difference between disruptions and innovations in the healthcare field, as advanced tools are positively affecting patient care. We must tap into our imaginative powers to meet and predict patient demands. However, our ability to implement innovative ideas throughout our whole health ministry is important.

This is the point at which disruptions can aid us in maintaining and enhancing community and individual health. Businesses may remain competitive in the market and meet client expectations by employing these technologies to hasten the development of new products and services.

## *Increased Scalability*

Teams that use AI and machine learning to automate processes might expand their operations without hiring more staff. Besides automating work, artificial intelligence aims to increase human intellect, facilitate better decision-making, and boost patient outcomes. Scalability is of utmost importance in the transformation of healthcare, as artificial intelligence will analyze enormous amounts of patient data across millions of patients instantaneously. Because of this greater scalability, businesses can concentrate on strategic projects and expansion prospects while boosting production and efficiency.

### Enhanced Security

Combining artificial intelligence and machine learning can speed up and improve the detection of potential security threats. Eric Topol, author of the book *Deep Medicine,* said, "As we continue to leverage the power of artificial intelligence in healthcare, we ensure we are not sacrificing security for innovation." The situation demands urgent action, as we must establish robust security protocols to shield patient privacy and thwart any data breaches. As an industry, we must work together to build trust and transparency in our AI systems, ensuring that patients and healthcare providers can trust their security. Using predictive algorithms, these technologies can alert teams to suspicious activity before an incident occurs, protecting data from malicious attacks.

### Competitive Advantage

By using AI, teams can benefit from increased productivity, cost savings, and improved customer results. Knowledge offers a significant and decisive advantage, but effort and passion matter. Organizations that leverage AI's capability to analyze copious amounts of healthcare data will gain a significant competitive edge in terms of patient outcomes, cost reduction, and improved quality of care. Besides the correct technology, we also need to have the right people, procedures, and strategies in place to optimize AI's impact. Keeping this in mind, businesses' performance in the upcoming years will depend on their ability to integrate AI.

### Diversity of Perspectives

A team with machine learning and artificial intelligence skills can improve creativity and problem-solving by bringing in different viewpoints and experiences. To broaden problem-solving, it is beneficial to have a diverse team of AI and machine learning experts on hand to bring perspectives and experience to the table. They can widen their critical thinking skills and produce innovative ideas that they may not have thought of otherwise by considering several approaches to the problem. A competent team may use those viewpoints to analyze data and extract relevant information—even crucial information—for original problem-solving and decision-making.

***

## How—Team Planning

Forming an AI team is different from following the fad or getting on board with it. We must first assess where we are now, assign expenses, identify the most pressing issues, and begin any outstanding pilot projects. These projects will define problems and issues that we must coordinate with trained teams.

Experimentation with AI integration, while concentrating on requirements for implementation and assessment, is vital to put into action. Healthcare as a business requires a detailed AI implementation plan that covers everything from setting up sound foundations to outlining future goals. Since assembling a trained and skilled AI team is not a simple operation, let us explore formal possibilities to do this.

- Establishing a team of AI experts within the company.
- Contracting out AI work.

Both approaches have drawbacks, since effective AI teams demand a variety of responsibilities and adaptable skill sets. Our AI team will also need to collaborate with other divisions within our company. We may then create a solution that satisfies the requirements of both professionals and patients.

While artificial intelligence and machine learning have the potential to ease many issues in healthcare, they can also introduce additional difficulties and obstacles. Overall, to help our healthcare business reach new heights, we must develop exceptional AI teams with great collaboration, teamwork, and planning in focus.

At BrainX, we have a remarkably diverse and multifaceted team of clinicians, researchers, AI experts, computer scientists, ethicists, and business professionals. We support developing solutions addressing all aspects of AI in healthcare development and implementation (Figures 3.1 and 3.2).

**Figure 3.1 The founders of BrainX, Brain Community, and BrainXAI ReSearch**
**Note: Standing left to right: Jacek B Cywinski, Frank Papay, Piyush Mathur, Kamal Maheshwari. Sitting left to right: Shreya Mishra, Raghav Awasthi.**

**Figure 3.2 Left to right: Ashish K Khanna, Piyush Mathur, Chintan Dave**

# Chapter 4

# WHO

## *Building a Team for AI/ML*

> I think what makes AI different from other technologies is that it's going to bring humans and machines closer together. AI is sometimes incorrectly framed as machines replacing humans. It's not about machines replacing humans, but machines augmenting humans. Humans and machines have different relative strengths and weaknesses, and it's about the combination of these two that will allow human intents and business processes to scale 10x, 100x, and beyond that in the coming years.
>
> **Robin Bordoli, former Chief Executive Officer, Figure Eight[1]**

As healthcare practitioners use data to forecast and prescribe ailments, enhance treatments, and potentially avert the onset of diseases, there is a notable surge in implementing AI and machine learning technologies. Nevertheless, recognizing that the core of machine learning and AI is individuals and teams is crucial to completely actualizing the capabilities of these technologies. As a result, we may expect an increase in the need for training and retraining, as well as the growth of proficient data technologists.

Since AI and machine learning use enormous volumes of data, teams and individuals with extensive training and expertise will be required to meet demand. This demand will positively affect the future of work, as AI technology will generate an abundance of employment prospects in a variety of industries. As expansion entails adjustment and transformation, there will be

DOI: 10.4324/9781003661627-6

an expanding need for robust collaboration that integrates diverse AI systems and processes.

Integrating AI into the healthcare profession requires teams and experienced technicians to learn and adapt to additional responsibilities. Teams will need to be adept in data analysis, machine learning, and other AI technologies, which will require retraining and upskilling programs. Employers must adopt new training programs, policies, and tactics to ensure a knowledgeable, productive, and engaged staff to coordinate efforts. Building a skilled team and suitably trained staff is critical for the successful implementation of training and upskilling.

Rajeev Ronanki, Chief Digital Officer at the healthcare organization Anthem, says the company has implemented AI and ML teams for tasks ranging from predicting a patient's health trajectory to resolving customer disputes. A machine learning team, for instance, can analyze years of healthcare data generated by patients with chronic conditions, such as diabetes or heart disease. Then, Anthem can predict the treatment outcome by cross-referencing with similar patients or their "digital twins."

Teams tasked with developing artificial intelligence must possess the knowledge and skills necessary to assess the technology's capabilities and hazards, execute it securely and effectively, and foresee any issues. To improve patient outcomes, enterprises, organizations, teams, and employees must all agree with the aims, objectives, precision, and effectiveness of AI.

For this reason, communication is vital. Organizations and businesses must develop tracking systems to stay abreast of the latest developments in AI for healthcare. The difficulty lies in locating, educating, and retaining AI specialists. For healthcare businesses to move seamlessly to using AI, they must allocate time and money toward discovering the ideal combination of personnel. This is a fundamental and important prerequisite.

AI has experienced tremendous growth, with adoption increasing by over 270 percent since 2010, according to Gartner, Inc. Thirty-seven percent of all business types currently employ artificial intelligence-powered technology, including but not limited to natural language processing, predictive analytics, machine learning, and robotic process automation.

Thus, it is essential to assemble well-rounded teams comprising individuals with varied backgrounds and skill sets, including those with non-technical responsibilities. BrainX is cognizant of the increasing necessity to assemble interdisciplinary teams comprising specialists from multiple fields, as opposed to relying solely on exceptionally intelligent individuals.

Collectively devising and executing state-of-the-art AI solutions, these groups frequently include professionals with varied expertise and experiences. We expect each function to encompass certain subcategories of expertise and skill sets with which it works in close collaboration. AI technicians and developers are, in most circumstances, responsible for the following four categories and functions:

- The ability to establish real-world scenarios and deliver value requires a solid understanding of business processes.
- Experts in analytics—machine learning, statistics, forecasting, and optimization—who apply the right techniques.
- Expert in data. A person who can answer the questions: where does it come from? Is the quality comparable? Is the data clean? Does managing it in a certain way preserve trust and security?
- A resolute AI architect who operationalizes analytics.

There are other prominent roles played by machine learning teams, as well as other types of contributors:

- Data Scientist.
- Machine Learning Engineer.
- AI Researcher.
- Natural Language Processing (NLP) Specialist.
- Robotics Engineer.
- AI Product/project manager.
- AI Ethicist.

## Data Scientists

Data scientists find data-driven solutions to business problems in the healthcare ecosystem. These experts provide expertise in data mining, predictive analytics, and machine learning. For example, they might analyze user data to identify distinct groups of users and create models to categorize them to improve the user experience (Figure 4.1). By tracking data science metrics, data science professionals are fast becoming a sophisticated, specialized, and sought-after workforce. Trained data science teams are fast becoming indispensable to healthcare organizations, as the demand has multiplied tenfold.

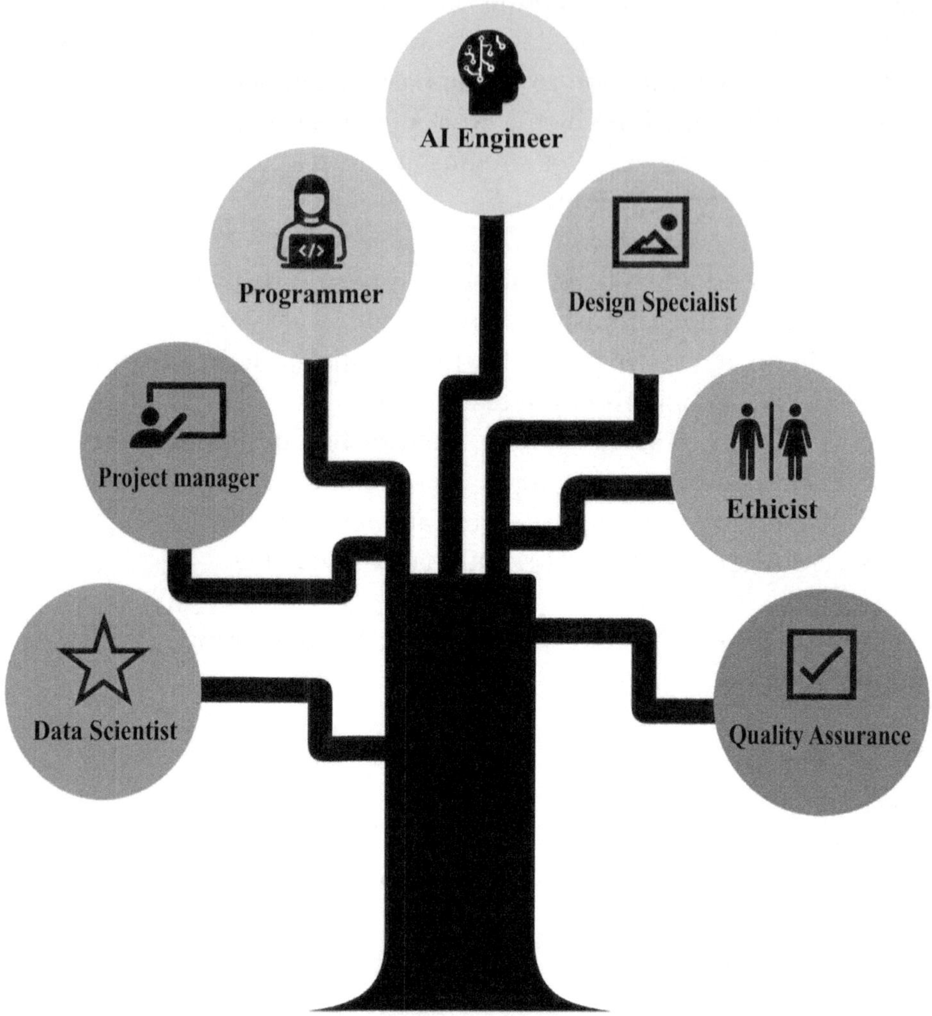


**Figure 4.1 Multidisciplinary expertise required to develop and implement AI solutions.**

With the emergence and rise of AI, data scientists actively develop data infrastructure and perform data mining and quality checking for many healthcare applications. Analyzing and interpreting data using statistical and machine-learning techniques, they collaborate with domain experts and data engineers to identify relevant data sources. DJ Patil, the former United States Chief Data Scientist, stated, "Data scientists are like artists. They transform raw data into something beautiful and meaningful." These scientists are the 21st century magicians, transforming any data into insights that drive business success. The backbone of AI is data scientists, who are digital-age storytellers who use data narratives for organizations to better understand patient needs and improve decisions for the best care and outcomes.

## Machine Learning Engineer

A machine learning engineer (MLE) creates and installs machine learning models for various AI applications. MLEs boost performing AI systems by applying algorithms to detect patterns and insights in massive datasets while also maintaining data pipelines that flow into the platform. Computer science, mathematics, and statistics form the solid foundation of an MLE's background.

The team is knowledgeable about programming languages such as Python, Java, and C++, as well as machine learning frameworks such as TensorFlow, Keras, and PyTorch. It also acquainted the team with data processing techniques, data visualization, and cloud computing. A machine learning engineer oversees data preparation and cleaning, feature engineering, model selection, tweaking, and deployment.

## Data Engineer

The data engineer in an AI team applies their talents to design strong and scalable AI systems while also maintaining the infrastructure required for storing, processing, and analyzing enormous volumes of data required to train and operate AI models. Cassie Kozyrkov, Google's Chief Decision Scientist, emphasizes this topic. "The unsung heroes of artificial intelligence are data engineers. They construct the infrastructure that allows data scientists and machine learning engineers to do their duties." Sound data engineers are architects in charge of designing, constructing, and maintaining the sophisticated infrastructure that enables organizations to store, process, and analyze massive volumes of data. We must construct AI models on a solid foundation of clean, well-organized data, which data engineers must ensure.

## Artificial Intelligence Researcher

Researchers in artificial intelligence challenge the limits of AI technology through pioneering investigations. They collaborate closely with data scientists and machine learning engineers to find innovative areas to develop new models and strategies to increase AI performance. Today, artificial intelligence researchers push the boundaries, emerging with breakthrough technologies as modern-day synthesists. Researchers transform data by constructing intelligent systems that are the catalyst for shaping our world for years to come.

## Natural Language Processing Specialist (NLP)

"NLP Specialists are the magicians of AI," says Dario Gil, Director of IBM Research. "They can help machines understand and respond to human language in ways that were previously considered impossible." As we have seen at BrainX, NLPs are language wizards, transforming words into knowledge and comprehensible AI applications. NLP experts enable machines to speak with people in a natural and intuitive manner, working like digital translators. NLPs assist machines in understanding and processing human language, transforming unstructured data into meaningful insights, unlocking the potential and complexities and diversity of human language.

## Robotics Engineer

AI applications developed by robotics engineers can interact with the physical world. Using AI and robotics, we can create machines that can learn from patient data, reduce errors, and provide personalized care. By working closely with data scientists and machine learning engineers, robotic engineers develop algorithms to control robotic systems, ensuring they can operate safely and efficiently. They collaborate with mechanical engineers to design and build robotic systems that can perform various tasks, from manufacturing to healthcare.

## AI Product/Project Manager

AI product managers oversee bringing AI solutions to life in the organization, but their duties differ from those of traditional IT product managers. Creating AI products requires a specific skill set. With increased demand, AI product managers must be both managers and leaders on a conceptual level. They must understand:

- A machine learning algorithm's training process: feature engineering and how it works.
- Types of AI approaches and techniques available (machine vision, predictive analytics, natural language processing)?
- Which industries can benefit from applying these approaches and techniques?
- Describe the lifecycle and phases of an AI project, including understanding business needs, understanding data, and assessing project requirements.

Product managers develop product strategy as part of their responsibilities by collaborating closely with the entire AI team to find possibilities for innovation and comprehend client requirements. Working in tandem with the sales and marketing departments, their primary aim is to develop engaging AI products and track the performance metrics required for the promotion and sale of those goods.

## AI Ethicists

As AI systems advance and become more sophisticated, we need to discuss and address ethical issues thoughtfully in an initiative-taking manner. A key role in resolving these concerns is that of the AI ethicist. As AI systems increase in influence and complexity, the requirement for AI ethics professionals rises.

Professionals in this domain possess a profound comprehension of the social, moral, and legal ramifications of artificial intelligence, besides their technological prowess. Increasingly acknowledged as a major priority by enterprises, the AI ethicist directs ethical principles in AI development and application. Further reading will go into the intricacies of defining AI ethicists, indicating their position in the contemporary AI-dominated society, and strategies for approaching the attainment of expertise in this specialized field.

As AI is being integrated into an expanding number of industries, the ethical considerations associated with its application have grown in importance.

Currently, organizations must employ committed AI ethicists to traverse this complicated environment securely, identify potential hazards, and act ethically.

Developing artificial intelligence is guided by ethical concerns; ethicists exert a substantial influence on the trajectory of AI research. They ensure ethical considerations are an integral part of the design process, as opposed to being supplemental components. AI ethicists assist in the reflection of cultural norms and values by ensuring that AI systems are consistent with moral and social standards. They direct their efforts toward mitigating biases in AI systems that may cause unjust or detrimental consequences. Compliance and assuring adherence to norms and regulations are vital to creating AI. Assisting organizations in navigating the intricate terrain of regulations and standards pertaining to—and absence of—artificial intelligence, AI ethicists ensure that the development of AI systems remains within lawful boundaries while also offering counsel to policymakers and legislators.

Artificial intelligence ethicists ensure that AI systems comply with industry standards and legal requirements. This assists businesses in avoiding legal hazards and preserving their reputations. In the absence of risk mitigation and potential harm assessment, irresponsible AI use can inflict substantial damage.

Making AI safer for all, AI ethicists assist organizations in identifying and mitigating these dangers.

Ethicists specializing in artificial intelligence function as a precursory mechanism for ethical concerns, recognizing and addressing them to prevent escalating ethical difficulties. This enables organizations to confront these concerns proactively, avoiding harm and controversy by identifying issues early. With healthcare, before an AI project goes live, AI ethicists need to be put in place to conduct reviews of AI programs to identify potential ethical issues and risks and safeguard compliance: they actively ensure projects comply with existing ethical guidelines and regulations.

AI ethicists collaborate closely with developers, product managers, legal experts, and other team members to integrate ethical considerations into every stage of AI development. To do so, AI ethicists educate team members about ethical AI practices, fostering a culture of responsibility and ethical consciousness within the organization.

## Additional AI/ML Roles

- Practitioners of data modeling.
- Experts in deep learning.
- Programmers and software engineers.

- Subject experts.
- Designers of consumer goods and products.
- AI sociologists and ethicists.

We will need additional expertise and critical roles on an AI team to work with our organization's data, including the following:

- Professionals in operations.
- Leaders in the IT industry.
- Business strategists and executives.
- Analysts of business operations.
- Statistical or mathematical experts.
- Engineers specializing in machine learning applications.
- Graphic or UX designer.
- Testers and QA specialists.
- Leaders in human resources.
- Attorney.

## Note

1. Bordoli Robin. Quote. Article. https://blog.oxigin.net/humans-and-ai-a-symbiotic-relationship-for-customer-success-a7d949fbe6ba.

# 3 THE WHAT (OF AI IN HEALTHCARE)

# Chapter 5

# Healthcare Value Proposition

> Artificial intelligence has the potential to transform healthcare by automating routine tasks and providing new insights into complex medical problems. From diagnosing diseases to predicting patient outcomes, AI is already making a significant impact on the healthcare field, and its potential is only beginning to be realized.
>
> **—Eric Topol, American cardiologist and author:** *Deep Medicine*[1]

DeepMind researchers developed an AI system to analyze retinal scans and detect early signs of age-related macular degeneration (AMD), a leading cause of blindness in older adults, in collaboration with Moorfields Eye Hospital in London in 2018. The AI system was a breakthrough in ophthalmology, producing excellent results. Millions of people worldwide suffer from AMD, which can lead to vision loss if left untreated. Doctors have struggled for years to detect early signs of the disease. Doctors can now see and diagnose AMD in its preliminary stages using the new AI system, giving patients a much better chance of success.

Dr. Emily Jones, an ophthalmologist at Moorfields Eye Hospital, was among the first to use the new AI system. She was skeptical of the results but was convinced after seeing them for herself. As a result, Dr. Jones could diagnose early-stage AMD in patients who learned they had perfect vision and begin treatment before the condition worsened. Dr. Jones's patients included John, who had been coming to Moorfield's Eye Hospital for routine eye exams for years. Even with perfect vision, Dr. Jones surprised John by revealing that his retinal scan revealed early signs of AMD. Because of the early detection, John received a variety of treatments over the next few

DOI: 10.4324/9781003661627-8

weeks, including injections and laser treatment. Despite his discomfort and anxiety, John was grateful for the early detection provided by AI and the opportunity to save his sight.

The creators initially developed the Google DeepMind neural network to learn how to play video games like humans. Along with video game exploration, DeepMind also developed a Neural Turing machine, which could access external memory like a Turing machine, mimicking the brain's short-term memory. By 2020, DeepMind had made considerable progress on protein folding with AlphaFold. The results were so profound that on July 20, 2022, AlphaFold announced the release of over 200 million predicted protein structures, representing all known proteins.

DeepMind posted a blog post in April 2022 about Flamingo, a single visual language model, which can describe a picture with just a few training images. The company merged with Google AI's Google Brain division to become Google DeepMind in April 2023.

As AI professionals collaborated closely with teams across Google Product Areas, they understood they could deliver AI products that dramatically improved billions of lives. Google DeepMind had the potential to transform industries, advance science, and serve diverse communities. A key aspect of Google DeepMind is the ability to build capable and general artificial intelligence safely and responsibly, to address the most complex challenges in science and engineering.

Using over 1,000 retinal scans, the AI system could accurately diagnose AMD in 94% of cases, significantly better than human experts. The system detected early signs of AMD before they were visible to humans, allowing earlier diagnosis and treatment.

After DeepMind's AI system at Moorfields Eye Hospital proved successful, DeepMind collaborated with other medical institutions, such as the Royal Free Hospital and University College London Hospital. The collaborations have shown the value of AI in healthcare and paved the way for further innovations.

Given the noteworthy progress in AI, it is crucial to consider its core benefits and potential to enhance healthcare opportunities.

To answer, we must understand both AI's positive and negative aspects as a solution. What can AI provide, and can we explain and work it out in the real world with actual patients? Can we point to or count its benefits, considering the harsh realities of front-line care? Is it making healthcare professionals' lives more difficult, or is it adding more work and cost to professionals and the healthcare system?

The offer's value differs depending on the healthcare industry participant, but for the end user, it is about engagement, improved clinical and patient outcomes, and accurate diagnosis. While AI, as an innovative technology, has unimaginable potential, we foresee a future in which humans and machines can partner together for the best possible outcomes in the healthcare arena. We are entering what we believe is a fourth industrial revolution in which new AI technologies have the potential to be the biggest thing to hit healthcare since the discovery of penicillin.

Dr. Eric Topol explained in a recent article for the *Wall Street Journal*, "Radical New Possibilities and Medical Care Are Not Some Far-off Fantasies." [2]

## The Concept of Proportional Value in AI Has Vast Monetary Implications

Take Microsoft, for example, which announced its investment in startup OpenAI in January 2023. It has added hundreds of billions of dollars in market value since Microsoft is the second-largest company in the S&P 500, making its performance influential. The AI boom has helped drive much of the S&P 500's gains this year, according to research from Société Générale. The bank estimates the S&P 500 would be down 2% in 2023 without stocks tied to AI, not up to almost 8%.

California and Wisconsin are trialing OpenAI's "GPT" generative artificial intelligence to read patient messages and draft doctor responses. Three health systems are testing whether AI will reduce the time medical staff spend replying to patients' online inquiries as part of a pilot program. UC San Diego Health and UW Health began evaluating the tool in April. For about a week, Dr. Marlene Millen, a primary care physician at UC San Diego Health, helped lead the AI test, evaluating GPT in her inbox. Her team has been working on improving AI-generated responses that need heavy editing.

We at BrainX want to investigate the propositional value of AI technologies and the value that we can expect to see in the future. While it is impossible to comprehend how quickly AI technology is growing, as we are about to discover, recent developments are shaping the world around us. Still, one aspect of its value is understanding the needs and benefits of AI, as well as the problems, issues, and disadvantages that it presents, so that we can deliver it in a more indirect manner.

***

Healthcare organizations around the country are working to improve the efficacy and efficiency of their workforces, as well as the quality of patient care in their operations and workforces. However, as the healthcare industry transitions to value-based care models that prioritize patient outcomes over patient volume, many are reaping the benefits of proportionate value by employing AI.

In contrast to common fears that machines will replace human labor, AI technology may be "re-humanizing" healthcare. As artificial intelligence tools have slowly made their way into the healthcare industry, many have voiced concerns that the technology will remove the human aspect of patient care, leaving individuals in the care of robots and machines. A report stated, "Healthcare institutions have been expecting the impact that artificial intelligence will have on the performance and efficiency of their operations and their workforces—and the quality of patient care." Despite common apprehensions that lack substantiation, the integration of AI technologies in healthcare holds the promise of revitalizing the human element in healthcare delivery. This coincides with adopting value-based care models, which prioritize patient outcomes over patient volume.

Researchers discovered providers are already using AI to improve data analysis, enabling better treatment and diagnosis, and minimizing administrative hassles—all of which free up physicians' time to undertake other activities, based on interviews with over 900 healthcare professionals.

AI offers benefits and inherent value, one of which is the capacity to automate tedious tasks like data entry, documentation, and appointment scheduling. This allows healthcare professionals to devote more attention to patient care. AI can evaluate massive volumes of medical data to help with disease and condition diagnosis with improved accuracy and timeliness, resulting in better patient outcomes. AI can adapt medicines to specific patients using patient data analysis, enhancing healthcare effectiveness. In addition, AI can forecast disease development, identify high-risk patients, and prescribe preventive actions, resulting in earlier interventions and lower healthcare expenditures.

AI has the potential to uncover hidden patterns and relationships in vast datasets, increasing medical knowledge and facilitating evidence-based decision-making. AI-powered devices can aid in remote patient monitoring, expanding healthcare access for individuals with limited mobility or in remote areas. AI can help hospitals improve their operations by optimizing processes, anticipating patient flow, and managing workers more efficiently, resulting in reduced wait times and improved healthcare delivery. AI has the potential to address a wide range of healthcare issues, enhance patient outcomes, and increase the quality and efficiency of healthcare services.

With current demands in AI's existing utility, more healthcare providers throughout the world are planning to develop a more robust healthcare ecosystem focused on achieving equitable health outcomes. This novel approach to healthcare delivery, known as "value-based care," prioritizes the patient. In today's healthcare delivery, value-based care using artificial intelligence is the new technique to promote patient-centricity and establish a resilient healthcare system. The goal is simple: to expand patient access to high-quality, timely, competitively priced, and easily accessible care. Since we are talking about value, introducing innovative technologies can assist organizations in overcoming the many hurdles associated with adopting the value-based care paradigm.

Understanding the demands of providers, payors, and patients, as well as how AI creates value for all, is critical as healthcare systems throughout the world transition away from traditional techniques and operations to a long-term strategic commitment. When done correctly, the benefits will be enormous. More healthcare organizations are using artificial intelligence to improve their services. They are doing this by adopting new strategies and tools, like cloud-based data platforms, microservices, API-enabled core apps, and AI. Even though it is a long-term commitment, we should concentrate on an organization's key strengths and shifting market trends. When done effectively, it can yield long-term benefits and value.

Many applications of AI in healthcare are implemented as a positioning value, with AI algorithms changing the medical imaging sector and the ability to evaluate X-rays, MRI scans, and CT scans, among others. These developments have the potential to increase diagnostic accuracy, treatment regimen efficiency, and patient outcomes. AI algorithms now empower radiologists to identify anomalies, enabling them to make more accurate diagnoses.

DeepMind, Google's AI-powered cancer detection system, has shown equal accuracy to human radiologists in diagnosing breast and colon cancer. Personalized medicine is a significant component of the need for artificial intelligence in healthcare. To personalize the optimal course of therapy, AI can be utilized to provide insights on biomarkers, genetic information, allergies, and psychological assessments. This information can predict a patient's response to various treatment approaches for a certain ailment. This can reduce negative effects and the cost of overpriced or needless treatment choices. With personalized treatment procedures, it can also cure genetic issues.

AI systems can analyze patient data such as medical history and test results to diagnose life-threatening illnesses such as cancer more precisely and early. This is an important aspect of AI that we should not disregard. AI systems can increase radiological imaging accuracy with a predictive year-over-year market growth of over 30%. The Medical Artificial Intelligence (MedAi) platform, for example, helps interpret and analyze medical imaging data from medical scans to identify various diseases and malignancies in patients faster and more accurately than human radiologists do. For example, IBM Watson uses NLP and machine learning algorithms to generate treatment regimens for cancer patients, and Pfizer has collaborated with various AI-based services to identify ailments.

Another advantage and utility of artificial intelligence is that it may find new R&D for drug discovery, therefore speeding up the process and reducing limits on drug discovery methods for novel chronic diseases. AI can also save millions of lives by accelerating drug testing and discovery, which saves both money and time. According to a McKinsey report, over 270 companies are engaged in AI-driven discoveries, with the United States accounting for more than half of them. The report also mentions Southeast Asia and Western Europe as potential hotspots in this region. For example, Merck & Co. is developing a revolutionary AI-based Alzheimer's treatment.

A notable eccentric advantage of AI in healthcare is pushing the boundaries of human performance, accomplishing things that even excellent human providers cannot do. For example, Google Health has created an algorithm that identifies acute kidney impairment two days in advance. Such algorithms have the potential to improve treatment beyond what humans can now deliver, but they are most effective when medical AI can accomplish tasks that humans, even outstanding ones, cannot.

One of the most significant benefits and proportional value of AI is its ability to democratize great medical knowledge and practice. Specialists can now collaborate and outperform providers who would not have been able to do so without artificial intelligence. Some applications employ images of the human eye to identify problems that require treatment by an ophthalmologist. General practitioners, technicians, and even patients can use these apps. The problem with this structure is that specialists, particularly those who are skilled, are difficult to find in many professions because of strong demand.

## Revenue for AI Solutions

Like billing codes for other aspects of care delivery in the United States, the American Medical Association (AMA) provides guidance for classifying various artificial intelligence/augmented intelligence applications that describe work associated with the use of AI-enabled medical services and/or procedures for reimbursement.

Three categories of AI applications, including assistive, augmentative, and autonomous, have been described in these guidelines. This classification is based on the clinical procedure or service provided to the patient and the work performed by the machine on behalf of the clinician.

## Assistive

The work performed by AI is to assist the clinician with detecting clinically relevant data without analysis or generating conclusions. A billing code example is computer-aided detection (CAD) imaging (CPT 77065-77067).

## Augmentative

The work performed by AI when the model analyzes and/or quantifies data clinically is meaningful. This still requires a clinician to review and report. Billing code example: continuous glucose monitoring (CPT 95251).

## Autonomous

The work performed by the AI for the clinician is autonomous when the machine interprets data and independently generates clinically meaningful conclusions without concurrent clinician involvement. Autonomous medical services and procedures include probing and analyzing data. The algorithm's work may or may not include data acquisition, preparation, and/or transmission. Billing code example: retinal imaging (CPT 92229). Billing for AI algorithms provides a pathway to reimbursement to implement and maintain value-based care delivery.

***

## Provides Real-Time Data

One key feature we perceive as an immediate requirement for AI is the vital element required in giving real-time information and data when diagnosing patients and treating any imminent medical difficulties. By applying quick and accurate AI data algorithms, doctors and other medical professionals use AI to speed up and optimize important clinical decision-making, enabling them to obtain accurate information quickly as an intrinsic benefit. More rapid and realistic results can lead to better preventive measures, financial savings, and shorter patient wait times.

## Real-Time Analytics

Real-time analytics can benefit the healthcare industry by strengthening doctor-patient relationships. Patients will be more engaged in their treatments if we make vital medical information available via mobile devices. Mobile alerts allow doctors and nurses to receive immediate updates on patient conditions and emergencies. Traditional medical organizations could never get as much data as AI technology improvements allow for.

## Saved Time and Resources

When medical practitioners automate critical activities, they have more time to study people and detect illnesses and maladies. Artificial intelligence is speeding up procedures and saving hospitals important production hours. In every sector, time is money. Artificial intelligence could bring about a substantial reduction in costs. The healthcare industry generates over $200 billion in waste annually, according to our estimates. This waste is attributed to unnecessary tests and treatment options.

Moreover, a sizable portion of these excessive fees arises due to administrative restrictions, including account submission, evaluation, and settlement. Identifying medical necessity is another area that needs improvement. In the traditional approach, it takes hours to thoroughly evaluate patient data and history for medical necessity. Doctors are now utilizing deep learning and natural language processing to analyze hospital cases and prevent denials. With the increased availability of productive hours and resources, medical practitioners can now dedicate more time to assisting and reaching out to patients.

## Assisting in Research and Data Acquisition

Through AI, researchers can amass extensive data from a range of sources. By having access to a vast and growing information database, one can effectively analyze dangerous illnesses. Research could benefit if real-time data knowledge is easily translatable. Medical research institutions are devising practical solutions to assist medical workers in effectively handling extensive data sets. The use of artificial intelligence has extended to the early detection and examination of symptoms in illnesses. Telehealth systems track patients' progress, gather vital diagnostic information, and contribute demographic data to shared networks.

## Reducing Practitioners Stress

According to recent research, most primary care physicians are on duty due to deadlines and other factors. Physician burnout is caused by the tedious tasks of data creation and input in electronic medical records, as well as the need for data retrieval and processing for prior authorization of tests and treatments.

AI eases medical staff workloads by streamlining processes, simplifying tasks, and facilitating instant data exchange. High patient volume and professional demands cause physician burnout. With AI assisting in tasks like explaining diagnoses, doctors may experience reduced stress levels. By assuming these tasks, caregivers can concentrate on their strengths: patient care and stress reduction.

BrainX acknowledges the immense practicality of artificial intelligence and embodies the propositional value of compassion. By providing AI solutions to challenges faced by hospitals and healthcare institutions, there is an opportunity to revolutionize the healthcare industry. AI has demonstrated its potential to assist healthcare professionals in analyzing health data, leading to more informed decisions about patient treatment. This becomes apparent when considering the value proposition of AI.

It seemed unimaginable that a machine could offer guidance in medical treatment. Yet, advancements in artificial intelligence have established this collection of technologies as a potent instrument for enhancing clinical and operational efficiency. As a result, medical professionals can provide better, more affordable, and increasingly personalized care to patients. Integrating AI solutions in back-end operations and patient care brings many advantages, such as improved diagnostic accuracy and more efficient workflow management.

Below are some additional benefits of value presented with AI in healthcare.

## *Workflow Optimization*

AI enables doctors to focus on technological advancements that improve diagnoses and treatments by optimizing workflows and operations. With the help of AI, referring physicians can enhance their efficiency in scheduling procedures and facilitate better patient access to specialists. AI improves diagnostic abilities and simplifies regulations and data by optimizing and automating processes. Our goal is to empower healthcare staff with valuable insights into utilizing and integrating AI technologies. Moreover, AI has enhanced efficiency in healthcare organizations, resulting in professionals redistributing their work hours to better accommodate caregiving responsibilities.

## *Reduction of Clinical Errors*

Although there is a significant reduction in clinical errors thanks to AI, a solution to clinical errors poses a challenge. Seventy-five percent of medical institutions have used AI to improve disease prognosis and clinical error management. Artificial intelligence can examine patient data to swiftly detect minor inconsistencies, leading to proactive or reactive responses, avoiding potential disasters.

## *Deeper Patient Bonds*

AI technologies enable clinicians to spend more time interacting with patients, fostering deeper connections and meaningful relationships. AI scheduling tools are revolutionizing job descriptions, improving resource capacity, simplifying scheduling, and empowering patients.

### *Less Clerical Tasks (Physicians)*

AI is helping doctors revive their medical ambitions. AI technology is replacing at least 10% of the time physicians spend on routine administrative tasks like updating electronic health records or taking notes, as reported by multiple respondents. With limited time, clinicians are increasingly prioritizing AI technologies to focus on the most critical aspects of their profession.

***

## Broadview of Value

The growth and development of artificial intelligence bring about a diverse array of advantages. The applications of artificial intelligence extend beyond the healthcare sector. AI has proven its worth and impact in the healthcare industry by using AI-powered tools to analyze copious amounts of medical data and provide valuable insights to practitioners. Patients see improved outcomes, practitioners achieve more accurate diagnoses, and treatments become personalized.

The rise of recent technologies defines our current era. AI is the future of healthcare, and emerging technologies have the potential to revolutionize the field, transforming it in ways not seen since the dawn of modern medicine.

## Important Points

- The value proposition of AI in healthcare is found in its capacity to raise patient satisfaction, lower costs, and improve patient outcomes.
- By automating mundane operations, AI can boost productivity and reduce costs, allowing healthcare workers to focus on complex tasks.
- AI can speed up and improve disease and condition diagnosis, enabling earlier interventions and better results.
- AI can also reduce the stress on healthcare professionals by reducing administrative work, allowing them to spend more time with patients.
  - The value proposition of AI is vast and needs to be taken seriously.
  - The advantages far outweigh the disadvantages.
- AI, as a valued technology, can lighten the load of caregivers, creating a stress-free environment.

## Notes

1. Topol Eric. *Deep Medicine.* Basic Books; 1st edition (March 12, 2019).
2. Topol Eric. Article. *Wall Street Journal.* https://www.wsj.com/articles/eric-topol-and-stephen-r-quake-a-stethoscope-for-the-next-200-years-1420242913.

# Chapter 6

# Limitations of AI in Medicine

There have been recent developments in artificial intelligence and machine learning. Even when creators and educators correctly develop and teach AI systems, machine bias remains a significant concern. Building these AI systems morally is critical, keeping biases and ethics in mind. The way we employ and openly deploy these technologies impacts their effectiveness. Carefully evaluating the diversity and representativeness of the training data is important to avoid bias in AI systems.

While applying AI has sparked interest, there are risks and challenges that our industry must overcome. Despite the advantages of AI, there are concerns that cannot be overlooked.

- Injuries and Error.
- Algorithm Bias.
- Technology Dependence.
- Privacy Issues.
- Lack of Transparency.
- Ethical and Legal Issues.
- Cost.

## Injuries and Error

One potential risk is that AI systems may make errors, leading to patient harm or other healthcare problems. If an AI system suggests the incorrect medication, overlooks a tumor on a radiological scan, or

DOI: 10.4324/9781003661627-9

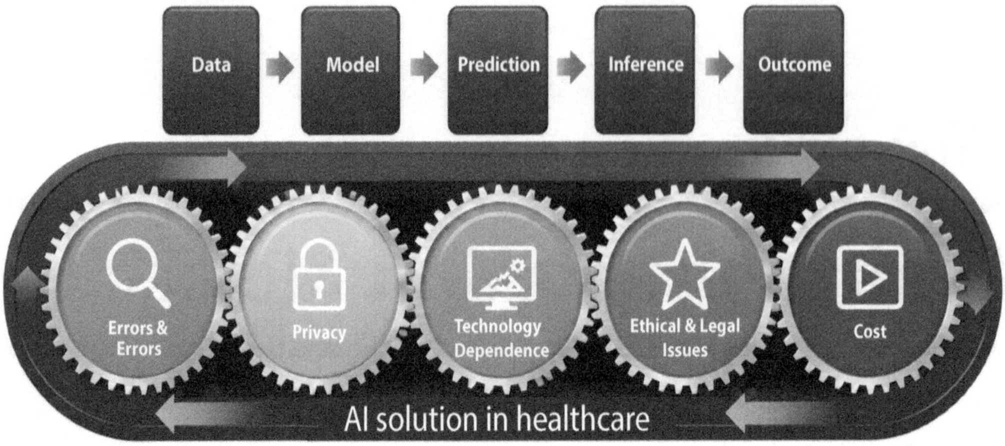


**Figure 6.1 Common challenges with AI in healthcare**

selects one patient over another based on an inaccurate prediction of who would benefit more, it could harm the patient. Even in the absence of AI, medical errors are responsible for many injuries in today's healthcare system.

At least two potential contrasts exist between human and AI failures (Figure 6.1). Injuries produced by software rather than human error may evoke different responses from patients and clinicians. If used extensively, one flaw in an AI system may harm thousands of patients instead of just a few patients affected by a single provider's error.

***

## Algorithm Bias

Large datasets are used to train AI systems, and the data quality influences the algorithm's effectiveness. If the data already contains biases, AI systems may increase them. For example, if they skew the data used to train the algorithm toward one demographic group, an AI system for identifying breast cancer may be less trustworthy for other demographic groups. Misdiagnosis and underdiagnosis could occur, both of which could be harmful.

## Technology Dependence

The reliance on technology could become excessive for healthcare providers as they increasingly use AI-powered tools and systems. This can lead to a decline in decision-making and critical thinking skills. In the event of technology failure, medical professionals may face delays in diagnosis and treatment because of a lack of backup plans.

## Privacy Issues

AI algorithms require extensive access to patient data. This collection contains sensitive information, including genetic data, personal details, and medical history. Unauthorized individuals may compromise and misuse the information, jeopardizing privacy and potentially harming patients.

## Lack of Transparency

Non-experts struggle to understand how AI algorithmic decision-making systems reach specific diagnoses or treatment strategies, which is why they are referred to as "black boxes." Healthcare providers might find it challenging to trust and rely on these systems.

## Ethical and Legal Issues

In healthcare, implementing AI creates many ethical and legal difficulties. Who has liability, for example, if an error committed by an AI program results in harm to a patient? Who uses and has authority over the data generated by systems powered by AI? There is still ongoing debate over these concerns, and we can provide no definitive answer.

## Cost

Building and implementing AI-powered systems can come with a high price tag. This expense may lead to increased healthcare costs, making it less affordable for those unable to pay.

## Human Monitoring and Surveillance

Despite AI advancements, human oversight remains critical in medical practice. Surgical robots, like their counterparts, prioritize logic over compassion. Healthcare practitioners can recognize critical behavioral cues to diagnose or prevent medical issues. AI might suggest a theoretically reasonable but impractical course of action due to logistical or economic limitations. Human intervention is necessary to minimize unnecessary operations and stop overprescribing drugs in these circumstances.

## May Not Consider Social Factors

Beyond their immediate physical concerns, patients often have additional needs. Specific patients may need personalized counseling that considers their social, economic, and historical backgrounds. Take, for instance, an AI system that can match patients to appropriate care facilities. Regrettably, this approach might not accommodate the patient's financial limitations or specific preferences.

Utilizing an AI system can compromise privacy, even if it offers the desired solution. Firms such as Amazon receive unrestricted autonomy in data collection and application. For example, hospitals may encounter unique challenges when transmitting data from mobile devices and desktops.

## Unemployment in the Healthcare Industry

In 2017, the UCSF Medical Center employed an artificial intelligence system to evaluate medical photographs and detect anomalies through utilizing a machine learning algorithm. It could detect abnormalities with the same precision as human radiologists, but at a faster rate and with fewer errors. This led to some layoffs at UCSF, as fewer radiologists were required to perform their duties.

Although AI can increase efficiency in healthcare and enhance patient care, it may also result in the loss of jobs.

With more healthcare organizations adopting AI systems, it is crucial to explore ways to retrain or reskill affected personnel. The World Economic

Forum's 2018 study predicts that AI will create 58 million alternative job opportunities by 2022. On the other hand, the research also shows that AI will eliminate or displace 75 million employees by 2025. As AI is integrated into various industries, jobs requiring repetitive labor will become outdated. AI has the potential to decrease costs and ease clinician stress, while also making certain roles unnecessary. Equity concerns may arise if this variable leads to the layoff of healthcare professionals who have invested in their education. The societal implications of AI in healthcare and medicine must be considered because of its potential to revolutionize these fields.

## Inaccuracies Are Still Possible

In 2020, researchers from Cambridge and Copenhagen Universities conducted a study to evaluate the accuracy of an AI application commonly used for diagnosing and prioritizing eye conditions. When compared to human ophthalmologists, researchers discovered the AI tool had a lower accuracy in identifying certain eye conditions. Observations made by the researchers show that particular illnesses in older individuals and women are more prone to misdiagnosis. Researchers observed that biases in the training data, which did not adequately represent a wide range of patients, contributed to the AI tool's inaccuracy.

Training AI algorithms on diverse and representative datasets is necessary to avoid biased and inaccurate conclusions. Although AI has the potential to reshape healthcare, these systems are unreliable and vulnerable to errors. Thus, healthcare professionals must thoroughly assess and scrutinize AI algorithms before using them in clinical settings to ensure safety and accuracy.

Cataloging millions of occurrences and collecting diagnosis data is essential for medical AI to function effectively. With no understanding of specific illnesses, populations, or environments, the likelihood of misdiagnosis increases significantly. When recommending a specific therapy, the importance of this aspect becomes clear because of the constant development and adaptation of AI to address data deficiencies. It is important to keep in mind that certain groups may be underrepresented. Spot-checking inaccuracies and inconsistencies will still require human involvement.

## Security Risk Susceptibility

The University of California, Berkeley conducted a study in 2019 that identified security risks in employing AI systems for X-rays and MRIs.

Researchers found these systems could be vulnerable to cyberattacks, leading to the manipulation of medical images and potentially resulting in incorrect diagnoses and treatments.

The absence of standardized encryption techniques and security policies led them to attribute the security flaws in AI medical imaging systems to the identified vulnerabilities in protecting patient information. Adequate cybersecurity protocols must be commonplace in healthcare institutions to prevent these attacks.

The study emphasizes the importance of prioritizing security measures when integrating AI systems and the role of cybersecurity in healthcare. Rigorous security standards and encryption techniques are crucial for accurate and safe AI-powered diagnoses and treatment plans. Moreover, the increasing use of AI-integrated medical devices presents additional difficulties.

Ensuring robust cybersecurity measures are present in healthcare is essential for the long-term success of offensive, initiative-taking AI applications. By leveraging AI's successes and failures, cyberattacks will become more complex in prediction and avoidance. This is analogous to how AI leverages data to improve the intelligence and precision of its systems. Once powerful attackers can bypass security measures, preventing attacks will become difficult.

AI's implementation in healthcare is expanding, increasing the utility and knowledge of technology, but not without facing and overcoming challenges and restrictions. AI alone may overlook social factors, lack knowledge about the population, and be vulnerable to advanced cyberattacks, so human control remains crucial.

## Data Complexity vs. Work Process Complexity

The success or failure of work process systems and data complexity on this AI journey relies on strategic planning and the effective selection, implementation, and optimization of AI technologies. AI's potential to transform healthcare lies in increasing efficiency of labor processes at lower costs. AI implementation allows providers to increase the accuracy and effectiveness of their processes, surpassing manual or non-AI options. When deploying AI in healthcare, it is necessary to factor in administrative and data operations.

Managing complex data sets, including health scans, patient reports, and medical records, is key to tackling the challenges presented by AI technologies.

It takes effort to develop models that can generate accurate results even with inadequate or inaccurate data inputs. These models should consider industry regulations and ever-changing factors. To accomplish this, it is important to understand the challenges posed by data and labor processes in healthcare AI applications.

# Chapter 7

# Setting Project Objectives

Like all other aspects of life, strategy is a highly intelligent and carefully planned course of action. Integrating AI in healthcare is not an outlier.

Without suitable objectives and guidelines, we will miss chances to define project scope, set expectations, and make informed decisions. To prevent implementation failure, the following considerations need examination when establishing project objectives for healthcare initiatives: the requirements of patients and healthcare professionals, the resources, and the broader implications for public health.

With daily announcements of new breakthroughs, artificial intelligence and machine learning are rapidly transforming the processes of research, patient care, systems, operations, purchasing, and implementing IT tools in the healthcare industry. As a result, we occupy thousands of healthcare organizations by staying abreast of the most recent offerings and innovative tools. This underscores the fundamental nature of objectives and planning.

Selecting a vendor for healthcare IT projects is inherently challenging, especially in a marketplace filled with optimism, enthusiasm, and grand ideas, which can make the process even more difficult. Incorporating AI into a workflow or service line has consequences that go beyond simple competition.

Organizations must integrate artificial intelligence in an initiative-taking, measurable, and step-by-step approach. Companies need a strategic plan to integrate AI into their clinical or operational processes and assess the impact on patient safety.

 DOI: 10.4324/9781003661627-10

What are the key factors that make up an AI strategy for healthcare development? How can provider companies mitigate risks when adopting emerging technologies in a fast-growing market?

Setting a simple use case leads to creating strategic objectives focused on advancement and enhancement. By using pilot programs, organizations can build and launch AI and machine learning solutions on a smaller scale. Implementing innovative technology in a restricted environment for testing and problem-solving before scaling up can benefit organizations.

A use case definition allows companies to determine required data and resulting capabilities accurately. Clearly defining what needs to be delivered can prevent getting involved too early with analytics, reports, and services that may not be available during AI strategy development. Comprehending the limits of our actions is of the utmost importance. To stay focused, we need to break down our options into smaller parts and not become distracted by temporary demands.

## Objective 1: Quality of Care

An inherent aim of integrating artificial intelligence into the healthcare sector is to augment the standard of care. This is of utmost importance in guaranteeing transparency, interpretability, and the absence of bias in AI systems. Regularly evaluating the efficacy of AI systems and incorporating healthcare professionals in their development and deployment can accomplish this.

## Objective 2: Clinical Workflows

Another goal is to improve the effectiveness of healthcare processes.

Utilizing AI-powered solutions can ease the workloads of healthcare workers by automating routine tasks and offering decision assistance. Preserving human judgment is essential in preventing AI systems from taking over completely.

Healthcare professionals should have the power to override AI advice when necessary and remain accountable for clinical decisions.

Designers need to prioritize user-friendliness and seamless integration with clinical workflows when designing AI systems for healthcare professionals. Well-designed clinical workflows should boost productivity, automate routine tasks, reduce errors, and improve patient outcomes.

## Objective 3: Patient Privacy

Besides enhancing quality care and optimizing clinical efficiency, it is essential to safeguard patient confidentiality. Ensuring patient privacy is vital and non-negotiable in the healthcare sector.

By using sophisticated algorithms, AI can aid healthcare personnel in securing patient data, especially when dealing with sensitive medical information like mental health diagnoses, life-or-death situations, and sexually transmitted diseases. To protect patient privacy, AI should automatically remove sensitive details from medical records, limiting access only to authorized healthcare professionals.

Creating AI-driven communication solutions that safeguard patient information privacy and enforce access restrictions relies on establishing secure communication platforms. Secure communication, encryption methods, and other precautions are essential for platforms to maintain patient-provider confidentiality and enable care.

Advancing this intended goal requires developing AI to ensure and deter privacy breaches in the future. It is of utmost importance to dedicate efforts toward enhancing AI systems in healthcare by identifying patterns and evaluating patient data that may present vulnerabilities. In the age of digital healthcare, where patient information is stored and shared electronically, we can prevent data breaches and ensure the protection of patient privacy by taking proactive measures.

Concerns have arisen about AI potentially using patient data for non-healthcare purposes, like insurance or marketing, leading to worries about other areas of patient privacy. Healthcare providers should ensure transparency regarding the usage of patient data in AI applications, and patients should have the ability to opt out of these programs if they prefer. To address these concerns, clear standards and rules governing the usage of AI must be established.

Healthcare providers can ensure the protection of patient information and compliance with regulations like HIPAA by implementing data security measures, obtaining patient consent for data use, and de-identifying data, as necessary. Patient privacy continues to be a paramount concern, and this purpose remains first in pursuing these advancements. AI can protect patient privacy by creating secure communication platforms, removing sensitive medical information, and identifying vulnerabilities. Governments and healthcare professionals must collaborate to establish clear protocols and standards to protect patient confidentiality and uphold their control over their medical data as AI evolves.

## Objective 4: Systems and Processes

Automation and augmentation are two distinct applications of artificial intelligence in healthcare. Both require implementation procedures and tasks. AI is now automating healthcare tasks that were previously manual tasks, including appointment scheduling, medical record maintenance, and insurance claim processing. Areas of automation comprise:

### *Electronic Health Records (EHRs)*

Electronic health records (EHRs) contain patient data such as medical history, treatments, and test results. AI can automate updating EHRs, allowing doctors and nurses to prioritize patient care.

### *Medical Billing*

AI can automate the medical billing process by identifying errors and inconsistencies in claims, reducing the risk of denied claims, and saving time and money.

### *Inventory Management*

AI can automate inventory management in hospitals and clinics since artificial intelligence replaces or complements human labor in regular tasks, like processing inventory and smoothing procurement and delivery.

### *Augmentation*

Augmentation, which is coordinated with medical records or appointment scheduling, entails applying artificial intelligence to enhance human capabilities, such as illness prognosis or diagnosis. The major distinction between these two methodologies is the extent to which artificial intelligence replaces or supports human labor. Automation may thus result in eliminating positions in certain fields, but augmentation enables healthcare professionals to allocate their efforts toward more intricate duties and critical decision-making. However, both methodologies might enhance healthcare delivery in terms of efficiency, accuracy, and patient outcomes. The decision to opt for automation or augmentation will be determined by the specific demands and objectives of individual healthcare facilities.

Augmentation offers various advantages, such as allowing AI to enhance human problem-solving and decision-making abilities by identifying illness patterns and other consequences that humans may miss. This might cause more precise prognostications or diagnoses for patients.

## Objective 5: Efficiency, Effectiveness, Innovation

Considering the ongoing global transformation, it is critical to recognize the paramount importance of adopting methods that optimize healthcare efficiency and stimulate innovation. We must implement this technology with forethought and efficacy, as its application can bring about a significant paradigm shift within the healthcare sector. To accomplish this purpose, stakeholders must design and build solutions intending to be used for an extended period across several healthcare sectors.

## Objective 6: Seamless Processes and Easier Communication

It might be challenging to provide patients with high-quality care because of the inefficiencies and complexities that frequently plague healthcare systems. As a potent instrument, artificial intelligence must improve communication and streamline operations in healthcare settings.

Streamlining patient intake and triage procedures is an area of focus. As intended goals, we ensure AI eliminates the laborious and time-consuming patient intake procedures that frequently depend on erroneous and delayed manual data entry. AI-powered intake systems should collect and process patient data automatically, enabling healthcare personnel to evaluate patient requirements promptly and distribute resources in a judicious manner. This approach not only enhances patient outcomes but also streamlines administrative processes and maximizes the use of resources.

Developers of artificial intelligence must prioritize easing communication among patients, organizations, and healthcare providers. Coordinated care frequently requires effective communication, but language difficulties and time-consuming paperwork frequently impede this. By implementing a robust course of action, we may leverage language translation and transcription services powered by artificial intelligence to surmount these obstacles, facilitating more effective communication and resulting in enhanced patient outcomes and satisfaction.

## Objective 7: Expert Strategy-Decision Making

AI can assist healthcare providers in making better-informed judgments, further enhancing communication and optimizing operations. AI systems can spot patterns and trends in vast quantities of patient data, enabling physicians to formulate precise diagnoses, devise efficacious treatment strategies, and give patients more individualized care.

Professional strategy is of utmost importance. Because of the potentially critical nature of the outcomes, physicians should have access to professional procedures that facilitate forming more informed and impartial judgments. The algorithms possess the capability to analyze and comprehend clinical factors through the use of machine learning. They are applied in hospitals across the globe and enable treating personnel to personalize and follow up with patients to decrease readmissions and hospital stays, hence reducing the overall cost of healthcare.

Despite their extensive training in diagnostic patterns and patient care, physicians can still be caught off guard by unexpected diagnoses. AI models can help clinicians identify these diagnoses from patient records. This can enable physicians to dive deeper into a patient's medical history and intervene to improve patient outcomes.

While maintaining a receptive attitude toward learning and experimenting with novel concepts—which are essential for the success of any healthcare AI-integrated undertaking—BrainX's mission is to foster and investigate evolving cultures. We go on this path not alone. Many healthcare companies remain receptive to experimenting with innovative strategies, gaining insight from errors, and concentrating on expansion that is scalable to any healthcare AI methodology or concept.

## Innovation Strategy through Identification of Unknown Correlations

Without exception, innovation is the cornerstone of the success of any industry, including healthcare. Indeed, innovation in healthcare is vital because it has the potential to improve the standard of treatment and save lives. Identifying unidentified relationships with the aid of AI is one method of fostering innovation; this can inspire originality and result in substantial advances in healthcare. AI implementation in healthcare is not novel. For several years, AI has been used in healthcare, mostly for diagnoses and therapy.

However, recent advancements in artificial intelligence have enabled the detection of previously unknown relationships. Given a result, we have presented healthcare with opportunities for innovation, as the relationships between several unknown variables remain unclear.

Applying AI has allowed healthcare to identify an association between a certain gene and a disease that might not have been recognized before. Healthcare experts may gain fresh perspectives on patient outcomes, therapies, and diseases by discerning these unidentified relationships. There is an ever-present need to develop new treatments.

# Chapter 8

# AI Regulation in Healthcare

> The promise of artificial intelligence in medicine is to provide composite, panoramic views of individuals' medical data; to improve decision making; to avoid errors such as misdiagnosis and unnecessary procedures; to help in the ordering and interpretation of appropriate tests; and to recommend treatment.
>
> —**Eric Topol,** *Deep Medicine: How Artificial Intelligence Can Make Healthcare Human Again*[1]

Open any webpage, device, or book and it would be a challenge not to see the impact of AI. However, with the surge of large language models for consumers, including the artificial intelligence sensation ChatGPT and competitors like Bloom and Stable Diffusion, the ever-present need for regulation is at the forefront. Since its debut in November 2022, ChatGPT has generated much excitement and recently surpassed over 100 million users worldwide. With the advent of AI across sectors, there have been challenges for regulating AI to be transparent, ethical, and unbiased. With this in focus, regulations and oversight in safe AI algorithm development are now at the top of the list.

Healthcare policy with AI is developing swiftly. This is a significant concern for lawmakers, Americans, and healthcare enterprises. There is an immediate need for a proper regulatory outlook. At BrainX, we recognize the role regulatory briefs play in helping healthcare organizations simplify complicated healthcare policy and regulatory issues. We need to move toward identifying important points, next steps in facilitating compliance, and directing strategic decision-making.

DOI: 10.4324/9781003661627-11

With the rapid expansion of AI in healthcare, policymakers should develop regulation updates covering both the public and private sectors as a matter of high-level importance. As policymakers establish new policy changes, it is vital to include strategic regulatory elements. This will enable leaders in the healthcare and life sciences industries to implement AI swiftly and decisively.

Recently, Elon Musk, the CEO of Tesla and SpaceX, advocated for governmental limits on artificial intelligence in the marketplace and across the industry. In an interview, Musk stated that artificial intelligence is "Possibly more destructive than nukes," and that "We need government control to safeguard public safety."[2] Musk has called for creating a regulatory agency to oversee the development and deployment of AI technology. He believes agencies should collaborate with experts in the field to address potential implications of AI on the labor market and safety issues. He wants to set safety norms and laws for implementing AI systems. According to his predictions, AI could evolve to the point where it can replace human labor, causing a large-scale unemployment problem.

However, not everyone agrees with government regulation of AI. Some argue that governmental overreach could stifle innovation and hinder progress in the industry. Governments need to create sustainable health systems, tackle inequality and bias, and improve the overall health of the world's population. We must ensure that we identify, engage, and treat the right patients early and assist governments worldwide in solving all these challenges.

In a published work in October 2021, Babylon developed a Code of Ethics and Standards for AI Integration. Inside the code, they made a public declaration of their mission with AI, stating,

> Babylon Health founded itself with a single purpose: to put an accessible, affordable health service into the hands of every person on earth. Everything else flows from this; our values, how we behave, what we expect, and how we collaborate with each other to deliver our mission.[3]

Decision-makers and business leaders must address AI's advantages and potential risks and collaborate to implement legislation to ensure responsible and safe usage.

As of early 2026, there are over 1200 U.S. FDA (Food and Drug Administration) approved algorithms available for application in healthcare. Most of these are for radiology, but the list is growing for other healthcare specialty applications, too. Understanding developing FDA and other regulations is important in the successful application of AI in healthcare.[4]

***

## Advantages of AI Regulation in Healthcare

With the creation of artificial intelligence, the healthcare sector has undergone a significant revolution. Applying AI raises issues with data privacy, patient safety, and prejudice. Therefore, AI regulation has countless benefits, which are urgently needed. Let us examine:

- Patient Data Safety.
- Bias and Discrimination.
- Transparency and Accountability.
- Innovation and Competition.

### *Patient Data Safety*

AI regulation can ensure patient safety. To do so, we must first leverage large-scale patient data analysis using AI in healthcare while remaining conscious of individual patient care decisions based on this data. To minimize errors that could harm patients, AI systems must be precise and trustworthy. Therefore, developers should adhere to strict safety requirements and conduct extensive testing before developing and implementing AI systems in healthcare. However, with AI regulation addressing data privacy and security issues, AI systems must rely on vast amounts of secure patient data, including sensitive personal information, such as medical histories and genetic data. The misuse or theft of this data can have severe consequences for patients, including identity theft, discrimination, and misdiagnosis. Therefore, AI regulations must establish precise guidelines for data collection, storage, security, and use to address these issues and ensure the protection of patient data. These securities should set guidelines on allowed use and purposes, ensuring patient data safety.[5]

### *Alleviate Bias and Discrimination*

AI legislation is critical for addressing issues of prejudice and discrimination. Subjective assessments and treatment may occur due to biased data, as AI systems are only as objective as the data they are trained on. We must implement strong and supportive norms to protect various patient groups, particularly those from marginalized communities, from disparities in healthcare outcomes. Developers must ensure that AI systems are fair and equitable under rigorous regulation by requiring the creation of unbiased algorithms and testing AI systems for bias. This will ensure that all patients have access to ethical healthcare.[6]

### *Transparency and Accountability*

Finally, AI regulation can improve transparency and accountability in the healthcare industry. We often see AI systems as "black boxes," and it is challenging to understand how they arrive at their decisions. This lack of transparency can make it challenging to hold healthcare providers accountable for their decisions and erode patient trust. AI regulation can require transparency in AI decision-making, ensuring that patients and healthcare providers understand how AI systems arrive at their decisions. This can help promote accountability and improve patient trust in the healthcare system.

### *Innovation and Competition Regulation*

The healthcare sector may gain significantly from AI regulation, as it encourages innovation and competition, patient safety, accountability, and improved provider trust. With careful consideration of the ethical implications of AI technology and implementation of the relevant legal frameworks, these benefits can be obtained while maintaining patient autonomy and privacy.

***

## Disadvantages of Regulation

During his recent visit to Sweden for a meeting with the EU-U.S. Trade and Technology Council, Anthony Blinken stated that the United States was working with European allies to develop artificial intelligence conduct codes. Along with Blinken, European Commission Vice President Margrethe Vestager said, "We need accountable artificial intelligence. Generative AI is a complete game changer."[7] According to the Associated Press, Blinken added, "The council has an important role to play in helping establish voluntary codes of conduct that would be open to all like-minded countries."[8]

Globally, the influence of artificial intelligence is expanding. In the United States, people are increasingly concerned about implementing algorithms in medical diagnosis and treatment. They recognize the need for a code of conduct for algorithmic decision-making systems in this field. While existing rules may detect adverse biases in these instruments, algorithmic decision-making systems and AI are progressively increasing within the medical domain.

The public and most physicians remain in the dark regarding the intricacies of the tools' development. This lack of transparency poses a risk of automating and worsening biases inside the healthcare system. The guidelines recently issued by the FDA significantly broaden the scope of instruments that fall under their regulatory purview. This revised recommendation emphasizes the urgency for additional measures to combat bias and promote equity, considering the increasing prevalence and utilization of AI and algorithmic tools.

The apprehensions expressed by prominent American CEOs and technology experts over the perils of artificial intelligence have brought to light that it has the potential to both advance and undermine civilizations. Regarding healthcare, a customized strategy is required, with regulations aiming to establish an AI-dedicated council that is well-versed in the benefits and drawbacks of AI and its various applications. Since our government is decades behind in this area, we cannot maximize this opportunity. Consumers and policymakers ought to exercise prudence when investigating developments in artificial intelligence and using it, asserting that existing AI models cause harm to human beings.

## *Bias in Medical and Public Health Tools*

According to a 2019 study, varying hospitals used clinical algorithms that prejudiced patients of specific racial and cultural backgrounds, considering them sicker than patients of other races advised of the same therapy. For instance, the algorithm used historical data to train and determine that African American patients historically had lower healthcare spending compared to Caucasian patients because of historical wealth and income differences.

Subsequently, they improved the algorithm because of this. However, even though researchers discovered and fixed the bias in this algorithm, the incident raised the possibility of enforcing strict controls in algorithm development.

Developing AI ethical and legal issues in healthcare presents problems and challenges. During the presidency of Barack Obama, the U.S. government released papers on artificial intelligence that addressed a range of subjects, including the use of AI for the public's benefit and concerns regarding justice, security, and governance. For instance, one conclusion highlighted is the need for developing moral AI while concurrently promoting fairness, transparency, and accountability by design. We have included our interpretation of the White House Bill of Rights with artificial intelligence below.

The White House Office of Science and Technology Policy has identified five principles that ought to govern the design, implementation, and utilization of automated systems designed to safeguard the American public in the era of artificial intelligence, intending to further President Biden's vision. An AI Bill of Rights serves as a blueprint for a future society in which technologies are used to uphold our highest values while safeguarding all individuals from these threats.

To develop this framework, researchers, technologists, advocates, journalists, and policymakers consulted and responded to the experiences of the American public. Our team offers a technical companion guidebook to assist individuals in their efforts to integrate these safeguards into policy and practice. They outline detailed procedures for incorporating these principles into the technological design process in the manual. These principles offer direction in situations where automated technologies have the potential to significantly affect the rights, opportunities, or access to essential necessities of the people.

In the age of artificial intelligence, the Blueprint for an AI Bill of Rights is a collection of five principles and associated practices that govern the design, implementation, and operation of automated systems to safeguard the rights of the American public. Formulated by comprehensive consultation with the American people, these principles serve as a roadmap for the construction and implementation of automated systems that safeguard civil liberties, privacy, and rights under democratic norms. The five principles contain concrete steps that organizations of all sizes and types—from governments to corporations—can implement to uphold these values.

Experts representing the private sector, governments, and international consortia have published the principles and frameworks directing the responsible utilization of automated systems. This framework offers a sector-neutral national values statement and toolkit to facilitate the incorporation of these safeguards into technological design, policy, and practice.

Current legislation and regulations do not advise whether sector-specific privacy laws and supervision obligations should apply to the Blueprint for an AI Bill of Rights.

The White House Office of Science and Technology Policy led a year-long effort to collect and synthesize input from individuals nationwide regarding algorithmic and data-driven harms and potential remedies. This effort was on behalf of policymakers throughout the Federal Government, affected communities, industry stakeholders, technology developers, and other experts from a variety of fields and sectors. Through panel discussions, public listening sessions, meetings, a formal request for information, and contributions to a widely publicized and publicly accessible email address, individuals from all over the United States, public servants from Federal agencies, and members of the international community engaged in dialogue regarding the potential benefits and drawbacks of these technologies. Their contributions significantly influenced the development of the Blueprint for an AI Bill of Rights.

We have reached a consensus about AI's transformative potential to enhance Americans' lives and the necessity and attainability of preventing the negative effects of these technologies, according to these discussions. The White House has identified Five Rights. They are the following: (1) safe and effective systems; (2) algorithmic discrimination protections; (3) data privacy; (4) notice and explanation; and (5) human alternatives, consideration, and fallback.

**Safe and Effective Systems**: Protection from inappropriate data use in the design, development, and deployment of automated systems, and the compounded harm of its reuse, is crucial. The domain-specific standards identify and mitigate unsafe outcomes through continuous monitoring of their intended use. Outcomes include deploying a system, removing a system from use, or protecting you from the harmful impacts of automated systems proactively.

An independent assessor should evaluate and report to confirm the system's safety and effectiveness, including steps taken to mitigate potential harm. We recommend publishing the findings of the evaluation.

**Algorithmic Discrimination Protections**: There should be no discrimination based on algorithmic performance, and the design and implementation of systems should be fair. Algorithmic discrimination transpires when automated systems inadvertently facilitate differential treatment or have adverse effects on individuals based on any legally protected classification, including but not limited to race, color, ethnicity, sex (including gender identity, intersex status, pregnancy, childbirth, and related medical conditions), religion, age, national origin, disability, veteran status, genetic information, and national origin. Violating legal protections may occur because of algorithmic discrimination, contingent upon the circumstances.

Those involved in creating automated systems must follow consistent and initiative-taking procedures to protect communities and individuals from algorithmic bias, while also ensuring the fair use and design of technologies. The safeguards should include assessing fairness during system design, protecting against using proxies for demographic information and using representative data, ensuring accessibility for people with disabilities throughout the design and development process, conducting testing to identify and address disparities before and during deployment, and maintaining transparent organizational oversight.

To validate the effectiveness of these safeguards, the organization should conduct an algorithmic impact assessment comprising plain language reporting and independent review. This assessment should include the outcomes of disparity testing and information on mitigation strategies.

**Data Privacy**: We should safeguard user data from abusive data practices through inherent protections, and users should have control over data utilization. By implementing design decisions that incorporate privacy protections by default, such as ensuring that data collection adheres to reasonable expectations and collects only the strictly necessary data for the context, we should safeguard individuals against privacy breaches.

To ensure the utmost respect for and handling of personal data, it is imperative that designers, developers, and deployers of automated systems obtain your consent and adhere to your decisions concerning its collection, use, access, transfer, and deletion. When it is not feasible to do so, designers, developers, and deployers of automated systems should implement alternative privacy-by-design safeguards. Systems should not make design choices that limit human autonomy or invade user privacy by default. Systems should only utilize consent to legitimize data gathering when users can grant it in a suitable and meaningful manner.

Consent requests must be succinct, comprehensible in everyday language, and afford the user control over data collection and the context of utilization. The existing cumbersome notice-and-choice procedures governing extensive data uses ought to be revised. Enhanced safeguards and limitations should apply to data and conclusions concerning sensitive sectors such as finance, health, employment, education, criminal justice, and youth-related information.

We should not permit unrestricted surveillance of individuals or communities. To safeguard civil rights and privacy, we must subject surveillance technologies to stricter control, including pre-deployment assessments of their potential harms and scope limitations. Continuous surveillance and monitoring ought to be avoided in housing, education, employment, and other settings where implementing such technology might restrict access, opportunities, or rights. We must grant individuals access to reporting that verifies abiding data decision-making on personal information and assesses the potential repercussions of surveillance technologies on their rights, opportunities, or access.

**Notice and Explanation**: You must know that an automated system is being used and comprehend how and why it influences results that influence you. It is imperative that designers, developers, and deployers of automated systems furnish documentation in plain language that is universally comprehensible. This documentation should be comprised of concise explanations of the system's operational principles, the function of automation, notification that the system is operational, identification of the accountable individual or organization, and timely, transparent, and easily understandable reports of system outcomes.

Keeping this notice current and informing those affected by the system of major changes to essential functionality or use must occur. You must understand the process and rationale behind determining any conclusion that affects you by an automated system, even if it is not the only input contributing to that outcome.

Automated system explanations should be context-adjusted to the amount of risk involved. They need to be technically valid, relevant, and valuable to you, operators, or others who need to comprehend the system. Automated system explanations should be adjusted to the context and the amount of risk involved.

**Human Alternatives, Consideration, and Fallback**: When applicable, you should be able to opt out and have access to a representative who can promptly address and resolve any issues you may have. If applicable, you should be able to deactivate automated systems in favor of a human alternative. Determining appropriateness in any setting should rely on realistic expectations, with an emphasis on safeguarding the public from particularly detrimental impacts and ensuring widespread accessibility. The law may require using a person or an alternate in certain circumstances.

We should grant users prompt human intervention and resolution through a fallback and escalation procedure if an automated system malfunctions, generates an error, or if they wish to appeal or question the consequences it has on them.

Besides maintaining accessibility, equity, and effectiveness, we should ensure human concern, followed by operator training. They should not place an undue strain on the general population. Proper functioning in critical sectors such as education, health, criminal justice, and employment should customize automated systems to their specific objectives, enable meaningful access for oversight, provide training for all individuals interacting with the system, and factor in human judgment when making adverse or high-risk decisions.

Whenever viable, we should make reporting public, including describing these human governance procedures and evaluating their timeliness, accessibility, outcomes, and efficacy.

However, there is considerable dispute regarding how the government should oversee technology and strongly regulate artificial intelligence. Mandatory regulation of AI in healthcare is crucial because of its prominence in the scientific community. Such regulation provides clinicians and caregivers with the limits to analyze patient data, make secure and accurate diagnoses, and identify trends and patterns that may inspire the development of innovative treatments.

Concerns over the potential for AI rules to disrupt markets, exacerbate inequality, and introduce additional hazards to public safety and national security are increasing in volume. Without regulatory help, we can exploit AI technology in healthcare for lethal or bad objectives, significantly complicating management efforts. AI development is susceptible to exploitation and disruption by both local and remote sources because of the system's usability and accessibility. Because of the significant potential for misuse, most healthcare organizations consider these AI technologies to be critical to individual and national security as geopolitical tensions escalate globally. Because of greater economic integration and interconnectedness, the consequences and implications of regulated technical developments are also more likely to spread across industries and nations globally.

To make the successful transition with artificial intelligence, there needs to be an ongoing effort to address fundamental values and principles. Relevant role players must present a unified vision of the values and principles—such as equity, equality, inclusivity, responsibility, transparency, and accountability—that certain technological advancements and the best ways to protect them may adversely affect. This task will require fresh thinking about how to ensure that certain technologies, such as biotechnology, predictive algorithms, or technologies that allow for the exploitation of resources and do not exacerbate already existing socioeconomic inequalities. Unfortunately, new threats accompany innovative technology, bringing the need for governmental regulation in healthcare.

In a recent paper in *The National Library of Medicine*, titled "Artificial Intelligence in Health Care: Accountability and Safety," the authors wrote,

> The prospect of patient harm caused by the decisions made by an artificial intelligence-based clinical tool is something to which current practices of moral accountability and safety assurance worldwide have not yet adjusted. Two focus implications of clinical decision-making involve artificial intelligence: moral accountability for harm to patients and safety assurance to protect patients against such liability.[9]

Moral responsibility concerning accountability is at the top of the list of significant matters. The systems described are examples of assistive artificial intelligence systems in health care, where, in such cases, human clinicians decide whether to act on the system's recommendations. Human clinicians meet both control and epistemic conditions regarding this final decision. Once the decision-making process begins, a clinician cannot directly alter the final decision once it has already started.

Unless regulated, clinicians cannot be confident that AI software is reaching conclusions that reflect their clinical intentions. There is also epistemic uncertainty about how the clinician reached the recommendation. In addition, broader structural and organizational factors will influence the decision to implement recommendations, such as the workload of clinicians and the development of automation.

We need to develop and implement new rules and regulations, passing new laws, to ensure the moral and responsible use of AI. And while the healthcare sector stands to profit from these laws over time, AI is helping doctors better than ever diagnose and treat illnesses and increase positive patient outcomes.

## Technology Advancement

The escalating institutional and governmental oversight of artificial intelligence in healthcare is serving as a catalyst for the remarkable technological progress within this domain. By imposing rigorous regulations on developing and deploying AI-powered healthcare solutions, regions establish a structure that promotes innovation while minimizing potential hazards. This development has yielded medical technologies that are more precise and effective in the diagnosis and treatment of ailments.

Given the considerable potential of artificial intelligence technology implementation in the healthcare industry, regulatory oversight is progressively growing in importance to guarantee the ethical and responsible utilization of such technologies. Even though regulation has some benefits, it also has several significant negatives.

### Stifling Innovation

A significant limitation of AI laws inside the healthcare industry is their potential to impede innovation. Organizations must show a substantial financial investment and a willingness to assume risks to create and deploy innovative AI solutions within the healthcare sector. Implementing innovative AI technologies might incur greater financial and temporal burdens, hence impeding the ability of smaller enterprises and entrepreneurs to contend. This could restrict investment in AI technologies to the most notable and well-funded corporations, stifling innovation and causing the sector to stagnate.

### Unintended Consequences

Unforeseen consequences represent an additional disadvantage of healthcare AI policy. Regulatory measures may hinder healthcare practitioners' capacity to diagnose and treat patients accurately, despite their role in guaranteeing the ethical implementation of AI technology and patient protection. One example of this would be if excessive regulation of AI technology forces healthcare providers to use less precise and effective methods of diagnosis and treatment. Many regulations that may hinder the progress of artificial intelligence technologies have the potential to significantly enhance patient outcomes.

### Lack of Standardization

A lack of uniformity may also come from regulating artificial intelligence in healthcare. It can be difficult for enterprises to navigate the regulatory environment and develop technologies that comply with all regulations because regulatory agencies and nations have their own internal regulations, which may clash. This may cause AI technology to offer limited availability, impeding patient access and diminishing the potential advantages associated with its use.

## *Compliance Increase*

Increased compliance costs represent a further disadvantage of AI regulation in healthcare. Developing and implementing methods to ensure that AI technologies comply with the criteria set by each regulatory body may be a costly and time-consuming endeavor for businesses. Certain restrictions may also cause supplementary personnel, such as specialized workers, to oversee the development and implementation of certain AI systems.

When implemented in a manner that violates the rights of American citizens, the use of technology, data, and automated processes represents one of the greatest threats to democracy in the twenty-first century. Too frequently, individuals employ these instruments to impede our opportunities and deny us access to essential products or services. An abundance of documentation exists regarding these issues. On a national and global scale, for instance, patient care support systems have been hazardous, ineffective, or biased. Hiring and credit decision-making algorithms may incorporate or sustain detrimental biases and discriminatory practices. Individuals have faced constrained prospects, encroachment upon their privacy and personal space, and monitoring of their activity—often without their awareness or agreement.

International regulatory bodies are developing benchmarks for implementing artificial intelligence in the healthcare sector, considering the imperative for robust AI oversight. As an illustration, Baymax, the robotic healthcare assistant and unanticipated hero from *Big Hero 6*, is an intriguing, animated persona and a fantasy portrayal of the future of technology.

Nevertheless, the Baymax figure represents an artificial intelligence system with astoundingly realistic prospective applications in the healthcare sector, fashioned by the creators. However, as artificial intelligence technology advances, how can authorities foster innovation while maintaining patient safety? It begins by acknowledging the imprecision of the term "AI," which is applied to systems capable of processing and responding to inputs in a manner akin to human cognition.

Because of the widespread application of AI in multiple sectors, including education, healthcare, and the military, healthcare professionals have used AI to increase efficiency and enhance patient care for years. Although the existing rules and regulations do not specifically address the use of AI in healthcare environments, healthcare professionals have implemented no legislation despite the industry's stringent regulations.

Using AI in healthcare has been the subject of discussion, and many nations and organizations, including the United States government, continue to build norms and regulations governing the application of AI beyond the healthcare sector. At present, there is no legislation in any country that specifically regulates AI-related data privacy concerns. However, industry-specific limitations and the introduction of more artificial intelligence solutions have prompted these products to enforce stricter regulations on "high-risk" AI applications.

One of the most pressing issues of the present day is the potential infringement upon the rights of the American people using technology, data, and automated systems. Media outlets have reported these concerns extensively.

Assistive systems intended to facilitate patient care have shown deficiencies in safety, efficacy, or impartiality domestically and internationally. We have discovered that algorithms in many industries and healthcare sectors replicate and reproduce existing disparities, besides ingraining new negative biases and discrimination. Without their knowledge or approval, unauthorized data collection has been used to invade privacy and track individuals' every move.

Despite the overwhelming negativity of these outcomes, they are avoidable. Using automated systems has resulted in remarkable advantages, encompassing algorithms for illness detection, computers that forecast the routes of storms, and equipment that aids farmers in cultivating food more efficiently. Presently, these technologies influence sector-wide decisions of considerable magnitude, while data helps to revolutionize global industries.

American innovation propels these instruments; regulation is imperative to guarantee the ethical and responsible development and implementation of AI in the healthcare sector. Besides ensuring patient safety and confidentiality, governmental bodies and institutions ought to establish AI standards that encompass transparency, accountability, and data privacy and security requirements. Doing so would aid in the prevention of unethical or malicious AI applications in healthcare. Collaboration between healthcare practitioners and AI developers is necessary, besides legislation. AI needs to be perceived not as a substitute for human expertise, but as a supplement that augments it. The development and testing of AI systems should involve healthcare professionals to guarantee they are effective and safe in all circumstances.

***

## Important Points

- International authorities are creating standards for the use of AI in healthcare to address the need for strong AI regulation.
- One of the greatest challenges today is using technology, data, and automated systems in ways that threaten the rights of the American people.
- International authorities are creating standards for AI use in healthcare in response to the need for strong AI regulation.

## Notes

1. Topol Eric. *Deep Medicine*. Basic Books; 1st edition (March 12, 2019).
2. https://www.cnbc.com/2018/03/13/elon-musk-at-sxsw-a-i-is-more-dangerous-than-nuclear-weapons.html.
3. Babylon Health. Code of Conduct. October 2021. https://www.sec.gov/Archives/edgar/data/1866390/000186639023000055/bbln-20221231.htm.
4. FDA. Medical Device Information and Software. https://www.fda.gov/medical-devices/software-medical-device-samd/artificial-intelligence-enabled-medical-devices.
5. General Data Protection Regulation. https://gdpr.eu/what-is-gdpr/.
6. Article. Artificial Intelligence. Europe. https://digital-strategy.ec.europa.eu/en/policies/european-approach-artificial-intelligence.
7. Vesteger Martha. Code of Conduct. https://www.reuters.com/technology/eus-vestager-sees-draft-code-conduct-ai-within-weeks-2023-05-31/.
8. Associated Press News. 2023. https://apnews.com/article/artificial-intelligence-voluntary-code-of-conduct-regulation-585f2aaff6bfbdbcee572b347fa97cff.
9. Habli I, Lawton T, Porter Z. Artificial intelligence in health care: Accountability and safety. *Bulletin of the World Health Organization*. 2020 Apr 1;98(4):251–256. https://doi.org/10.2471/BLT.19.237487. Epub 2020 Feb 25. PMID: 32284648; PMCID: PMC7133468.s

# Chapter 9

# AI and Intellectual Property

> The pace of progress in artificial intelligence (I'm not referring to narrow AI) is incredibly fast. Unless you have direct exposure to groups like DeepMind, you have no idea how fast—it is growing at a pace close to exponential. The risk of something seriously dangerous happening is in the five-year time frame. Ten years at most.
>
> **—Elon Musk: Comment on Edge.org**[1]

In January 2015, the late Stephen Hawking once wrote in his open letter from "Research Priorities for Robust and Beneficial Artificial Intelligence,"

> The establishment of shared theoretical frameworks, combined with obtaining data and processing power, has yielded remarkable successes in various component tasks such as speech recognition, image classification, autonomous vehicles, machine translation, legged locomotion, and question-answering system capabilities in these areas and others cross the threshold from laboratory research to economically valuable technologies, a virtuous cycle takes hold whereby even small performance improvements are worth large sums of money, prompting greater investments in research. There is a broad consensus that AI research is progressing and that its impact on society will increase…because of the enormous potential of AI, it is important to research how to reap its benefits while avoiding potential pitfalls.[2]

Hawking was right. One of the many pitfalls in AI is prizing research and strategic intellectual property (IP) patents protecting ideation within AI


DOI: 10.4324/9781003661627-12

circles. Artificial intelligence could significantly increase the efficiency of the current economy. Still, it has proven to have a more significant impact by acting as a new "method of invention" that can alter the structure of research and development, patent protection, and innovation processes in many healthcare fields.

BrainX has endeavored to distinguish between advancements in "deep learning" to serve as a general-purpose method of invention. We additionally recognize that future research output and innovation-focused competition may rely heavily on policies promoting transparency, IP protection, and sharing critical statistics between the public and private sectors.

The United States Patent and Trademark Office (USPTO) has developed specific web pages and reports, portraying emerging AI across America's industry sectors. Recently, the USPTO issued a report entitled "Public Opinions on Artificial Intelligence and Intellectual Property Policy," which examines, in-depth, the wide range of perspectives regarding the impact of artificial intelligence on the intellectual property landscape, including patent, trademark, copyright, and trade secret policy, as well as emerging issues regarding database protection. The new report shows the agency's unwavering commitment to keeping up with this critical and rapidly developing technology to speed up American innovation.

According to the report, regarding AI and intellectual property,

> A key priority of the United States Patent and Trademark Office is to maintain United States leadership in innovation, especially in emerging technologies, including artificial intelligence. To further this goal, the USPTO actively engages with the innovation community and AI experts to promote the understanding and reliability of IP rights concerning AI technology. The USPTO ensures IP incentives are in place to encourage further innovation in and around this critical area.[3,]

Wilbur Ross, U.S. Secretary of Commerce, stated that on February 11, 2019, President Trump signed Executive Order 13859 announcing the American Artificial Intelligence Initiative, the nation's strategy for artificial intelligence. "As artificial intelligence technologies continue to advance, the United States will not cede its global innovation leadership. The Department of Commerce acknowledges signifying utilizing American ingenuity to advance and safeguard our economic security."

There are several ways in which a natural person can contribute to conceiving an AI invention and be credited as an inventor. For instance, designing the algorithm and weighting adaptations, structuring the data on which the algorithm will operate, executing the AI algorithm on the data, and getting the results. As with other technological fields, AI may offer opportunities for innovation. For instance, designing an AI algorithm, implementing specific hardware to improve an AI algorithm, or applying methods for preparing inputs for an AI algorithm may raise patent issues. Many innovators in an AI system could generate a pool or chain of invention rights. As with many AI algorithms, there is the possibility that multiple individuals could play a role in the innovation of the AI system.

Article 35 of the United States Constitution (35 U.S.C 100) defines "inventor" as "the person or, with a joint invention, the individuals collectively who invented or discovered the subject of the invention." The law requires making a specific determination of the person or persons who have legally contributed to conceiving an AI invention and can be credited as an inventor. In addition, Article 35 U.S.C 116 states that two or more people may jointly invent something even if they did not work together physically, each did not make the same type or amount of contribution, or each did not contribute to each patent claim.

Many governmental agencies recognize the urgency to address the many challenges with AI implementation, and the Federal Government has now prioritized AI-related research and development activities addressing AI's ethical, legal, and societal implications. There is an urgency to address the safety and security of AI systems. For instance, in collaboration with a major technology company, the National Science Foundation's (NSF) Program on Fairness in Artificial Intelligence supports research on fairness in AI to contribute to trustworthy AI systems readily accepted and deployed to address society's challenges of bias and ethics. The NSF collaborated with a non-profit to fund early concept grants for exploratory research on AI and society to better understand AI technology's social challenges and encourage scientific contributions to their resolution. With patients and doctors in a close-knit relationship with privacy and HIPAA, the importance of providing AI systems with explainability mechanisms that help human users comprehend the reasoning behind AI outputs is crucial in research and development, and strong intellectual property protection for developing trustworthy AI.

The writers of the Constitution and Patent Act could not have foreseen that the dramatic rise of AI and the increasing ability to devise innovative solutions would challenge the limits of U.S. patent law. The dramatic rise of AI has raised a glaring question: can we recognize AI as an "inventor" under U.S. patent law for otherwise patentable inventions, or is this status reserved only for humans?

In 2019, the United States Patent and Trademark Office (USPTO) published a Request for Comments on Patenting Artificial Intelligence Inventions. The notice raised concerns regarding whether current patent laws adequately address inventorship for AI-created inventions that are typically developed without human involvement. Soliciting feedback by the USPTO also included the potential impact of allowing AI systems to be named inventors on the patent system and AI-related innovation. The responses to the USPTO's request reflected a wide range of opinions on issues of AI patent inventorship. Still, many commenters agreed that existing laws are not equipped to handle AI-generated inventions, and new policies must ensure recognition and protection for such innovations.

In two patent applications filed in 2019, Stephen Thaler, the developer of the AI system DABUS (Device for the Autonomous Bootstrapping of Unified Sentience), listed DABUS as the inventor. However, without a valid inventor, the USPTO rejected the applications as inadequate. The USPTO determined that the Patent Act restricts inventorship to natural persons, citing opinions of the U.S. Court of Appeals for the Federal Circuit, which reached similar conclusions in denying states and corporations inventor status with machines.

Dr. Thaler requested a review of the decision, but the district court concurred with the USPTO's conclusion and denied DABUS inventor status. The court determined Congress intended to limit defining "inventor" to natural persons based on "overwhelming evidence." The court also cited findings from the USPTO's 2019 Federal Register notice to emphasize that many commentators disagreed with Dr. Thaler's position that we should consider AI machines as inventors. Dr. Thaler filed an appeal in 2022 because he was unsatisfied.

In his case, the Federal Circuit for the first time tackled the question of whether the Patent Act could consider an AI as an "inventor." Dr. Thaler argued that AI authorship would encourage developing AI capable of inventing and provide incentives for the commercialization and disclosure of information for human- and AI-generated inventions.

## Copyright Law and AI in Healthcare

Copyright and intellectual property are essential components of artificial intelligence in healthcare because they ensure the ownership and protection of medical data, algorithms, and software development. Applying AI in medicine has ushered in a new era of innovation and technological progress. With this advancement, however, come questions of ownership and protection, as the data produced by AI systems is valuable and sensitive. It is essential to implement safeguards for the intellectual property of AI in healthcare.

The Copyright Act of 1976 is a United States copyright law. It remains the primary basis of copyright law in the United States, despite being amended by several subsequently enacted copyright provisions. The act outlines the fundamental rights of copyright holders, codifies the doctrine of "fair use," and adopts, for the newest copyrights, a unitary term based on the date of the author's death, as opposed to the previous scheme of fixed initial and renewal terms. On October 19, 1976, it became Public Law 94-553 and went into effect on January 1, 1978.

Besides technological advancements, the primary reason for passing the 1976 Act was the United States' participation in the Universal Copyright Convention (UCC) (and its expected participation in the Berne Convention). While the United States became a signatory to the UCC in 1955, the government machinery was slow to update U.S. copyright law to conform to its standards.

AI algorithms and systems can generate vast quantities of data, such as patient records, diagnostic images, and medical research data. This information is commercially and scientifically valuable, and can develop new treatments, enhance patient outcomes, and optimize healthcare delivery. However, we must contemplate the complex issue of copyright ownership for this data, as it involves ethical, legal, and regulatory considerations.

Within this copyright umbrella, AI algorithms and software developers have the exclusive right to use, reproduce, and distribute their creations. In addition, these laws allow them to license their work to third parties, generate revenue, and safeguard their investment in R&D.

Since AI algorithms and software can improve the precision and efficacy of medical diagnosis, treatment planning, and patient monitoring, the value of these applications lies in the intellectual property embodied in the software and algorithms. Therefore, protecting the creators' intellectual property rights along with copyrights is essential, as it ensures they will continue to innovate and develop novel solutions.

Intellectual property protection encourages collaboration and innovation in the healthcare sector. There needs to be a concerted effort among entities. By motivating creators to invest in research and development, these protections promote industry expansion and medical knowledge advancement. Entities should attempt to ensure the safeguarding of medical data, instilling confidence in patients regarding the security and privacy of their information.

Who owns the intellectual property rights to works generated by AI algorithms without human intervention? The software's author (as a literary work) is the person who creates it, and the author is the first owner of the work unless an employee created it during their employment, in which case the employer is the first owner. These operational terms are fraught with practical difficulty. To date, no significant case law has clarified creating a work absent a human author, so the increasing prevalence of AI algorithms is likely to lead to clarifying these terms by the courts. Parties to AI algorithm system development and use agreements that could create new copyright-protected works should include any necessary explicit terms regarding ownership, assignment, and licensing. We should consider a variety of issues, including addressing and recording.

## Database Rights

Database rights is an independent legal concept that pertains solely to the database developer. This individual possesses the sole authority to prohibit unauthorized retrieval and repurposing of the database's materials.

Database rights are a critical element of intellectual property rights, particularly in healthcare AI. These rights provide legal protection for database developers, considering the comeback of innovative AI algorithm development and database deployment across diverse healthcare domains. This enables companies to regulate the use of their database and hinder illicit duplication or dissemination, which would otherwise circumvent safeguards and rights associated with the innovation.

Database rights manage certain data permissions; in AI in healthcare, these permissions may be crucial. The effective incorporation of artificial intelligence into clinical environments relies heavily on the accessibility and authorization of high-quality datasets, considering the growing utilization of AI in medical diagnosis and research. The databases under consideration may contain voluminous medical data, including patient records, clinical trial results, and genetic testing outcomes.

Through legal safeguards, database rights encourage financial commitments toward the establishment and upkeep of databases. This process possesses the capacity to generate exhaustive and accurate datasets, hence enhancing the precision of AI-driven diagnostic tools and medicines. Managing database permissions can aid in protecting sensitive medical data. AI algorithms necessitate vast amounts of data for learning and training purposes; hence, this information must stay confidential.

## Confidential Information and Trade Secrets

BrainX has detected a substantial risk associated with the unauthorized utilization of algorithmic programs developed and manufactured by third parties for machine-learning models via cloning. This conclusion is based on clinical trials, research, and our expert medical judgment. BrainX has engaged the services of attorneys, analysts, and AI startup employees to gain a comprehensive understanding of the legal landscape pertaining to generative AI. These professionals have been consulted regarding the imminent risk of copyright and intellectual property infringements, which have the potential to generate substantial legal conflicts.

AI software and algorithms will certainly make up the developer's confidential knowledge and trade secrets. This secrecy gives additional IP protection. Examples of sensitive information and data that are critical to operating AI systems in healthcare include patient data and medical records. The protections can guard such data.

Particularly critical in the healthcare sector—where proprietary data and technologies must remain secure and confidential—is preventing competitors from duplicating or mimicking sensitive information. Healthcare organizations must maintain the confidentiality and security of their inventions and breakthroughs to maintain a competitive edge.

Trade secrets and confidential information serve as protective measures for sensitive patient data. Healthcare institutions often comply with rigorous regulations and legislation that control the handling and divulgence of patient information, as HIPAA mandates. Organizations can guarantee the privacy and security of patient data by employing trade secrets and confidential information.

This contributes to developing confidence in the healthcare system and encourages patients to exercise caution by disclosing sensitive information only to medical professionals.

To achieve this aim, we must implement a framework of protocols and guidelines governing the exchange of confidential data and trade to protect sensitive patient information. To properly implement these initiatives, organizations and the laws and rights defined by intellectual property and copyright law will need to collaborate. This may entail implementing encryption techniques, utilizing specially designed secure software, and implementing additional precautions to safeguard data. Corporations can enforce rigorous internal policies and laws that dictate the way they use and distribute sensitive information and trade secrets.

To establish a resilient framework for safeguarding trade secrets and confidential information, healthcare organizations must initially find out which data is pivotal to operating their artificial intelligence systems. This may encompass proprietary technologies and algorithms, patient data, medical records, and research and development endeavors. Once they identify this information, they can protect it in several ways to guarantee its security and privacy. Protecting confidential information and trade secrets is critical. Healthcare organizations can harness the potential of artificial intelligence to enhance patient outcomes and advance medical research while upholding the confidence and trust of stakeholders and patients by implementing rigorous safeguards for such data.

## AI and Patent Law in Healthcare

At BrainX, we witness the healthcare industry rapidly adopting artificial intelligence to enhance patient care, reduce healthcare costs, and streamline medical processes. However, with the increasing use of AI in healthcare, patent law faces new challenges. Today, the healthcare industry is more focused than ever on developing new and innovative technologies to improve patient outcomes, reduce the cost of medical care, analyze copious amounts of medical data, identify patterns, and make treatment decisions that are more informed.

This has led to a surge in AI-related patent applications in the healthcare industry. The United States Patent and Trademark Office (USPTO) has reported a 27% increase in applications for AI-related patents in the past year. This surge in AI innovation has raised important questions about applying patent law in the healthcare industry, along with patent protection for their inventions in multiple countries. Every country has its own set of patent laws and regulations, and patent time frames, making it essential for healthcare companies to collaboratively understand the nuances of patent laws in other countries.

According to the World Intellectual Property Organization (WIPO), the United States, Japan, and China are the top three countries in terms of the number of patents issued in 2019. The United States led the way with over 600,000 patents granted, followed by Japan with over 300,000 and China with 200,000.

In Europe, the European Patent Convention (EPC) provides a unified patent system for its member states. This means that a single patent application can cause a patent to be granted in many European countries. However, countries outside of the EPC, such as Switzerland, have their own patent laws and regulations. In India, the Patents Act of 1970 governs the patent system, but the law was amended in 2005 to align it with international standards. However, getting a patent in India can be lengthy, with an average processing time of approximately five years.

Brazil has a unique approach to patent laws. The country allows for compulsory licensing, so it can grant licenses to third parties to produce patented inventions without the consent of the patent holder. This occurs in the interest of public health and safety, particularly with pharmaceuticals. As stated by the Brazilian Ministry of Health, "Compulsory licensing is a legitimate instrument of the Brazilian government to guarantee access to medicines and treatments for the population."

While the United States is reputed for being a patent-friendly country, recent changes in patent laws have made it more difficult to obtain and enforce patents. The America Invents Act (AIA) of 2011 shifted the U.S. patent system from a "first-to-invent" to a "first-inventor-to-file" system, which has made the patent application process more complex. Additionally, the U.S. Supreme Court has issued several decisions in recent years that have made it harder to enforce patents, including the landmark case of *Alice Corp. v. CLS Bank International*, which made it more difficult to obtain patents for software and other abstract ideas.

Despite the challenges in obtaining and enforcing patents in different countries, companies must continue to navigate these laws to protect their intellectual property. Companies should tailor their patent strategy to their business objectives, which requires a thorough understanding of the patent laws and procedures in the countries where they operate. Since we understand every country has its own set of patent laws and regulations, it is essential for healthcare organizations to understand the differences to protect their intellectual property.

For example, from the United States' considerable number of patents granted to Brazil's unique approach to compulsory licensing, navigating international patent laws can be a complex and challenging process. However, by collaborating with experienced attorneys and patent agents, companies can develop tailored patent strategies that align with their business objectives and protect their inventions around the world. Grasping the intricacies of patent legislation across various nations can pose a challenge; however, it is imperative for enterprises aiming to thrive in the international market.

Since AI and algorithms are developed software with data and varying sequences, we must discuss patenting AI technology. There are two ways to patent AI technology. First, we can patent it as a method or process of treatment, diagnosis, or medical condition monitoring. Second, we can patent it as an apparatus or system that uses AI technology. It must meet three requirements for an invention to obtain a patent:

- Novelty.
- Non-Obviousness.
- Usefulness.

The same criteria apply to AI technology in healthcare as they do to any other form of innovation. In the healthcare industry, determining the level of inventiveness and creativity necessary for an AI innovation to be deemed novel and non-obvious is one of the most significant difficulties for patent law. Given the quick rate of AI progress in healthcare and the fact that many AI solutions are built on existing algorithms and data, it is challenging.

Developing patent law incorporates additional criteria for establishing the patentability of AI technology in response to these problems. As an example, the USPTO has instructed patent examiners to assess patent applications involving artificial intelligence using the appropriate criteria of novelty and non-obviousness. A further crucial aspect pertaining to patent law in the healthcare sector is ownership. As an illustration, the USPTO has issued directives to patent examiners to ensure that they assess patent applications, including artificial intelligence, according to the standards of novelty and non-obviousness. However, at the forefront are patent and intellectual property ownership.

When developing AI technology, copious quantities of medical data may be owned by multiple parties, including patients, healthcare providers, and research institutions. This raises important questions regarding the ownership of intellectual property rights of developed data. Patent law has developed new standards for determining ownership of AI-related inventions to address this issue. The individual or group that created the AI technology may define ownership, and ownership may also be determined by the owner of the data used to create the AI technology.

Patent law is not the sole legal framework that applies to AI technology in healthcare; we must acknowledge this. Additional legislative structures, such as those governing medical devices and data protection, are crucial in overseeing the implementation of artificial intelligence in the healthcare sector.

The ever-increasing use of AI in healthcare has prompted important questions about applying patent law in this industry. The patentability of AI technology is being challenged, as new standards determine the patentability of AI technology using an abundance of medical data owned by multiple parties.

Ownership may be determined based on the individual or entity that created the AI technology, or the ownership of the underlying data used to develop it.

## AI and Trademarks in Healthcare

Medical advancements inspire immense optimism and hope for the cure or improvement of patients' lives. Given this context, it may be necessary to implement governance innovations encompassing copyrights, legislation, trademarks, policy, and ethics to ensure that society benefits from medical advancements while also avoiding their drawbacks. The rapid advancement of artificial intelligence has prompted scientists from diverse fields to express concerns regarding AI in health, which will require regulatory interventions to ensure a proper equilibrium. The legislation governing patents and trademarks enters this context.

Patent law and trademarks are vital components of AI in the healthcare industry. Patent law is a legal system that grants inventors temporary exclusive rights to their innovations. Conversely, trademarks are exclusive marks, logos, or names that distinguish one brand from another. Patents and trademarks in healthcare protect inventions and prevent unnecessary competition, allowing healthcare providers to focus on providing the highest quality care without fear of losing their unique approach to a particular treatment.

According to the Strathmore University Center for Intellectual Property and Information Technology Law, and the World Intellectual Property Organization,

> Trademark registration confers an exclusive right to the use of the registered trademark. This implies that only the owner of the trademark can use it or license it to another party in exchange for payment. Registration provides legal certainty and reinforces the position of the right holder.[4]

In healthcare, AI relates to the administration of trademark laws and its capacity to streamline administrative tasks relating to registration, searches, opposing marks, and other procedures.

## AI and the Trademark Search

Through the analysis of a vast array of variables related to the search process, such as sound, visual traits, sights, and classification of goods and services, and other trademark attributes, such as descriptiveness, AI enables trademark owners to search for and identify potential trademarks for registration. The analysis can also incorporate other external factors, such as identifying potential growth areas, obstacles to trademarks, goodwill, and similar trademarks. In trademark searches, we can utilize AI to classify goods and services, where AI algorithms automatically suggest classes for goods and services in trademark applications. We create algorithms to evaluate the conceptual similarity between marks based on shared or opposing meanings.

Since AI has played a significant role in patent law and trademarks, AI algorithm developers need to search for potential patent and trademark infringement cases in real-time by analyzing existing data along with pertinent patents and trademarks. Developers can easily research patents and trademarks through the USPTO (www.USPTO.Gov) or Google Patents (www.google.com/patents), which is designed for ease of use in intellectual property protection. This enables healthcare providers to remain current on patent and trademark infringement cases and to take swift action to protect their intellectual property.

Healthcare organizations must implement strategies to avoid inadvertently violating existing patents and save time and money on costly legal disputes. To accomplish this, we can use artificial intelligence to monitor the market for potential infringers, identify them, and notify the patent holder, allowing the safeguard of intellectual property against unauthorized use.

There are also potential disadvantages to applying AI in patent law and trademark law within the healthcare industry. For instance, AI algorithms are not foolproof and may overlook potential patent infringement cases, resulting in legal disputes. In addition, it could abuse AI technology to file frivolous patents to monopolize the market of certain companies. Another problem is that AI may inhibit innovation. As AI simplifies the detection and enforcement of patents, some healthcare providers may be hesitant to create innovative technology or treatments for fear of infringing on existing patents. This has the potential to impede progress and hinder innovation within the healthcare sector.

Another potential disadvantage is that it exacerbates the legal complexities of AI because privacy laws differ from one country to the next. The Health Insurance Portability and Accountability Act (HIPAA) of the United States establishes standards for protecting patient health information, but other countries may have different laws and regulations. This can make it difficult for businesses to develop AI-generated inventions that can have global use.

Many medical organizations are adopting blockchain technology to manage the legal complications of AI-generated inventions to overcome these issues. Blockchain technology enables the storage of patient information in a transparent and safe manner while maintaining its privacy and confidentiality. Blockchain empowers patients with greater privacy control by permitting them to manage who has access to their data. Fundamentally, the lack of transparency around data utilization will impede our ability to establish confidence among patients and the wider healthcare community.

As AI technology advances, healthcare organizations must ensure compliance with the law. In doing so, businesses will be required to maintain current privacy policies and change them as required. We will maximize the benefits that AI-generated innovations can provide to advance medical treatments and enhance patient outcomes. We must achieve a delicate equilibrium between the advantages offered by medical innovation and the safeguarding of personal privacy and autonomy. We can guarantee that inventions developed by AI are not just efficient, but also ethical and accountable.

## Software Challenges

One of the most prominent areas where AI is making a significant impact is in medical software development and application, by adding measures to protect software and data from cyberattack. According to a recent report by the International Association of Privacy Professionals, the healthcare industry accounts for 30% of all data breaches, making it the most vulnerable to cyber threats. This statistic highlights the pressing need for robust data protection measures and strong software development. A balance is needed between innovation and security. There is no either-or choice.

Concerns about the safety of AI software are growing with the potential for AI to be used in everything from self-driving cars to medical diagnoses. It is critical to ensure that we develop this technology safely. This can be difficult because of the complexity and difficulty in predicting how the AI technology will behave in specific situations. The rapid pace of technological innovation has nearly outpaced the ability of developers, regulators, and other stakeholders to control deployment and use. Therefore, safely and responsibly developing AI is crucial.

Transparency and accountability are key to ensuring the safety of AI software. As AI systems become more integrated, this requires developers to make AI systems transparent, providing users with information about how decisions are made and what data is used. Transparency is key to building trust in AI software systems. Developers must be accountable. It is necessary to implement logical lines of responsibility and create mechanisms for addressing any errors or biases that are discovered.

Overall, modern healthcare is becoming increasingly dependent on connectivity, with ever-increasing quantities of data generated and exchanged between systems at an accelerating rate. The software involved in such interconnected systems may be patentable, but it is essential to consider what it does to ensure patient privacy and safety.

## Notes

1. Musk Elon. Interview. Edge. http://www.edge.org.
2. Hawking Stephen Open Letter. Wikipedia. 2015. https://en.wikipedia.org/wiki/Open_letter_on_artificial_intelligence_(2015).
3. USPTO Report. 2020. https://www.uspto.gov/sites/default/files/documents/USPTO_AI-Report_2020-10-07.pdf.
4. WIPO. Trademarks. https://www.wipo.int/en/web/trademarks.

# Chapter 10

# Data and Purposes in AI

> We must address, individually and collectively, moral and ethical issues raised by cutting-edge research in artificial intelligence and biotechnology, which will enable significant life extension, designer babies, and memory extraction.
>
> **—Klaus Schwab** [1]

In 2017, Amazon made headlines with its patent application for a new algorithmic feature, which allows its voice assistant, Alexa, to detect when users are sick. In May 2017, Amazon filed the patent titled "Voice-Based Determination of Physical and Emotional Characteristics of Users" with the United States Patent and Trademark Office. According to the patent application, Alexa would use voice recognition, cough detection, and other physical cues to determine whether a user is sick.

The system listens for tone, pitch, and rhythm alterations in the user's voice that suggest disease or illness. Alexa recognizes coughing and other bodily indications using a microphone, alerting Amazon to potential products to present to the end user. While the advantages of this technology are enormous, it begs the question: is this a borderline data breach, breaking privacy issues with patients and consumers alike?

With this security issue as a concern, Alexa's ability to detect illness could have broader public health implications by helping health officials track the spread of sickness and diseases like the common cold, the flu, or varying strains of COVID-19. This AI technology could be beneficial during outbreaks or pandemics. However, many in the healthcare industry have raised concerns about the potential privacy implications of Alexa's ability to detect

 DOI: 10.4324/9781003661627-13

illness without the user's consent. Critics worry that the data collection driving the technology could collect sensitive health information without the user's permission. People are concerned about using and sharing this data with third parties.

Amazon states it will only use this data for healthcare-related purposes. However, like any innovative technology, there are concerns about the potential effects on privacy and safeguarding sensitive data. Since AI data sets are developed and enhanced over time, and technology is expanding, we will need to overcome difficulties and challenges.

## Creation of a Data Sandbox

By description, a data sandbox is a virtual environment that allows healthcare organizations to experiment with data and analytics without risking production systems or patient safety. A sandbox can test data and training models for AI applications in developing new AI algorithms and exploring new use cases and data sets.

In the past few years, the amount of data generated from multiple sources, such as electronic health records, medical imaging, and data supplied by patients via wearables and mobile devices, has grown in the healthcare industry. According to reports, experts forecast a rapid increase in the total amount of data created, captured, copied, and consumed globally, reaching 64.2 zettabytes in 2020. Over the next five years, they project global data creation to grow to over 180 zettabytes.

First, the sandbox enables the development of specific AI models and algorithms using real-world data, which can be challenging because of data security and privacy concerns in the real world. Second, it allows experimentation with varying algorithms without risking the integrity of their production systems or disrupting their current operations. Third, the sandbox enables the training of AI models on large, diverse data sets to improve the accuracy and efficacy of predictive models.

As we explore data sandboxes, in line with the vigorous growth of the data volume, they forecast the installed base of storage capacity to increase, growing at a compound annual growth rate of 19.2% over the forecast period from 2020 to 2025. In 2020, the installed storage capacity reached 6.7 zettabytes.[2] Data proliferation has enabled artificial intelligence to improve healthcare outcomes and reduce costs. To effectively use AI in healthcare, stakeholders must establish a data sandbox that promotes safe and secure testing of AI algorithms.

Amazon Web Services (AWS), which provides an assortment of open-source tools and services, serves as an illustration of a functional data sandbox. The Elastic Compute Cloud (EC2) is one such solution that offers developers and companies cost-effective and scalable computing resources. The AWS Code Toolkit, which provides development integrations for many platforms and programming languages, and the AWS SDKs for Java and .NET, are two further open-source developer tools provided by AWS. Open-source developers and Amazon customers convene at the AWS Open, an event hosted by AWS that provides insights into novel AWS technologies and services.

## Identifying Data Sources

To construct effective data sandboxes, it is imperative to establish and distinguish the data sources and sets that will be used in one of the sandbox's former jobs. Medical imaging, electronic health records, and patient-generated data from wearables and mobile devices are some of these sources. Following the identification of data sources, it is critical to ensure that the data is obtained in compliance with privacy regulations such as the General Data Protection Regulation (GDPR) and the Health Insurance Portability and Accountability Act (HIPAA). In the healthcare business, an AI data sandbox would enable engineers to test AI algorithms on actual patient data in an ethical and secure manner. To guarantee that the collection, storage, and use of data adhere to ethical and regulatory standards.

## Secure Data Storage

The healthcare industry has increasingly turned to cloud services and artificial intelligence in recent years for more efficient and effective data storage and analysis. Cerner Corporation, a healthcare provider, is one prime example. It implemented a cloud-based platform for managing patient data, which resulted in a 50% reduction in data center costs. Another example is the AI algorithm developed by the University of California, San Francisco, which can predict the onset of Alzheimer's disease with 100% accuracy up to six years in advance.

Cloud services also allow for more collaborative and streamlined data sharing between healthcare providers, leading to improved patient outcomes. According to a study by the University of Pennsylvania, the use of cloud-based electronic health records (EHRs) is linked to a 30% reduction in hospital readmission rates.

In terms of data storage, Sage Intacct is a popular cloud-based accounting software used by healthcare organizations. The platform allows for real-time financial reporting and analysis, as well as customizable dashboards for tracking key performance indicators. With its open API and integration capabilities, Sage Intacct can also integrate with other healthcare software systems such as EHRs, enabling seamless data flow and analysis.

Cornerstone Healthcare Group is one healthcare provider that has seen significant benefits from using Sage Intacct. Cornerstone could reduce its monthly accounting close process from 30 days to just five days by implementing the platform, while also increasing visibility into financial performance and improving budgeting and forecasting accuracy.

Applying AI in healthcare is also transforming the analysis and utilization of patient data. For example, the company Zebra Medical Vision has developed an AI algorithm that can detect breast cancer with 90% accuracy, compared to a human radiologist's average of 77%. PathAI, another company, is using artificial intelligence to improve the accuracy and speed of cancer diagnosis through its automated pathology analysis platform.

With the increasing use of cloud services and AI in healthcare, the industry is moving toward a more data-driven and efficient model. According to a report by *Grand View Research*, it was expected that the global healthcare cloud computing market would reach $350 billion by 2022, with a compound annual growth rate of 20.1% from 2015 to 2022. The report highlights the increasing demand for data storage and analysis and the need for better care coordination and patient engagement.

## Preprocess the Data

Data preprocessing is a crucial component in establishing a robust data sandbox. This process includes data cleansing, transformation into a structured format, and preparation for analysis. To clean and structure the data, we need to use preprocessing techniques and feature engineering to develop new features for analysis and personalized treatment plans for patients based on medical history and test results, using clean data.

A recent survey found that approximately 80% of data scientists allocate a substantial amount of effort to data preparation. This underscores the importance of this stage within the workflow for data analysis. Preprocessing guarantees data accuracy and consistency while mitigating bias and enhancing the precision of analyses. It conserves resources and time by removing the requirement for redundant data processing. Establishing a solid data sandbox through preprocessing data is vital for generating insightful observations and facilitating improved decision-making.

Considering the growing significance of data-driven insights in the contemporary business environment, it is critical for businesses to allocate resources to implement appropriate data preparation methodologies to guarantee the precision, consistency, and dependability of their data. By doing so, they can save time and resources, improve the efficacy of their analyses, and gain a competitive edge in their respective sectors.

## Testing and Development of Data

Implementing AI algorithms in a production environment presents a unique array of obstacles. Prioritizing testing and development is crucial to achieving successful deployment in the data sandbox. By utilizing data sandboxes in healthcare, it is possible to ensure that AI algorithms function as intended and do not harm patients.

Duke University Medical Center researchers conducted one study on testing when they created an artificial intelligence model that could precisely forecast the likelihood that a patient will require readmission within 30 days after their discharge. The model underwent rigorous testing, refinement, and implementation in a production environment, yielding hospital cost savings of $400,000 and a notable 20% reduction in readmissions. Following this, Stanford University researchers created an artificial intelligence model capable of pinpointing sepsis for a period of 12 hours prior to its clinical diagnosis.

Researchers at Stanford University evaluated the model using real-time patient data and demonstrated its 85% accuracy rate in identifying sepsis. Patients received therapy and intervention at an earlier stage, which reduced mortality rates by 60% and generated savings of $20,000 per patient.

Implementing AI algorithms in a healthcare setting necessitates extensive testing to ensure patient safety. To address these concerns, healthcare settings must rigorously assess and validate AI algorithms before deploying them in a production setting. This includes evaluating the algorithms on real-world patient data to ensure accuracy and identifying any potential biases in the data that could affect the algorithm's performance. Regularly monitoring the algorithm's performance and updating it as needed is also critical to ensure its proper functioning and prevent harm to patients.

Besides testing and validation, healthcare professionals must be involved in the development and deployment of AI algorithms. Collaboration among data scientists, clinicians, and other healthcare professionals is required to ensure that the algorithm meets the needs of patients and healthcare providers.

## Data Protection

Healthcare is a sector renowned for its high data intensity, as it consistently generates and manages substantial quantities of confidential information. This data includes personal and medical information of patients, research data, and administrative records. Thus, data protection is of the utmost importance, ensuring its safety, security, and confidentiality to safeguard the privacy of patients and deliver optimal healthcare. Data sandboxes serve to safeguard data within a controlled setting, enabling researchers, analysts, and data scientists to manipulate health-related information without jeopardizing personally identifiable information.

The first step in data protection is implementing robust security measures, such as encryption of data at rest and in transit, multi-factor authentication, and stringent access controls to guarantee that only authorized individuals have access to the data prior to its release to the public. Artificial intelligence advancements have enabled researchers to examine healthcare data in innovative ways, hence enhancing knowledge of testing and security before public release. This has resulted in improved patient care, health outcomes, and research capabilities.

Nevertheless, as AI strengthens its presence in healthcare, serious issues will need consideration, such as misuse or improper treatment of extremely sensitive and confidential data. There are unknown repercussions for patients, healthcare professionals, and organizations as we deploy data protection with the idea of protecting patient privacy, data integrity, and compliance with legal and regulatory standards.

How can we safeguard it and use it to improve patient care? Initially, there is encryption. Encryption is one of the main methods of converting data into code. Authorized systems or individuals must complete decryption. Healthcare organizations must employ encryption techniques to protect sensitive patient information, such as medical records, triage data, patient intake forms, and assessments. The encrypted data may only be accessed by authorized individuals who possess the decryption key. This ensures that the data will stay secure and unreadable to any entity that does not possess the decryption key, even during a data breach.

Additionally, we must consider access control. Healthcare businesses must implement access control so that only authorized personnel can retrieve sensitive data required to perform their jobs. This requires role-based access control, in which individuals' access privileges to certain data are determined by their organizational position. In contrast to a nurse, who may only see specific elements of a patient's medical information, a physician has unrestricted access to those records.

Besides implementing access control and encryption, healthcare organizations must also possess data masking. Data masking disguises sensitive information by substituting it with illegitimate data, destroying the original data. Social security numbers, dates of birth, or other sensitive information that need protection do not require data masking. Healthcare institutions can securely exchange data with external researchers or other organizations, while data masking protects the confidentiality of sensitive information.

Besides conducting risk assessments, healthcare organizations must establish policies and procedures to preserve data protection as part of a data protection program. It is important to constantly update data protection policies and provide mandatory training for staff on data protection and best practices. These procedures ensure every employee is cognizant of their responsibilities and obligations regarding safeguarding data. Healthcare organizations can leverage robust data protection protocols to identify patterns, predict health outcomes, and establish trustworthiness and integrity to improve patient outcomes, develop tailored treatment approaches, and detect illnesses at an early stage.

## Data Ownership

As AI increases the value of data as a resource in the healthcare industry, concerns over data ownership have become important. The process of determining data ownership in the healthcare sector can be intricate and challenging. One approach to ascertaining data ownership is through the utilization and execution of patient consent forms, which enable individuals to express their level of comfort with the study application of their data. According to a study conducted by the National Institutes of Health, 67% of patients at a medical institution consented to using their data for research. While this illustrates the willingness of many patients to disclose their information, it also underscores the criticality of acquiring informed permission.

In healthcare, determining data ownership is not always straightforward. There are instances where patients may be uninformed regarding the collection of their personal information, let alone the entity that possesses it. This particularly applies when individuals gather data using linked devices or wearable technology. A study by Accenture revealed that a mere 2% of patients possessed an awareness of the entirety of the data gathered by their wearable devices. This emphasizes the significance of improved ownership and data-gathering transparency in healthcare.

Navigating the intricate web of regulations and legislation governing data protection is vital when verifying data ownership. Prior chapters covered how HIPAA regulations apply to healthcare data in the United States, putting stringent restrictions on the use and disclosure of patient data. Sharing data with researchers or other allowed parties may pose a challenge for healthcare companies.

Adhering to these rules while protecting the confidentiality of patient information is possible by implementing de-identification methods to eliminate individually identifiable details from data. This facilitates the exchange of data for research among organizations in adherence to HIPAA laws. University of Texas researchers improved patient care by sharing patient data for research using de-identification techniques.

Establishing data ownership in the healthcare sector requires a comprehensive strategy encompassing patient permission, implementing technical advancements like blockchain, and navigating intricate regulatory frameworks.

Transparency and patient privacy must be the highest priorities for healthcare organizations and researchers in all facets of data collection and utilization, as signifying data in healthcare increases. They can ensure that they inform patients about how their data is used and that such utilization adheres to ethical standards; doing so will improve patient care.

Data ownership presents a disadvantage due to the possibility of purposeful or inadvertent mismanagement or misuse, necessitating addressing heightened issues on multiple levels. For instance, we could market data to third-party companies or use it to discriminate against individuals based on their health status. To safeguard patients' rights and ensure the ethical and efficient management of data, it is critical to determine ownership of the data and adhere to established lines of ownership.

## Cleaning and Preparing Data

Utilizing unbiased data underscores the criticality of data cleansing and preparation as a determinant of effective AI adoption. The increasing volume of data created in the healthcare industry can pose difficulties in data cleansing and preparation for analysis. However, AI can assist in a variety of operations, offering a promising solution to these challenges. When employing AI for data preparation and cleansing, we must give ethical considerations careful attention. AI systems may perpetuate data biases, leading to outcomes that are erroneous or unjust. By being mindful of these potential pitfalls, we can ensure that AI is a force for good in the healthcare sector, driving us toward more accurate and just outcomes.

For instance, if a predictive model is built with biased data that pertains to specific communities, it might treat these populations unjustly. To maintain fairness, healthcare institutions must be honest about the data they use and conduct routine audits and monitoring of their AI systems. This commitment to honesty and transparency is not just a best practice but a moral imperative in the healthcare sector. By being open about our data usage and regularly reviewing our AI systems, we can build trust with our patients and ensure that our practices are always in their best interests.

Researchers previously explored natural language processing (NLP) as one technique for retrieving pertinent information from unstructured data such as text documents and notes. For instance, Stanford University identified patients with sepsis by analyzing a collection of electronic medical records using NLP. The researchers successfully identified patients with a high probability of developing sepsis by applying machine-learning techniques.

When data preparation and cleansing occur, we can recognize trends in massive datasets using predictive modeling. Sorting these patterns eliminates undesirable or even biased code from the dataset. Researchers from the University of California, Los Angeles, who employed predictive modeling to identify individuals who were at an increased risk of developing type 2 diabetes, analyzed an electronic health record dataset. After cleaning and preprocessing the data, they developed a model that properly identified which patients had the highest probability of developing the condition using enhanced machine learning methods. This enabled treatment and intervention to occur early.

Healthcare organizations may enhance patient outcomes and progress medical research by ensuring their datasets are correct, full, and up to date, using AI for data preparation and cleansing. Data cleansing and preparation improve the ability to identify and rectify errors, populate missing values, and eliminate inconsistencies. Data cleansing increases productivity and efficiency. By automating tedious and time-consuming processes like data purification, standardization, and integration, healthcare practitioners can allocate their efforts toward value-adding endeavors such as data interpretation, analysis, and decision-making. This improves patient outcomes, delivers accurate and timely diagnosis, and minimizes expenses.

## De-identifying Data

PhysioNet is among the most influential narratives and practices around the de-identification of data. The HIPAA Privacy Rule restricts sharing medical data containing protected health information (PHI) in the United States. Any information that could identify the individuals from whom the data were taken is considered PHI. Researchers who wish to utilize PHI-containing data must adhere to rigorous requirements, including obtaining Institutional Review Board (IRB) or comparable clearances for data utilization, as stipulated in data use agreements.

The HIPAA Privacy Rule exempts medical data that does not contain PHI, allowing for its free sharing. This category includes the data on PhysioNet. Many of the research data sets currently collected by PhysioNet contain PHI, and removing this PHI ("de-identification" in HIPAA speak, or "anonymization") is time-consuming and error-prone. The cost of de-identification is a significant barrier to data sharing for research projects.

At PhysioNet, their MIMIC II project has spent several years developing and testing software capable of removing PHI from text and, where appropriate, replacing it with realistic surrogate PHI. For example, they replaced patient names, medical record numbers, dates, and geographic locations with fictitious information.

The MIMIC II project contributed to PhysioNet its de-identification software, which may be useful to other researchers who need to remove PHI from their own data. It also contributed a large quantity of text drawn from ICU nursing notes, which were collected concurrently with the signals, trends, laboratory reports, discharge summaries, and other data in the MIMIC II clinical and waveform databases.

The importance of de-identifying data using AI in healthcare is growing because of the sensitivity of medical information. This is necessary to protect patient privacy while allowing medical data to be used for research and analysis purposes. Traditional methods of de-identification, such as removing individuals' names and addresses from medical records, may not consistently provide sufficient protection of privacy. For example, someone could re-identify individuals by using additional medical history information, such as gender, age, and medical conditions.

AI technology has the potential to significantly improve the accuracy and effectiveness of de-identification methods. AI can analyze vast databases in search of patterns that may aid in the re-identification of individuals and the removal of sensitive data by employing machine learning algorithms. Accuracy is improved, while time and money are saved over manual de-identification. Consequently, releasing the data used for training AI systems publicly becomes necessary, and continuous inspection of the de-identified data for any bias is required. Ethical and legal concerns must be considered; it is critical that the use of AI adheres to all applicable laws and regulations governing data security and privacy.

## BrainX Data

At BrainX, we support viable and clean data availability and strongly promote data usage for scientific research and discovery. We curate substantial amounts of published data to provide insightful information on AI to inform and educate about AI-related material in various healthcare publications. With over 10,000 reads annually, our healthcare publications deliver the needed information to push AI successfully within the healthcare industry. Filtered based on healthcare specialty and interest, users can visit BrainX and sort through the world's largest repository of links to open-source healthcare datasets to promote research related to AI applications in healthcare. https://brainxai.org/data/

## Notes

1. Schwab Klaus. World Economic Forum. Davos Summit in 2018.
2. Worldwide Data Statistics. Statista. https://www.statista.com/statistics/871513/worldwide-data-created/.

# THE HOW (OF AI IN HEALTHCARE)

# 4

# Chapter 11

# Algorithm Development Strategy

> Algorithms are the new stethoscope. They will be incredibly powerful in helping us diagnose and treat conditions.
>
> **—Eric Topol**

DeepMind, a division of Google, announced its first significant health initiative in 2016: a collaboration with the Royal Free London NHS Foundation Trust to aid in the management of acute kidney injury, which included an advanced algorithmic data set. This was a significant advancement in modern healthcare. Emerging new corporate players, such as Google, Microsoft, IBM, Apple, and other companies, have bid on developing robust algorithms for the future of healthcare and other sectors of global healthcare.

With AI's urgency high, algorithm development for healthcare applications has advanced significantly. Developing strategic and practical algorithms is vital, as big data and machine learning significantly affect most aspects of contemporary life, such as entertainment, commerce, and, most of all, healthcare.

With the increase in artificial intelligence adoption in the healthcare sector, it is evident that strategic algorithm development strategies are employed to achieve a wide range of applications, including administrative workflow support, patient outreach, image analysis, medical device automation, and patient monitoring.

To improve patient care and outcomes, it is necessary to develop effective algorithmic solutions. This underscores the importance for the healthcare

DOI: 10.4324/9781003661627-15

industry to embrace a strategic approach to algorithmic development, which considers critical factors and strategies to support and enhance patient care, in addition to potential challenges and benefits.

Strategically, vital algorithmic development will reduce costs across the board. By 2026, AI technologies will enable the United States to save $150 billion annually on healthcare expenditures. These cost savings are primarily because of transforming a reactive to an initiative-taking healthcare model, emphasizing health management rather than disease treatment. While this is expected to lead to a decline in hospital stays, medical visits, and treatments, strategic AI-based technology will significantly help individuals maintain their health by ensuring earlier diagnosis, individualized therapies, and more effective follow-up care.

## Development-Defining the Problem

Determining the problem through strategic algorithm creation is critical in healthcare to guarantee the efficacy of any given system or procedure. Algorithms are mathematical models that are employed to forecast decisions by utilizing certain data inputs. Consequently, in the absence of a precise definition of the problem, the algorithm's ability to resolve it may be compromised, resulting in unintended or detrimental consequences.

Developers and an organization must do a comprehensive examination of the data inputs and outputs, including a review of the data types utilized, their collection methods, and their analysis processes, to describe the issue. Healthcare professionals can identify potential areas of improvement for medication management through the analysis of data inputs such as a patient's medical history, current medications, and other pertinent health factors. This analysis enables the development of strategic algorithms that facilitate enhanced patient care.

Case studies can be utilized to refine the focus of algorithm development and delineate the issue. As an illustration, a recent case study involving implementing a patient triage algorithm demonstrated the repercussions of inadequately identifying the problem. Prioritizing patients according to their medical requirements, the algorithm failed to account for the patients' personal situations or preferences. Subsequently, patients were frequently reassigned to unsuitable care pathways, which led to deteriorating health outcomes and escalated hospital expenditures.

In conjunction with case studies, statistics should be applied to the construction of strategic algorithms. For instance, according to a recent study, fifty percent of medical diagnoses are erroneous due to inadequate analysis or misinterpretation of the data. Healthcare personnel can mitigate the likelihood of misdiagnosis by creating algorithms that precisely detect and scrutinize pertinent data. Such advancements would lead to improved patient outcomes and decreased expenditure on healthcare.

Determining the problem that the algorithm will address necessitates an unwavering comprehension of the subject and its foundational elements. Once the problem has been identified, it must be decomposed into smaller, more manageable components to facilitate developing a gradual-implementation algorithmic solution approach. This is why it is crucial:

**Complexity**: Healthcare issues often possess a complex nature, encompassing a multitude of variables, aspects, and interdependencies. Simultaneously attempting to handle the full issue may result in confusion and ineffectual solutions. A component-by-component breakdown facilitates comprehension and individual attention to each area.

**Scalability**: In the healthcare domain, scalability pertains to the capacity of algorithms to accept expanding datasets and increasing levels of complexity. Scalable algorithms are simpler to build when the problem is split, as each component may be evaluated and optimized independently for efficiency.

**Iterative Development**: The algorithm development process is iterative. By decomposing the issue, one can concentrate on constructing and honing more manageable components of the resolution, so enabling ongoing refinement and adjustment prior to their integration into the entirety.

**Risk Management:** Implementing algorithmic solutions in healthcare necessitates careful consideration of potential risks. By dividing the problem into smaller pieces, risk assessment and management can be conducted more effectively, thereby minimizing the potential impact of failure or error on the entire system.

**Collaboration**: Collaboration occurs frequently between various healthcare stakeholders, such as medical professionals, researchers, and software engineers. The ability of each group to concentrate on its area of expertise is enhanced by decomposing the problem into manageable components. This collaboration yields a more comprehensive and viable algorithmic solution.

Algorithmic development allows for a systematic and manageable approach. It simplifies complexity, enables scalability, facilitates risk management, supports iterative development, and promotes effective stakeholder collaboration.

Strategic storyboarding is a technique that integrates AI into algorithm development and issue-solving. Across millennia, storytelling has continued to be a core component of human society. Humans have been enthralled by stories from the earliest cave art to the most recent Hollywood blockbuster.

Storytelling has undergone a substantial transformation in recent years because of technological advances. A graphic depiction of a narrative, storyboards are generated by artificial intelligence; each panel represents an individual scene or sequence of events. Storyboards are implemented in various domains, including animation, advertising, video games, healthcare applications, and the filmmaking process.

In the healthcare industry, AI and storyboarding entail developing visual narratives or sequences that depict a variety of procedures, user experiences, or scenarios. The standard procedure for storyboarding with AI in healthcare is as follows:

**Identify the Purpose**: Determine the specific goal or objective of the storyboard. For example, it could be to illustrate the patient's journey, demonstrate the use of a medical device, or explain a treatment process.

**Define the Target Audience**: Identify the primary audience for the storyboard, such as healthcare professionals, patients, or caregivers. Understanding the audience helps tailor the content and language appropriately.

**Gather Information**: Collect relevant information, such as medical knowledge, patient data, healthcare guidelines, or AI-generated insights. This information supports the storyboard's content.

**Plan the Structure**: Determine the overall structure and flow of the storyboard. Divide the content into scenes depicting various steps, actions, or interactions related to the healthcare process.

**Create Visuals**: Based on each scene, create visual representations using AI-based tools or software. These visuals could include illustrations, diagrams, charts, or animations to communicate the information effectively.

**Add Text and Narration**: Include concise and clear text or narration that complements the visuals. Make sure the language used is understandable and relevant to the target audience.

**Iterate and Refine**: Review the storyboard and seek feedback from stakeholders, including healthcare professionals or subject matter experts. Based on the feedback, iterate on the design and content, ensuring accuracy and clarity.

**Use the Storyboard**: Once finalized, the storyboard can be utilized for various purposes, such as training healthcare professionals, patient education, presenting research findings, or communicating AI-based solutions to stakeholders.

Utilizing AI in the storyboard creation process enhances collaboration, communication, improves understanding of complex concepts, and facilitates adopting further AI technologies. As an example, consider creating an AI system to aid physicians in diagnosing rare diseases; we have illustrated and organized a sample AI solution's potential workflows using storyboards:

## *Scene 1*

**Visual:** An AI-powered interface displayed on a doctor's computer screen.
**Text:** "Meet Dr. Smith, an experienced physician who encounters challenging cases daily."
**Narration:** Explains the difficulty of diagnosing rare diseases due to the complexity of symptoms and limited medical expertise in some cases.

## *Scene 2*

**Visual:** Dr. Smith inputs patient data (symptoms, medical history) into the AI system.
**Text:** "Dr. Smith enters relevant patient information effortlessly."
**Narration:** Highlights how the AI system can quickly analyze vast amounts of patient data.

## *Scene 3*

**Visual:** The AI system processes the data and displays potential diagnoses ranked by probability.
**Text:** "The AI system generates a list of diagnoses, prioritized by likelihood."
**Narration:** Emphasizes the AI system's ability to expedite the diagnostic process and suggest potential rare diseases.

### *Scene 4*

**Visual:** Dr. Smith reviews the AI-generated list of diagnoses and selects a few to investigate further.
**Text:** "Dr. Smith uses the AI recommendations to delve deeper into potential rare diseases."
**Narration:** Illustrates how the AI system is a helpful tool for doctors, providing insights for further analysis.

### *Scene 5*

**Visual:** Dr. Smith examines additional patient information and compares it to the AI-generated suggestions.
**Text:** "Dr. Smith combines AI insights with medical expertise for accurate diagnosis."
**Narration:** Highlights the importance of human input and expertise in the final diagnosis process.

### *Scene 6*

**Visual:** Dr. Smith arrives at a diagnosis and discusses treatment options with the patient.
**Text:** "The AI system contributes to a successful diagnosis, leading to personalized treatment."
**Narration:** Conveys the benefits of AI-assisted diagnosis in improving patient care and outcomes.
This type of storyboard could be used in presentations, conferences, or educational materials to showcase an AI system that integrates with the diagnostic workflow, enabling more accurate and timely diagnoses of rare diseases.

## AI Development-Collection of Data

In healthcare, the use of AI is heavily reliant on the collection and analysis of data. Sources such as medical records, laboratory findings, and treatment particulars are gathered and organized as part of these collection processes.

Analyzing the obtained data is necessary to discern patterns, comprehend medical decision-making, and gain insights into patient health outcomes. By analyzing data, medical professionals can optimize patient care, enhance results, and decrease expenditures.

Prior to beginning the algorithm-building process, it is imperative to establish clear objectives for manipulating the collected data. Precise, quantifiable, attainable, relevant, and time-bound objectives are required. Regarding artificial intelligence in healthcare, SMART objectives are specific, measurable, attainable, relevant, and time-bound. With the intention of improving patient care, diagnostic precision, medical process optimization, and healthcare research, these aims will guide the development and deployment of artificial intelligence technology.

**Specific**: Smart goals in AI healthcare focus on addressing particular problems or objectives within the healthcare industry. For example, developing an artificial intelligence system that accurately detects and diagnoses early-stage cancer or unexpected diseases such as diabetes or retinopathy. If the issue is medication errors, the goal may be to reduce medication errors by 50% over the next year. Defining specific objectives guarantees that the algorithm development process is efficient and well-directed.

**Measurable**: The goals of artificial intelligence in healthcare should be quantifiable so that progress can be measured. This can be accomplished by establishing clear metrics or benchmarks for measuring the performance of AI algorithms and systems.

**Attainable**: The goals must be reasonable and realizable within the constraints of the available technology and resources. While attempting to revolutionize healthcare is essential, it is also vital to establish attainable goals that can be accomplished with the current expertise and infrastructure.

**Relevant**: The goals must be reasonable and realizable within the constraints of the available technology and resources. While attempting to revolutionize healthcare is essential, it is also necessary to establish attainable goals that can be accomplished with the current expertise and infrastructure.

**Time-bound**: Setting a deadline or timeline for achieving the objectives is essential. This facilitates maintaining focus and propelling progress toward the desired outcome. By establishing intelligent AI goals in healthcare, researchers and developers can ensure that their efforts are targeted and effectively contribute to improving the quality and efficacy of healthcare services.

## Curate and Preprocess the Data

After the data is filtered and collected, it is curated. Data curation involves selecting and gathering relevant data sources, cleaning and organizing the data, and ensuring that the data is of the highest quality. Because the accuracy and effectiveness of the algorithm are determined by the quality and applicability of the data utilized, these phases are crucial to algorithm creation.

Preprocessing is a prerequisite for analysis. It involves converting unprocessed data into a format suitable for analysis. This is achieved by operations including feature extraction, feature scaling, and data normalization. Preprocessing facilitates accurate and efficient data analysis, which strengthens the curation of data to precisely define our aims. We must establish these objectives by posing appropriate questions and obtaining answers that are essential to any investigation.

The subsequent phase entails data extraction from a multitude of sources, such as clinical data warehouses, electronic health records (EHRs), and claims databases, after curation and element identification. By implementing data validation criteria, the accuracy and quality of data sets can be assessed by detecting and removing errors, duplications, and missing information.

At BrainX, we have realized methods used for data analysis and strategic data collection, including statistical analysis and predictive analytics. However, collecting and analyzing data is challenging due to the vast amounts of data involved and the need for secure and compliant data storage and management.

There are two primary domains of interest at the forefront of data collection: personal health records and electronic health records. These consist of payer claims and reimbursement data, patient portal information, and patient profiles derived from patient portals. An additional endeavor to facilitate the transfer and consolidation of data among care partners is the Health Information

Exchange. Additional data sources, such as wearables, fitness monitors, and on-body sensors, offer valuable insights and recommendations for enhancing the quality and efficacy of healthcare. These recommendations specifically target people at the highest risk for illness prevention and early detection.

As anticipated, amassing such a vast amount of data and utilizing it to formulate judgments is not devoid of obstacles. Patient expectations, ever-changing data, fragmented data, and privacy/security requirements are the four most critical data-gathering difficulties currently facing the healthcare business.

## Fragmented Data

In healthcare, fragmented data refers to the problem of having inadequate or unorganized information across different systems, which results in lower accuracy, efficiency, and quality of healthcare delivery. Artificial intelligence assists in addressing this issue by providing data integration and analytics, allowing the healthcare industry to consolidate and organize data from multiple sources, as well as draw insights to improve decision-making processes, improving patient care. To begin, there are several sources and forms for healthcare data, including structured data, paper, digital, photos, and videos. With all of this in mind, data collection and aggregation communities are equally dispersed, making data extraction and integration a daunting issue.

## Ever-Changing Data

Physicians and patients, like the general populace, undergo life transitions such as relocation, career and name changes, retirement, and mortality.

Relocations, establishment of new locations, and mergers are all viable options for organizations. Additionally, implementing novel pharmaceuticals, tailored care models, and therapies disrupts data gathering and service provision, posing difficulties in the maintenance of accurate, comprehensive, and current health care information. A close correlation exists between information latency, member experience, and their economic sustainability, and outdated data and information. As a result, the implementation of novel treatment alternatives is postponed, healthcare initiatives elicit an unsatisfactory response, and participation and expertise are lacking.

## Privacy and Security Regulations

Maintaining patient trust is essential for establishing an efficient healthcare ecosystem. Patient confidentiality is based on HIPAA2 compliance and the use of electronic health records. Keeping data sets and activities compliant can be tough, given the ever-changing legal standards. Inadequate data quality and strategy prohibit firms from satisfying new regulatory standards, while also raising auditing and reporting costs. Improving overall population health until data security and compliance issues are effectively addressed must remain a priority.

## Data Collection—Patient Expectations

As an industry leader, BrainX anticipates that the healthcare system is on the verge of a perfect storm, with the aging Baby Boomer population putting the system to the test, while Millennials and Generation Z pressure healthcare organizations to adopt newer forms of engagement. As data is collected, organizations in the healthcare industry must adapt to a new age, member volume, and demographic. The sector must comprehend its members' shifting needs and preferences to provide lifestyle-aligned solutions.

We must have a cohesive data collection strategy that combines patient profile data, such as EHR/EMR, lab results, omnichannel interactions, transactions, and claims/reimbursement information, into a single and reliable data foundation. This will allow healthcare organizations to provide better and more personalized care. The data collected must be reliable, precise, and representative of the patient population.

## Data Analysis

W. Edwards Deming, an American engineer and author, stated, "Without data, you're just another person with an opinion." Data analysis is critical in healthcare for making well-informed decisions that can lead to better patient outcomes and more efficient operations. The ability to examine enormous amounts of data has become more powerful with emerging artificial intelligence, as AI can efficiently assess healthcare data. It is critical that we properly understand the data we are evaluating, including its sources, how it was acquired and kept, and any potential restrictions or biases. Without this knowledge, it is difficult to make precise inferences from the data.

After gaining a thorough comprehension of the data, the next step is to choose the most suitable artificial intelligence algorithms for the analysis. An array of algorithms exists, each possessing distinct merits and demerits. For example, decision trees are utilized to assess intricate data sets comprising several variables, while neural networks are more suitable for detecting patterns within extensive data sets.

## Choose the Algorithm

By choosing the most suitable algorithm for our problem, we can advance toward a robust and strategic implementation in the healthcare sector. BrainX is well-versed in a variety of algorithms, including logistic regression, neural networks, and decision trees; hence, it is critical that we comprehend the benefits and drawbacks of each method and choose the one that best fits our specific scenario. The healthcare institution must select the most suitable algorithm under its aims, missions, regulatory rules, and core values, following thorough testing and review. It must be verified and credible, with scientific data substantiating its effectiveness. After being chosen, an effort must be made to monitor the system's immediate and long-term efficacy in terms of patient outcomes, workflow, and expenses.

Creating a framework for ongoing assessment and development entails regularly reviewing and auditing the algorithm's performance and getting feedback from stakeholders, including patients and healthcare professionals. This approach requires open communication, and the healthcare organization needs to be transparent about any problems, obstacles, or advancements.

## Build Algorithms and Test Results

At Babylon, researchers used a new AI symptom checker approach, known as *causal machine learning*, to function as an "imagination" so AI could consider what symptoms it might see if the patient had an illness different from the one it was considering. The peer-reviewed research published in *Nature* showed that disentangling correlation from causation makes AI significantly more accurate. For example, this was the method of building and evaluating a specific algorithm for a particular treatment.

At Babylon, they gave an AI with a powerful algorithm the ability to imagine alternate realities and consider if this symptom would be present if the disease were different. As a result, the AI could diagnose probable sickness reasons in patients and outperform more than 70% of physicians on these written test cases. During testing, 1,671 actual written medical cases with typical and unusual symptoms for over 350 diseases were developed by a team of more than 20 general practitioners from Babylon.

A single doctor wrote each case, and it was subsequently evaluated by several doctors to make sure it accurately depicted a diagnostic circumstance. At least 50 written cases were presented to a panel of 44 Babylon GPs for assessment.

The physicians enumerated the most likely illnesses (on average, returning 2.58 potential diseases for each diagnosis). Their accuracy was gauged by the proportion of cases in which they accurately diagnosed the illness. The same tests were given to Babylon's AI, which used the newer causal algorithm in addition to an older approach based on correlations specifically designed for this study.

Creating dependable algorithms and experimental results is an essential element of healthcare technology. The results of the tests are used to determine whether a software application meets the necessary quality standards before it is released for commercial use. It is impossible to overstate prizing developing algorithms for scalable, trustworthy, and secure software applications, given that faulty or unreliable software and algorithmic programs can result in life-threatening complications such as misdiagnosis, delayed treatment, or mortality. Furthermore, testing outcomes are employed to detect software vulnerabilities or weaknesses, and algorithm creation and testing must align with user requirements and expectations. Potential issues can only be detected and resolved by conducting comprehensive testing of the results.

Developing unbiased and error-free algorithms is vital to guarantee the proper functioning, productivity, and efficiency of the software. Clear rules are necessary for developers to guarantee the proper compilation of source code and the optimization of the final product for optimal performance within the healthcare sector. Correctly created and executed building algorithms can reduce the risk of human error in patient-centered procedures, operational systems, and resources, in addition to automating various processes, operations, and systems.

## Modify and Train

IBM employed a comprehensive testing procedure in which algorithms are subjected to rigorous simulations and benchmarking to identify any weaknesses or improvement opportunities. The IBM team works closely with data scientists and engineers to modify and improve algorithms based on test results. This approach enables them to continuously enhance their algorithms iteratively.

Similarly, at Google DeepMind, the team extensively assesses and modifies algorithms before deploying them in the consumer sector. They use a combination of real-world data and simulated environments to thoroughly evaluate the algorithm before deployment. After careful consideration and analysis, we must train and modify the selected algorithm to analyze and interpret data effectively.

This is a crucial step in the data analysis procedure because it allows adjustments to the algorithm's parameters and settings to improve its accuracy and efficiency. The training process involves feeding the algorithm a set of data and allowing it to learn from this data, thereby enabling the algorithm to make more precise predictions and interpretations.

Additionally, modifications may be necessary to adjust the algorithm's behavior in response to unexpected data patterns. This requires a thorough understanding of the algorithm's underlying mechanics and the ability to make informed decisions about modifying its settings. We must devote the necessary time and resources to the training and modification process, which includes feeding the algorithm the data and allowing it to learn from it, as well as evaluating and modifying the algorithm's parameters to minimize discrepancies between its predictions and the actual outcomes in the data.

## External Validation

External validation guarantees the accuracy and dependability of the algorithm and the consistency and accuracy of the test findings. The need for external validation of these algorithms and the test findings corresponds with their escalating size and complexity. A thorough baseline should include patient demographics, clinical features, and illness prevalence data as we assess the external parameters.

Furthermore, the algorithm's precision can be evaluated by looking at its sensitivity, specificity, and positive and negative predictive values. These metrics assess how well the algorithm minimizes false positives and negatives while identifying patients with the disease of interest. Once the baseline is formulated, the next step is establishing a gold standard or reference standard in external validation. The gold standard compares the algorithm's output and determines its accuracy and reliability. Once we specify the gold standard, we must consistently apply it to all patients and samples.

Before furthering the AI project, it is imperative to ascertain the patient population. To accomplish this, it is necessary to identify and investigate the target demography of the algorithm, or a representative sample thereof, to perform an additional external validation. To ensure enough statistical power for the analysis and to account for variations in patient demographics, clinical characteristics, and disease prevalence, the study sample should be suitably large and varied in scope. This ensures that the algorithm is evaluated on various patient populations and that they can implement the results in actual healthcare settings.

Our objective with external validation is to present the results and conclusions clearly and straightforwardly by employing suitable statistical approaches for data analysis. Upon publication, the results ought to be substantiated through statistical analysis that is grounded in the gathered data and assessed criteria. It is imperative to ascertain any study constraints, including any selection or sample size biases, and suggest further research avenues. In the healthcare industry, external validation is crucial for verifying the precision and dependability of algorithms and test findings. By precisely following the prescribed methods and steps defined above, healthcare practitioners can have assurance in the validity of these algorithms and the subsequent test outcomes.

This will lead to enhanced healthcare delivery and improved patient outcomes.

## Deployment

Following the examination of external validation, curation, and preprocessing of AI data, we should deploy the algorithm in the population as the next logical step. Following the selection of an appropriate algorithm, we train it using accessible data.

Once the model is complete, it must be validated to ensure its optimal performance. The AI technology can then be included in the healthcare delivery system. Ongoing evaluation, monitoring, and model updates guarantee the efficient and effective implementation of AI in the healthcare sector.

The Department of Health and Human Services (HHS) is entrusted with advancing responsible AI innovation, development, deployment, and utilization. It also mitigates the hazards of AI-enabled healthcare technology and drug development.

President Biden's October 30, 2023, Executive Order, Safe, Secure, and Trustworthy Development and Use of Artificial Intelligence, provides substantial support for the notion that deployment is a critical phase. The Executive Order instructs HHS to establish an AI task force, develop an AI assurance policy, devise measures to enhance compliance with non-discrimination laws, establish an AI safety program, devise a strategy for incorporating AI into drug development, and award grants and prizes to encourage responsible AI development and use. The Executive Order instructs HHS to oversee the implementation of AI in technologies beyond the Food and Drug Administration's purview and supplements the FDA's existing regulatory initiatives.

Progress and the use of AI in the healthcare sector are outpacing efforts by the government to regulate its usage, like other industries. For example, the FDA received applications in 2021 for more than one hundred pharmaceuticals and biologicals that used AI/ML in one or more research phases. The Food and Drug Administration had inspected 171 medical devices incorporating AI/ML as of October 19, 2023. It has mandated the monitoring of AI-enabled technologies to ensure their long-term safety and performance in real-world scenarios; the integration of equity principles into AI-enabled technologies; the incorporation of safety, privacy, and security standards throughout the software development lifecycle; and the consideration of a customized approach when assessing the role of AI/ML in drug development. The EO is responsible for issuing directions concerning each of these matters.

Organizations should consider the complex interrelationships among the system, the actions it will govern, and the overall advantages of adopting AI while making the decision regarding its implementation. Furthermore, for enterprises to implement AI systems, they must have a well-defined set of criteria to assess whether the system will fulfill the business's predetermined objectives, a transparent data strategy, and a method for testing the system prior to purchase.

We should only deploy the system after evaluating the data and algorithms for improved safety, cost-effectiveness, speed, and efficiency in relation to their implementation. If not, it serves no use.

According to recent McKinsey research, innovative technologies like artificial intelligence are gradually being incorporated into and used in healthcare business models. As an illustration, certain AIs will increase organizational effectiveness by performing menial jobs like billing severity code assignments. AI systems may improve patient access to care.

AI systems may guarantee that we assign patients to the appropriate specialist and that they receive necessary testing before their initial appointment. Shah claims that doctors far too frequently waste patients' initial appointments by instructing them to obtain five tests and return in two weeks. "AI technology might bypass that. Physicians can see more patients by avoiding these pointless trips."[1]

AI deployment in healthcare is a complicated process that needs a well-thought-out plan to be implemented successfully. Deployment needs a defined data strategy, which includes a plan with defined metrics to assess when it is safe and ready. Since AI can only be as good as the data it uses to learn, it is essential to collect diverse data, properly label and clean it, and preserve it. Without a data strategy, deploying AI successfully is impossible.

Typically, clinician information technology interfaces implement algorithms powered by artificial intelligence. These interfaces comprise image viewers, electronic health records, and gadgets. Deploying and comprehending these interfaces is necessary to guarantee that they operate under the anticipated workflow between professionals and patients.

For implementing algorithms provided by suppliers to be secure and effective, meticulous deliberation is required. Variables to consider include whether to develop a pilot or allow them to function passively in the background as agents, where to deploy them (on servers or in the cloud), and how to install them efficiently in collaboration with the existing IT staff. Every deployment initiative may require the evaluation of cost-effectiveness and success, in addition to key performance indicators of successful deployment. The IT staff should coordinate with the deployment team to create instructional handbooks, in-service training for clinical user groups, and round-the-clock availability of deployment teams to address any issues.

## Maintain and Manage

AI initiatives are only the beginning of the journey toward achieving long-lasting and satisfactory outcomes. Once we deploy an AI initiative, we need to manage and maintain it appropriately to ensure its continued success. There are several effective methods that healthcare organizations can use to manage and maintain their AI initiatives. One method of managing and maintaining AI initiatives is through continuous monitoring. This involves regularly monitoring

the performance of the AI system to ensure that it is functioning as intended and to identify any issues that may arise. For example, the University of California, San Francisco (UCSF) used continuous monitoring to manage their AI system to predict patient deterioration. By monitoring the system continuously, they could identify issues with the accuracy of the predictions, which they could then address and improve.

Companies can also implement and sustain AI efforts through routine upgrades and updates. To maintain the efficacy of AI systems, it is imperative to consistently update and improve them, considering emerging technologies and obtaining new data. To illustrate, a prominent healthcare firm enhanced the precision of its AI system, responsible for identifying the potential for sepsis, through consistent updates. They could increase the efficacy of patient treatment by reducing the number of false alarms and enhancing the system's precision through consistent updates.

Healthcare institutions may also provide continuing education and training for personnel who interface with AI systems, in addition to implementing frequent upgrades and updates. Employees must possess a comprehensive understanding of the operational mechanisms, constraints, and interpretation of the outcomes generated by such intricate AI systems. To enhance its personnel's understanding of the AI system utilized for respiratory failure detection, the Hospital Corporation of America (HCA) Healthcare system, for instance, provided education and training. This comprehensive training made the personnel more proficient at deciphering system outcomes and formulating well-informed judgments concerning patient care.

Managing and maintaining AI initiatives in the healthcare ecosystem is necessary to continue providing valuable insights and improving patient outcomes. As AI technology evolves, healthcare organizations must remain vigilant in managing and maintaining their AI systems to stay ahead of the curve and drive better patient care.

## Post Deployment-Mining for Insights

Machine learning (ML) and artificial intelligence algorithms may mine the deployed clinical data for insights that improve patient outcomes. Nevertheless, these exceedingly intricate systems are vulnerable to a decline in efficiency and are highly responsive to fluctuations in their immediate surroundings. After effective integration into clinical practice, ML/AI algorithms should be subject to ongoing surveillance and revisions to guarantee their sustained safety and effectiveness.

BrainX acknowledges that we can adapt the methods used for decades in hospital quality assurance and quality improvement domains to oversee static machine learning algorithms. However, processes for continuous model updates are still in their infancy. We understand the critical considerations that need to be taken into account when choosing between existing technologies. MLOps is a valuable technique in developing high-quality machine learning and artificial intelligence solutions.

Data scientists and machine learning engineers can work together more quickly on model development and production by using an MLOps strategy to build continuous integration and deployment (CI/CD) procedures with appropriate ML model monitoring, validation, and governance. Machine learning is challenging to produce. The process of machine learning involves intricate elements, including data preparation, explainability, deployment, training, tweaking, and monitoring of the model, among many others. Additionally, it necessitates cooperation and handoffs between teams—Data Science, Data Engineering, and ML Engineering. Keeping all these processes synchronized and operating simultaneously naturally requires strict operational discipline. The machine learning lifecycle's experimentation, iteration, and continual improvement are all included in MLOps.

AI monitoring aims to alert teams when a special-cause deviation occurs and provide support in identifying required model adjustments or data gathering process refinements. Performance can be negatively impacted by both common-cause and special-cause variation; thus, statistical approaches must distinguish between the two. Statistical control charts are a customary Statistical Process Control (SPC) instrument utilized to identify and represent diverse forms of shifts.

As an illustration, a conventional control chart utilized in monitoring algorithms represents a succession of observations as a time-sum statistic. It exhibits control limits to highlight the standard range of values for this statistic. It generated an alarm when the chart statistic is above the control boundaries, suggesting the probable existence of special-cause variation. The hospital should investigate the underlying reason to determine whether corrective steps are required following the activation of an alarm. This involves the collaboration of stakeholders, including statisticians, healthcare providers, IT specialists, and the designer of the original model.

Several studies have suggested utilizing ML explainability measures, such as variable importance, for monitoring, considering the intricate nature of ML algorithms. The purpose of these measures is to offer a more intuitive depiction of the data. Nonetheless, it is critical to avoid over-interpreting these graphs. Because most metrics defined in the ML literature quantify the significance attributed to each feature by the current model, changes in these metrics merely signify a modification in the input variable distribution and do not inherently suggest a modification in the relationship between the input and target variables.

The relevance and currency of algorithms and data necessitate frequent maintenance and updates. Due to technological and medical advancements, algorithms and data can rapidly become obsolete; thus, it is critical to maintain an accurate knowledge base. Consistent updates additionally contribute to error prevention and improve the accuracy of clinical decision-making. Healthcare professionals must monitor and secure patient information to prevent unauthorized access or disclosure. To safeguard the privacy of patient information, healthcare providers should adopt access controls, encryption, and secure data storage.

An algorithm, a set of directives that delineate the procedures to resolve a given issue, ought to be developed, computed, and resolved meticulously and accurately. This guarantees that we duly contemplate and incorporate each facet of the problem. To effectively resolve a problem, it is vital to comprehend its fundamental causes and contributing aspects. For example, a high number of hospital readmissions, inadequate patient education, non-adherence to medication, and a dearth of social support may all be contributory causes. After recognizing the problem, we must gather additional information through surveys, reviews of medical records, and analyses of hospital data. Analysis of the gathered data is necessary to identify patterns and trends that can guide the algorithm's development.

## Note

1. Clark E, Singhal S, Weber K. The future of healthcare: Value creation through next-generation business models. McKinsey & Company. 2021 Jan 4. https://www.mckinsey.com/industries/healthcare/our-insights/the-future-of-healthcare-value-creation-through-next-generation-business-models

# Chapter 12

# From Vectors to Algorithms

Since its 2019 acquisition of GitHub, Microsoft has endeavored to keep the project collaboration platform's "developer-first" ethos. The vector's search strategy, embodied by the Space Partition Tree and Graph algorithm, attempted to address the fact that rising data volumes rendered keyword searches "brittle."

Using models of deep learning, the algorithm could search a "vector" of information in milliseconds. Vector database searches are more than just identifying words or phrases. They incorporate the "meanings" of each word or phrase into their neural network.

Rangan Majumder, Microsoft's program manager for Bing search and AI, stated, "As deep learning became more prevalent, we applied it to some of these issues where keyword search was ineffective." Using vectors, or numerical representations of a data point, word, or image pixel, the aim was to deliver relevant results more quickly.

Deep learning models are applied to these vectors to better comprehend and represent a search's intent, considering ambiguities such as words with multiple meanings. Besides applying deep learning models, the vector search initiative involved indexing over 150 billion pieces of data by the search engine to improve traditional keyword matching. The indexed data included web page content, complete queries, and other media types, besides single characters and words, to strengthen an otherwise fragile strategy. The search engine then examined its indexed vectors to find a relevant match.

Vectors in AI, particularly healthcare algorithms, are numerical representations of distinct entities or objects. In healthcare, vectors play a crucial

 DOI: 10.4324/9781003661627-16

role, frequently used to represent a variety of patients, diseases, treatments, and outcome characteristics. For example, in a machine learning algorithm designed to predict patient outcomes, vectors can represent individual patient attributes such as age, gender, medical history, and vital signs. The vectors were fed into the algorithm, which uses them to make predictions and decisions, such as identifying high-risk patients or recommending personalized treatment plans.

Using vectors in AI algorithms provides a way to organize and process complex data sets by converting information into numerical representations. In contrast to storyboarding, which focuses on the sequence of steps required to solve a problem, vector diagramming visualizes data flow and decision-making within an algorithm.

In vector diagrams, a node represents each algorithmic step, and arrows show the data flow or decisions between nodes. This enables the development team to understand better how the algorithm will operate in real-world situations and identify potential areas for improvement or optimization. Identifying potential errors or inefficiencies before implementation is one of the primary advantages of vector diagramming.

Vectors play a significant role in identifying any potential bottlenecks or sources of error with the intended algorithms. This allows them to make informed decisions about optimizing the algorithm to improve patient outcomes and streamline processes. Here are examples of how vectors and algorithms work together:

**Medical Imaging**: Medical images, such as CT scans and MRI scans, are represented as vectors in radiology. Algorithms can analyze these vectors to detect anomalies, segment organs and tissues, and diagnose diseases.

**Patient Monitoring**: Vectors can represent vital signs that have been obtained from patients at various times, such as blood pressure, heart rate, and respiration rate. These vectors are processed by algorithms to find patterns, spot abnormalities, and estimate the chance of deterioration.

**Predictive Analytics**: Algorithms can use machine learning techniques to create predictive models by describing patient data as vectors. These models can identify patients who are at elevated risk, forecast the course of diseases, and improve treatment strategies.

**Genomic Analysis**: Personalized medicine is a complicated and gradually developing field in healthcare. The various obstacles that keep customized treatments out of reach can eclipse the great promise of Precision Medicine.

The primary barrier lies in the unavailability of resources to gather, analyze, and apply patient genetic information. Healthcare providers can use genetic information with clinical, pharmacological, and lifestyle data to assist in the identification of early disease symptoms or an individual's susceptibility to developing a certain ailment. Genomics enables identifying the fundamental causes of clinical changes, which may lead to developing more effective and personalized treatments. Genomics research is advancing rapidly, and this information is intricate. Because many health systems continue to struggle to give physicians genomic data in a clear and comprehensible manner at the time of service, Precision Medicine remains theoretical.

According to our findings at BrainX, many types of data have been transformed by techniques associated with artificial intelligence and machine learning. Considering the enormous size of the genome, artificial intelligence methods can aid in detecting latent patterns within the data.

Although the complexity of genetic information makes it an ideal domain for advanced analytical methods, there are now barriers that could hinder the progress of targeted therapeutic interventions. Utilizing AI for the analysis of genomic data in healthcare is not without its share of potential biases, errors, and instructional deficiencies. To accomplish the goal of individualized medicine, the industry must surmount certain challenges.

Transforming genomic data from an incomprehensible resource to a valuable medicinal asset makes up the initial stage. Vectors may represent genetic data, including DNA sequences and gene expression levels, which would be impossible to convey without artificial intelligence. By analyzing these vectors, algorithms can gain insights into population genetics, identify disease-associated genetic variants, and tailor treatment strategies accordingly. Integrating vectors and algorithms offers substantial room for improvement in patient care, research, and healthcare administration.

It is critical to ensure the ethical application of data, maintain confidentiality and integrity, and address any potential biases or limitations in the employed algorithms. In summary, algorithms contribute computational power, while vectors furnish a mathematical depiction of healthcare data. These two elements collaborate synergistically to establish a robust framework for decision-making guided by data, personalized medicine, and the enhancement of healthcare practices.

## From Algorithms to Coding

DeepMind developed an artificial intelligence system called AlphaCode, which claims, "It 'Writes' computer programs at a competitive level." The Alphabet subsidiary assessed its system against coding challenges used in human competitions and discovered its program placed it in the top fifty-four percent of human coders.

According to DeepMind, the outcome is a significant step forward for autonomous coding, although its abilities do not represent the average programmer's programming tasks. Converting an algorithm into executable code involves several processes and mechanics. The complex procedure requires distinct mechanics and processes that organizations must adopt and implement.

## Choose a Programming Language

One must choose a programming language before converting an algorithm into executable code. There is an extensive range of programming languages, each with its own set of rules and grammar. The programming environment, the accessibility of libraries and tools, the characteristics of the task at hand, and the programmer's preferences influence the programming language choice.

## Translate the Algorithm

To translate an algorithm into a programming language, we must decompose the algorithm into smaller, more manageable components, each of which is then mapped to a corresponding construct in the target language. For example, we can translate an algorithmic loop into a "for" loop implemented in Python, C, Java, or an alternative programming language.

## Compilation

Once the code has been transformed, compiled, or interpreted into machine language, the code must remain understandable and functional for the computer's processor. The evident and indispensable procedure involves executing the code line by line and converting it into machine language with the aid of an interpreter program.

## Testing and Debugging

To ensure that the code generates the desired outcomes and is devoid of any faults or malicious components, developers need to debug and evaluate it through tests after development and decomposition. Assessing the functionality and dependability of the code through debugging is vital and time-consuming, as it involves locating and correcting any flaws or defects.

## Deployment

After testing and debugging the code, we can deploy it in a production environment. This involves putting the code into use and making it available to users, with the necessity to monitor the code and gather user feedback to ensure that it works as intended, identifying any issues that may arise.

## *Chapter 13*

# Modular Approach to Algorithm and AI Development

> AI is a tool, an instrument to help humans. We need to build AI systems that assist and augment human intelligence and make us better.
>
> **—Demis Hassabis**

DeepMind, a Google research division, uses a modular approach to building artificial intelligence solutions, demonstrating the strength and usefulness of this methodology. This method entails breaking down big systems into smaller, independent modules that may be created and optimized independently before being integrated into larger AI frameworks.

DeepMind extensively leverages modular components across many AI areas as proof of a modular strategy, allowing its researchers to solve tough challenges more precisely and efficiently. DeepMind engineers can focus on improving and refining these components, increasing their performance and reliability by concerted efforts in isolating individual functionality or tasks into distinct modules. This architecture for modular development provides them with the flexibility required to upgrade the individual building blocks of their AI systems continuously.

DeepMind's use of the modular approach in AI development represents a paradigm shift, empowering researchers to tackle complex challenges with granularity and precision. By diligently constructing and refining

DOI: 10.4324/9781003661627-17

these building blocks, DeepMind pioneers breakthroughs, amplifying performance, adaptability, and interdisciplinary collaboration. This approach not only pushes the boundaries of what AI can achieve but also holds the potential for us to grow and advance in our own work, inspiring us to consider its adoption.

Modular AI is an artificial intelligence paradigm comprising numerous specialized algorithms or modules, each engineered to execute a distinct function. This strategy is specialized to specific medical applications in the healthcare business, including medical imaging, drug discovery, and patient diagnostics.

Many instant results and advantages accompany modular growth (Figure 13.1). One potential approach to enhancing the efficiency, effectiveness, and velocity of medical diagnosis, treatment, research, and decision-making is through developing expert systems that support healthcare practitioners in rendering rapid and accurate diagnoses. Modular AI can additionally aid providers in identifying potential health issues, predicting outcomes, and developing tailored treatment programs through finely tuned analysis of medical records, test findings, and other clinical data.

As we deploy more modular development and predictive models, we should expect enhanced predictive analytics to help us foresee and avoid health problems before they arise. Modular AI can uncover patterns and risk factors for preventive care by evaluating massive datasets in patient

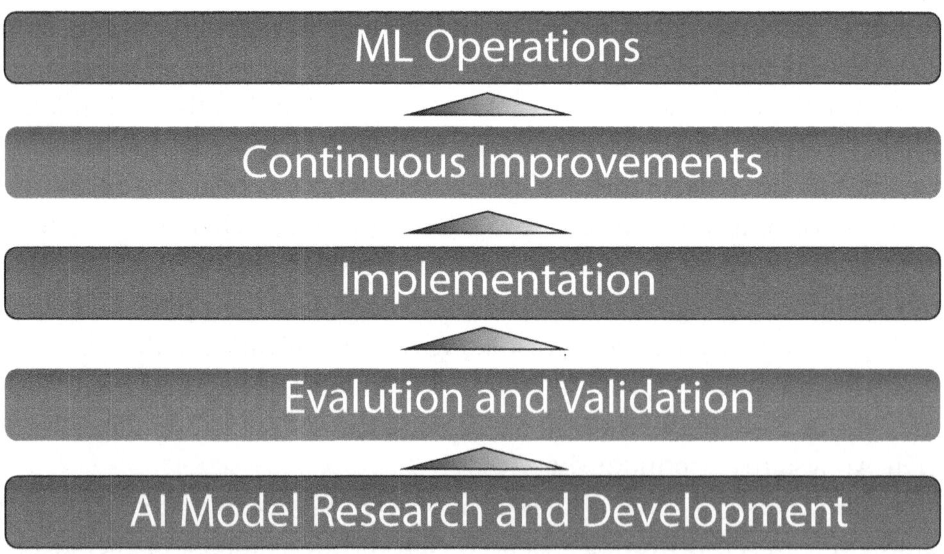


**Figure 13.1 Modular development and implementation of AI**

information, such as genetics, medical history, lifestyle factors, and environmental factors.

Precision medicine benefits from modular AI since personalized treatment regimens are produced based on a person's unique genetic makeup, lifestyle, and medical history. By examining a patient's genomic data and other clinical information, modular AI can discover the most effective treatment options and dosages while reducing negative effects.

At BrainX, we undertake research in a variety of healthcare industries and studies, and have observed that using a modular strategy results in a vastly better arena of medical study. By analyzing large datasets of medical records, clinical trial results, and genomic data, modular AI speeds up medical research by automating data analysis and assisting researchers in identifying new treatment targets, validating existing hypotheses, and speeding up the discovery of new drugs and therapies. Here are a few insights into the inner workings of modular development in healthcare artificial intelligence:

**Dividing AI Tasks into Modules**: Healthcare AI tasks necessitate diverse algorithms and models. Modular development entails identifying these activities and dividing them into individual modules. Individual modules, for example, might manage medical image analysis, patient diagnostics, natural language processing for medical records, and drug discovery.

**Independent Development and Testing**: Each module was created independently, with a specific goal in mind. This enables developers to work on many modules, saving time and effort. We can thoroughly examine individual modules in isolation to ensure their accuracy and effectiveness.

**Standardized Interfaces**: Modules in modular AI development conform to standardized interfaces to facilitate easy integration. Modules connect with one another using standardized protocols and data formats, allowing for effective collaboration.

**Reusability and Flexibility**: A significant benefit of modular development is its reusability. Once developers successfully develop and assess a module, they can reuse it for multiple AI applications. If enhancements or updates are required, developers can focus on a single module without affecting the entire AI system.

**Interoperability**: AI systems must frequently interact with existing medical infrastructure and electronic health record systems, and interoperability is necessary to allow seamless integration with various healthcare IT systems.

**Scalability and Maintenance**: Modular development enables scalability. We can introduce additional modules into the existing AI system as healthcare needs grow or expand. This adaptability also makes maintenance easier because developers may update or replace specific modules without disrupting the entire system.

AI and algorithms can benefit from modular software development in terms of scalability, cost savings, development time, and problem fixes. By separating tasks into modules, programmers may update the system without having to rewrite the code from scratch for each new feature or component, resulting in enhanced scalability. By doing so, we can maximize the potential of each application while minimizing expenditures.

***

## Application and Outcomes

Sergey Brin, a well-known computer scientist and entrepreneur who immigrated to the United States at an early age, co-founded Google with Larry Page. Before Google, he earned a bachelor's degree in mathematics and computer science from the University of Maryland and a doctorate in computer science from Stanford University. During his time at Stanford, Brin met Larry Page for the first time, and together, they developed and applied the algorithmic approach, serving as the foundational basis for Google's search engine, which is currently one of the most successful and influential technologies in existence.

Respectful use of AI requires us to be open to specific outcomes after applying the modules. For example, drug discovery is another application of modular AI, which analyzes data on genetic sequences, chemical compounds, and molecular structures with specialized modules. Researchers can identify potential drug candidates and develop new treatments more efficiently by doing so. Along with drug discovery, various areas of AI modular development exist, allowing for granular optimization and facilitating breakthroughs in performance in healthcare.

A notable example is robotics. As surgeons and physicians, we understand that robotics work entails employing modularity to manage various aspects of robot control and decision-making. By modularizing activities like vision, grasping, and locomotion, we may improve the adaptability of robot systems. With modularization, developers can improve and optimize each module individually, resulting in more robust and efficient robotic systems.

***

## Modular Approach Broad Perspective

Recent Microsoft AI initiatives have significantly contributed to the healthcare industry with the Microsoft Healthcare Bot. It is a recent example of using the modular approach and development with AI after the Coronavirus pandemic, when Copenhagen's emergency medical services received an influx of calls.

The organization, which provides emergency care to approximately one-third of Denmark's population, received approximately 2,000 calls from concerned individuals with COVID-19 symptoms or questions about the disease after the outbreak began. To answer the volume of calls, the company opened a second call center to manage the inquiries, but it was insufficient.

The Microsoft Bot is a modular AI-powered chatbot platform that enables healthcare organizations to build and deploy virtual assistants for various healthcare-related tasks, such as appointment scheduling, symptom checking, and patient education. The modular approach allows organizations to customize and extend the chatbot's functionality by integrating specific modules for different healthcare services.

Modularity in AI and healthcare algorithms provides advantages, including scalability and savings. For instance, modular systems are more trustworthy than monolithic options because updating a single module does not affect the rest of the system's functionality.

One of the primary reasons for the success of ChatGPT's modular approach in healthcare settings was its adaptability and ability to accommodate various healthcare contexts. ChatGPT could better comprehend and address healthcare concerns by dissecting complex circumstances into smaller modules.

By employing the appropriate diagnostic module, ChatGPT accurately identifies the underlying medical conditions of patients presenting a specific set of symptoms, enabling efficient and precise diagnosis, thereby reducing the possibility of misdiagnosis.

## Modular Approach Advantages

A survey of healthcare leaders in the United States found that 41% reported their AI use was fully functional as of 2021. A further 26% said their AI system was moderately functional, although 5% indicated they had not yet incorporated an AI system.[1] According to a recent article in the *National Library of Medicine*, "Modular development and Chatbots are natural language processing systems that are part of AI devices acting as virtual conversational agents mimicking human interactions."[2] While this technology is still in its developmental phase, health chatbots could potentially increase access to healthcare, improve doctor-patient and clinic–patient communication, or help manage the increasing demand for health services via remote testing, medication adherence monitoring, or teleconsultations.

The chatbot technology enables specific health surveys, creating personal health-related reminders, communicating with clinical teams, scheduling appointments, retrieving and analyzing health data, and translating diagnostic patterns that consider behavioral indicators such as physical activity, sleep, and nutrition. This technology can potentially alter the delivery of healthcare systems, thereby increasing the uptake, equity, and cost-effectiveness of health services while narrowing the health and well-being gap; however, these hypotheses require additional investigation.

We have implemented chatbots in health education, diagnostics, and mental health. A 40-page article review of conversational agents defines chatbot taxonomy, identifies the primary challenges, and defines the types and contexts of chatbots in health. As presented by the internet-based Doc-Bot, which is delivered via mobile phone or a Messenger-based chatbot for outpatient and translational medicine, chatbots can provide instantaneous responses to health-related questions from patients while searching for specific patterns of symptoms to predict disease.[3]

This demonstrates the opportunity for a modular approach to develop AI-powered applications and algorithms. Here are the benefits of using a modular system in healthcare:

### *Improved Collaboration*

With ongoing modular AI development, the American Diabetes Association, in partnership with Microsoft, is developing AI solutions for improved patient care. This collaboration among varying healthcare studies and sectors has seen success, as they have customized and extended the functionality of their chatbots by integrating specific, individualized modules for different healthcare services.

With AI, our industry faces an ever-increasing demand for better and more efficient algorithms. However, algorithm development has historically occurred in a siloed environment, with each team operating independently of the others. This method frequently causes unnecessary work and poor coordination, which causes projects to be delayed or even canceled.

However, working together is essential when creating modular algorithms. Separating algorithms into smaller, more manageable pieces allows for concurrent development without compromising the integrity of any team's efforts. This method shortens the development cycle and improves the overall quality of the algorithm, as developers can refine and evaluate each component separately before incorporating it into the whole.

Creating useful healthcare algorithms can be difficult and requires understanding from various areas, including computer science, data science, and medicine. Using a modular technique, you can build a team of professionals from several disciplines to work on a single component. Working together, we may develop a more robust application or algorithm that meets the interests of all parties by providing benefits.

## *Increased Flexibility*

The healthcare industry constantly evolves, and implementing a modular approach to development can help healthcare organizations be more agile and respond quickly to these changes. By breaking down algorithms, developers can create new modules and seamlessly integrate them into the system without disrupting the existing ones. This enables easier adaptation to changing conditions.

## *Increased Transparency*

How AI-powered applications and algorithms reached their results or made recommendations is not always evident. A modular approach can help increase transparency by breaking down the system to function with sensitive patient information, which helps create trust in the system among patients and staff.

### *Enhanced Diagnostics with AI and Algorithms*

Diagnostics is one of the key applications of the modular approach. Since AI-powered algorithms manage massive volumes of medical data, such as patient records, lab findings, imaging scans, and genetic data, by modularizing, we as providers can make accurate and quicker diagnoses. Modular diagnostic systems can detect symptoms, compare patient data to current medical knowledge, and make reliable recommendations, supporting physicians in difficult decision-making processes.

### *Precision Treatment Planning and Personalized Medicine*

Precision treatment planning and tailored medicine rely heavily on modular systems. By merging patient-specific data with modularized AI algorithms, healthcare providers can find the best treatment courses, anticipate drug reactions, and assess potential side effects or consequences. This personalized approach to medicine improves patient outcomes, reduces adverse effects, and aids in the tailoring of treatment regimens based on genetic profiles, lifestyle, and environmental factors.

### *Real-Time Remote Patient Monitoring*

Modular healthcare systems make real-time remote patient monitoring possible. These systems may track vital signs, detect problems, and securely transfer data to healthcare providers by merging wearable devices and IoT sensors. Advanced algorithms examine incoming data and alert medical personnel to unusual trends or changes. Overall, remote monitoring improves patient safety, allows for early intervention, and lessens the burden on healthcare facilities.

## Modular Approach Disadvantages

While the modular method has enormous potential, it has drawbacks and limitations. Data privacy and security are huge barriers. Because modular systems rely on copious amounts of sensitive patient data, we must set suitable privacy safeguards and rigorous security processes in place to prevent data breaches and illegal access. Furthermore, guaranteeing interoperability and compatibility between various modules and systems is critical for fostering smooth integration and preventing fragmentation. Using a modular approach in healthcare confronts the following difficulties:

### *Integration Complexity*

Integrating multiple modules into a comprehensive system can be complicated and difficult, necessitating careful planning and coordination. If not done carefully, integration can lead to errors and inconsistencies, jeopardizing the system's precision and dependability.

### *Data Integration*

As previously noted, successful AI-powered applications and algorithms need massive amounts of clean data. However, integrating data from many sources can be complex and time-consuming, needing an understanding of data administration and analysis.

### *Standardization*

Modular development causes an elevated level of standardization to ensure that diverse modules function together effortlessly. In healthcare, where systems and practices differ between organizations and areas, standardization can be difficult and remains one of the steepest challenges.

### *Ethical Considerations and Bias*

Implementing AI and algorithms in healthcare raises significant ethical issues. To ensure accuracy and dependability, algorithms must be rigorously validated, preventing potential biases from influencing diagnoses or treatment plans. In addition, healthcare providers must prioritize transparency, accountability, and clear communication to build patients' trust and address their concerns about using AI and algorithms in their care.

### *Future Perspectives and Integration*

As efforts are ongoing to integrate AI and algorithms seamlessly into healthcare systems, the modular approach relies upon technological advances; we can expect increased integration, precision, and patient outcomes. As we address implementation and integration challenges, it is essential to continue investing in research and push for a wider and more sophisticated collaboration effort, along with robust regulatory measures, to maximize the potential benefits.

## Security Breaches

One negative as we move toward algorithm modularization is the increased chance of security breaches. Multiple teams typically create modular algorithms that can share sensitive data access. This can make maintaining consistent security protocols challenging, raising the risk of illegal access and data breaches.

## Comprehension and Retention

Understanding and implementing modular algorithms may be more difficult for healthcare practitioners. A modular algorithm approach may have multiple components, increasing the algorithm's complexity and the difficulty that healthcare professionals experience in properly interpreting and executing the algorithm.

***

### *Vignette: Personal Note from Dr. Frank Papay*

"In any risky venture, working from the awareness of potential failure develops a platform of confidence and resilience to prepare and react to whatever happens. With any implementing innovation, such as AI or risky new surgical procedures, where there is a lot of risk, you include risk failure factors in the design, simulating, predicting, and preemptively mitigating them as you would for a rocket launch. It is not the innovation itself, but the execution of the innovation that reveals the most risk!"

***

Although modular algorithm development can simplify the expansion and maintenance of complex healthcare algorithms, it is essential to consider the potential drawbacks of this strategy. Healthcare organizations must adopt effective measures to manage module dependencies, integrate systems seamlessly, ensure consistent security protocols, and train healthcare professionals to use modular algorithms effectively to mitigate risks and difficulties.

The modular approach to AI in healthcare contributes to the goal of democratizing AI. By dividing AI systems into modular components, developers can design reusable and flexible modules that can be easily implemented in multiple healthcare settings, regardless of technical knowledge. This ease of access promotes AI adoption, allowing healthcare companies of many sizes and resources to benefit from its promise, unlocking the full potential of this approach. While obstacles exist, the modular approach has clear advantages. Continued efforts are necessary to advance AI in healthcare to benefit patients and healthcare providers around the globe.

***

## Important Points

- The modular AI and algorithm development approach can revolutionize healthcare by improving diagnostics, facilitating personalized medicine, and remote patient monitoring.
- As an organization or healthcare provider, we remember that the modular approach improves the explainability and transparency of AI algorithms.
- Most people often refer to conventional AI systems as black boxes, making it challenging to comprehend how decisions are made and emphasizing the need for transparency.
- As modular systems rely on vast quantities of sensitive patient data, organizations must implement appropriate privacy measures and robust security protocols to protect against data breaches and unauthorized access.
- It is essential to continue investing in research, collaboration, and regulatory measures to maximize the potential benefits of the modular approach.

## Notes

1. Stewart Connor. Article. Use of AI in healthcare in the US. https://www.statista.com/statistics/1256531/use-of-ai-in-healthcare-in-the-us/.

2. Nadarzynski T, Miles O, Cowie A, Ridge D. Acceptability of artificial intelligence (AI)-led chatbot services in healthcare: A mixed-methods study. *Digit Health*. 2019 Aug 21;5:2055207619871808.
3. Nadarzynski T, Miles O, Cowie A, Ridge D. Acceptability of artificial intelligence (AI)-led chatbot services in healthcare: A mixed-methods study. *Digit Health*. 2019 Aug 21;5:2055207619871808. https://doi.org/10.1177/2055207619871808.

# Chapter 14

# Generative Artificial Intelligence

> When Steve Jobs made the computer say, "Hello," it changed everything. Similarly, ChatGPT has made AI say "Hello" to the masses and is set to change anything and everything.
>
> **—Piyush Mathur, Co-founder, BrainX and BrainX Community**

Large Language Models (LLMs) are language models with hundreds of millions to billions of parameters that feature unsupervised pre-training and supervised fine-tuning. LLMs are useful in various applications, such as representation learning, machine translation, and text production. Recently, generative LLMs have taken the Computer Science and AI research communities by storm, with models like LLaMA and Stable Diffusion gaining widespread use, and ChatGPT reaching over 100 million active users in just two months after its release.

Prompting introduces a unique paradigm where downstream tasks can be modeled similarly to the ones solved during pre-training through a textual prompt. We might view this as an alternative to the traditional paradigms of unsupervised pre-training and supervised fine-tuning. We strongly relate the act of prompting to the concept of in-context learning, in which we provide a language model with an input consisting of training instances and a test instance.

In recent years, BrainX has seen an increase in companies incorporating generative AI into their products. ChatGPT and other large language models are being added to Notion, Salesforce, Shopify, Quizlet, and others

DOI: 10.4324/9781003661627-18

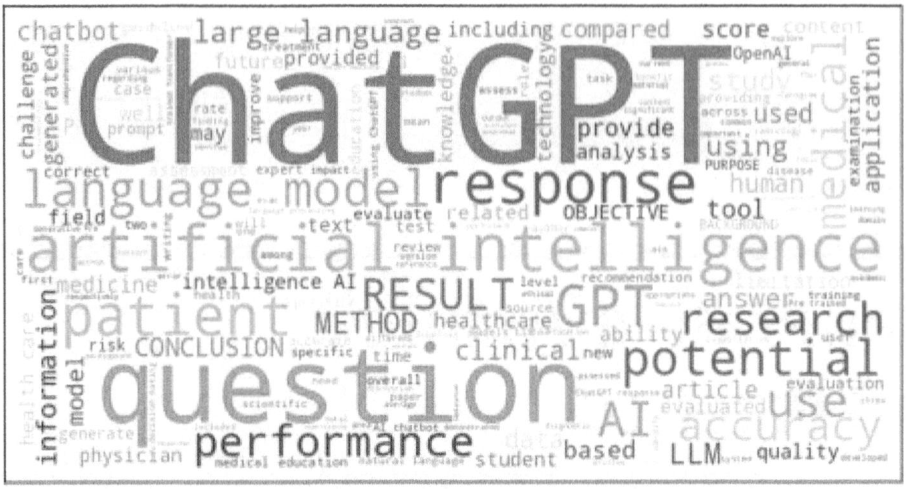


**Figure 14.1 Word cloud of large language models**

(Figure 14.1). What effect will it have on healthcare? It will help us go the last mile with our patients. This is significant because involving patients improves outcomes. LLMs will save lives.

Large language models have been around for a while, with their development and popularity skyrocketing since the mid-2010s. Large-scale neural networks and advances in natural language processing (NLP) techniques have enabled the creation of increasingly powerful language models. All these models are known as transformers and were first introduced in 2017. Since then, we have seen emerging ChatGPT-4 and others that have recently dominated our public discussion and interest. However, ChatGPT-4 is not the only one that can transform with other well-known models that include GPT, BERT, Chinchilla, Gopher, Bloom, PaLM, and LLaMA.

Large Language Models are distinct from "traditional" machine learning models (Figure 14.2). Traditional AI is used to recommend your next Netflix movie or determine whether an email is spam. However, large multimodal models in healthcare predict disease progression or assist in cancer detection using different data types, with vastly different results.

We can use LLMs for tasks that more conventional models previously performed, but with better outputs; many are indistinguishable from how humans would perform or report. While those traditional models may have good predictive accuracy and work with multimodal data, the major impact in healthcare will be that we are about to change the way human-AI interaction will work.

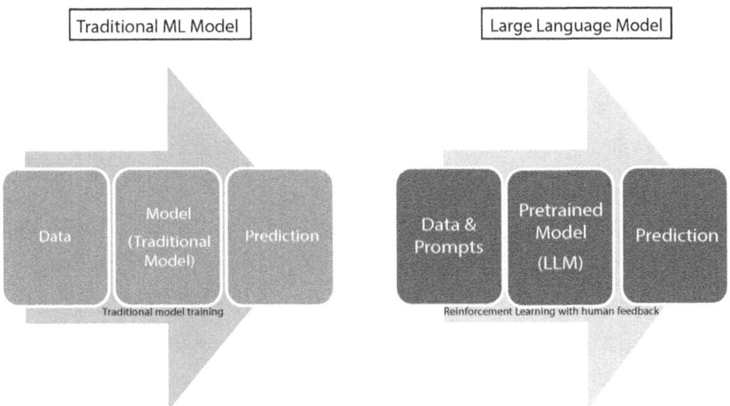


**Figure 14.2 Key differences in the development of traditional machine learning models versus large language models**

LLMs enable a unique way of interacting with technology. For example, we can look at Microsoft's new AI-powered copilot. "We are here today to talk about something fundamental to human experience, the way we work," Satya Nadella said in his announcement. "Most notably, the way we interact with computers. In fact, we have been on a never-ending quest for human-computer symbiosis for decades."

Since the field of generative artificial intelligence has seen a rapid acceleration of innovation in recent months, large language models are capturing academic, media, and public attention. GPT-3, BERT, and ChatGPT are examples of LLMs trained on large swaths of the internet to respond impressively to human queries (Figure 14.2). The ability of these generalized LLMs to write fiction, develop computer code, and speculate on the future has led to the realization that we are approaching artificial general intelligence for the first time.

Because of the copious amounts of free-text information available for training models, we have already proposed that LLMs, such as ChatGPT, could have applications in the healthcare field. We have proposed that models could aid in writing discharge letters by summarizing a patient's hospital stay after reading their medical records. We have also suggested using LLMs in medical research, supported by the empirical example of GatorTron, an LLM trained on over 90 billion words of text from electronic health records.

We evaluated the same model for its ability to respond to medical questions in natural language. These capabilities have sparked speculation about using LLMs as a medical triage service or as an application to provide plain English answers to medical questions from the public. However, we should note that such technologies, in their current form, have the potential to cause harm. It has well documented this effect occurs in mental health, where natural language processing algorithms have shown biases relating to religion, race, gender, nationality, sexuality, and age.

However, LLMs are still in their infancy despite widespread speculation about their future potential. Current constraints include the amount of computer power required for LLMs to function, which is frequently expensive. LLMs also require massive amounts of data to be trained effectively, which may necessitate data sharing between institutions to train algorithms. Strict data privacy laws and institutional data protection agreements contribute to data silos, making such data sharing a unique challenge in healthcare. Solutions such as federated learning or synthetic data are emerging to allow cross-border data sharing.

While these methods have demonstrated efficacy in different fields, their suitability for LLMs remains uncertain. The uncertainty surrounding the future of this research does not preclude its possibility or remoteness. We cannot overstate the importance of large language and multimodal models in facilitating decision-making and healthcare delivery. Because we routinely applied machine learning to health sector problems, particularly clinical decision support, it has typically limited its application to single-modal data. In the medical domain of machine learning, endeavors to enhance prognostication and emulate the multimodal processing of expert clinical decision-making have faced the integration of heterogeneous data.

At BrainX, we have been investigating the use of various transformer-based models and LLMs since their inception in healthcare. These models clearly have demonstrated superiority, flexibility, ease of use, and efficiency over prior NLP techniques. At BrainX, we are researching the optimal training and implementation methods to use these LLMs. Their implementation has challenges, including cost, the need for evaluation, and significant computer infrastructure.

We are studying the areas in healthcare where they truly can affect the quality-of-care delivery and demonstrate a clear value proposition (Figure 14.3). We have proposed HumanELY (human evaluation of Large Language Model Yield) as a human evaluation method. It is a freely available web tool for evaluating LLM outputs.[1]

Through large language models, we intend to depict the flow of information from hospitals/care centers that generate disparate data.

Computational modeling and information fusion facilitate outcomes of interest, such as drug and treatment targets, at the patient level. According

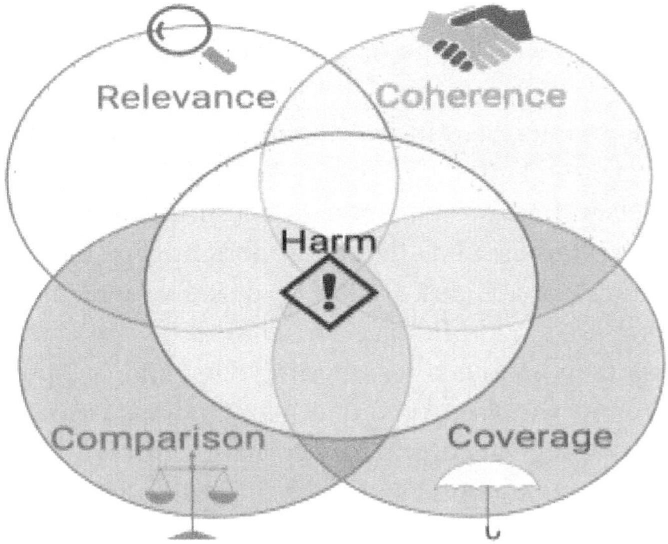


**Figure 14.3 Key metrics of human evaluation of large language model outputs**

to a recent report by the Healthcare Information and Management Systems Society (HIMSS), they project large language models in artificial intelligence and machine learning in healthcare to grow at a compound annual growth rate of 44.9% between 2018 and 2025.

Large language models and multi-model data delivery support data fusion underpinned by information theory. In machine learning, we expect data fusion efforts to improve predictive power and thus provide more reliable results in potentially low-validity settings.

The advantage of data fusion is that modeling results become inherently more robust by relying on various informational factors rather than a single type. However, the combinatory information methodology has drawbacks; it complicates model specification and reduces the interpretability of the results.

Although we understand at BrainX that most data from various sources and file formats are rarely consistent, this is especially true for clinical data. Data sets, for example, can have varying naming conventions and units of measurement or represent varying local population biases. It is critical to search for and correct systematic differences between large datasets and assess their degree of interoperability.

A balance is required to allow information to work in harmony and maintain data purity regarding information correspondence. Fusion is successful when data harmonization techniques are used to ensure the quality control of the integration process. Harmonization of clinical data necessitates multidisciplinary research involving medicine, biology, and computer science.

***

Many people are interested in developing foundation models for electronic medical records (EMRs) that resemble the successful ChatGPT and AlphaFold models to improve patient care and hospital management. However, recent enthusiasm has hidden important gaps in our understanding of these models' capabilities. BrainX analyzed various models that were trained using non-imaging EMR data (i.e., clinical text and structured data).

By classifying their architectures, training data, and prospective use cases in a taxonomy, we discovered that many models train on either vast, publicly available biological corpora or on small, narrowly focused clinical datasets. Their evaluation consists of tasks that fail to yield significant information regarding their practicality within health systems. Considering these findings, we put up an enhanced evaluation methodology that establishes a closer connection between healthcare measures and clinical foundation models to assess their benefits.

Foundation models (FMs), according to a recent study published in *Nature Digital Medicine*, are machine learning models capable of performing tasks after being trained on large, typically unlabeled datasets. FMs are changing the way machine learning models are developed, representing a paradigm shift. Instead of creating a bespoke model for each specific use case (as was traditionally done), we can reuse a single FM across a wide range of downstream tasks with minimal adaptation or retraining needed per task. FMs have gotten much attention because of their impressive capabilities in various domains, from text generation and video editing to protein folding and robotics.

## Application of Multimodal Models in Healthcare

The implementation of multimodal models in the healthcare sector presents a variety of novel resolutions to overcome obstacles. According to a recent study by MarketsandMarkets, the global natural language processing market is anticipated to increase at a compound annual growth rate of 20.1%, from $10.2 billion in 2019 to $26.4 billion in 2024.[2]

The primary catalyst for this expansion is the progress made in artificial intelligence and machine learning. These technologies have enabled the creation of exceptionally powerful algorithms that can analyze and interpret substantial quantities of patient data.

In pursuit of cost reduction and improved patient outcomes, healthcare providers are progressively using multimodal models to optimize operations, facilitate decision-making, and streamline processes. These models exhibit notable efficacy in the provision of virtual assistants for patients and the interpretation of medical imaging data.

Through the analysis of pictures obtained from sources such as CT scans and MRIs, these models have the capability to detect minute patterns and anomalies that human radiologists would fail to see. By enhancing the precision of diagnoses and conserving time and resources, this enables medical practitioners to administer more effective patient treatment.

According to a report by Accenture, virtual health assistants may potentially save the healthcare industry as much as $20 billion annually by 2021.[3] Nonetheless, there are industry-wide apprehensions regarding regulation and the ethical ramifications associated with implementing multimodal models in healthcare.

Of particular significance is the possibility of algorithmic bias, which may result in inequitable patient care based on race or gender. The privacy and security of patient data are paramount in this context, given that these models necessitate access to extensive quantities of sensitive information.

The advantages of large language and multimodal models in healthcare are evident, notwithstanding any issues arising over their application. These models provide us with the capability to accomplish tasks and uncover previously unattainable insights, performing on an unparalleled level.

The healthcare sector will witness an expansion of complex and sophisticated implementations of these models in the coming years as artificial intelligence and machine learning continue to develop. Considering the escalating expenses and the complexities posed by an aging workforce, healthcare providers may find multimodal models to be an effective remedy for the sector's most critical concerns.

## Medical Research and Drug Discovery and LLMs

Google's DeepMind is currently exploring using large language models for drug discovery and medical research. They combine AI with domain expertise, allowing DeepMind's models to analyze molecular structures, predict properties, and identify potential drug candidates. This approach promises to accelerate the drug discovery process, reducing costs and increasing the chances of finding effective treatments for various diseases such as

Alzheimer's, cancer, and diabetes. According to the *Journal of the American Medical Association*, deep learning algorithms can accurately predict Alzheimer's disease up to six years before symptoms appear.

DeepMind's work in medical research and drug discovery is improving diagnosis, treatment, and patient outcomes using large language multimodal models, enabling researchers and healthcare professionals to gain new insights and make more informed decisions.

Large language models revolutionize how we approach disease diagnosis and treatment in medical research and drug discovery. These models can identify drug targets and develop new treatments by analyzing vast quantities of medical literature and identifying patterns and connections that humans may not notice.

Additionally, they can assist in developing personalized medicine by analyzing genetic data and medical histories to predict patient outcomes and tailor treatments to individual patients. However, it should be noted that natural language processing algorithms in their current state have exposed biases in LLM technologies, particularly around mental and emotional health. These biases may cause potential harm based on age, religion, race, gender, nationality, and sexual orientation. This demonstrates that despite extensive speculation about their future potential, LLMs are still in their infancy. Existing limitations include the usually expensive amount of computer power required for LLMs to work. Effective training of LLMs also necessitates sharing huge volumes of data, which may require institutions to collaborate to train algorithms.

Due to the presence of institutional data protection agreements and stringent data privacy rules, which contribute to data silos, such data sharing in healthcare presents a particular problem. Synthetic data and federated learning are emerging to facilitate data exchange across national borders. While these methods have demonstrated efficacy in different fields, their suitability for LLMs remains unknown, and the trajectory of this investigation is unpredictable. Although it is neither inconceivable nor remote, the day when we achieve optimal patient outcomes will not remain in the distant future.

## Technical Capabilities and Limitations

Despite their potential in multiple healthcare applications, technical constraints must be considered before their implementation in healthcare environments. One of the most vital technical skills of big language and multimodal models is their capacity to process and draw insights from vast volumes of data in real time.

For instance, natural language processing models can extract essential information from clinical notes to enhance patient care. Despite the myriad technical possibilities, constraints must be considered when using multimodal and large language models.

A substantial constraint arises from their dependence on sizable quantities of data. To attain optimal levels of accuracy, these models necessitate an ample amount of training data, owing to apprehensions regarding data privacy and security. Additionally, these models may compromise their accuracy when faced with intricate medical data or uncommon illnesses. An investigation that was published in the *Journal of Medical Internet Research* revealed that the accuracy of a machine-learning model intended to forecast sepsis in infants was a mere 51%.

Another constraint of these models is their interpretability. The methodology employed by language and multimodal models is frequently characterized as "black boxes" due to the inherent complexity in comprehending their results. In healthcare settings, where the decisions made by these models might significantly impact patient care, this can be problematic. To solve this issue, researchers are developing methods to render these models more interpretable, including creating visualization tools that illustrate the process by which the model reached its results.

## Overall Benefits of LLM Usage

Given the challenges and obstacles associated with large language models, it is worth noting that one of the most substantial advantages of multimodal and large language models is their capacity to analyze unstructured data, including patient surveys, doctors' reports, and medical records. This facilitates identifying patterns and insights by caregivers that could otherwise remain undetected, hence leading to the creation of treatment plans and diagnoses that are more precise.

Significant linguistic and multimodal models provide patients with numerous benefits. Research has demonstrated that patients who are more engaged in their care are more inclined to comply with treatment plans, thereby surmounting language barriers that might otherwise hinder certain patients from obtaining appropriate medical attention.

Multimodal and broad language models give underserved people more access to care, reduce costs, and enhance patient outcomes. Although implementing these technologies presents considerable obstacles, healthcare practitioners must strive to overcome them to fully leverage the capabilities of AI and ML platforms. To guarantee that they can deliver optimal patient care, healthcare providers must remain informed about the most recent developments in broad language and multimodal models as technology progresses. By doing so, healthcare providers can facilitate more inexpensive and accessible care and effect significant industry-wide change.

***

## Important Points

- The advent of large language and multimodal models in healthcare has improved patient outcomes, reduced costs, and increased access to care for underserved groups.
- Signifying large language and multimodal models in advancing healthcare delivery and decision-making is vital.
- Machine learning is frequently being leveraged for use in clinical decision support.
- Historically, researchers have focused large language models on single-modal data, but now they are expanding exponentially.
- We must be mindful of harmful bias and corrupted datasets.

## Notes


1. Awasthi R, Mishra S, Mahapatra D, Khanna A, Maheshwari K, Cywinski J, Papay F, Mathur P. HumanELY: Human evaluation of LLM yield, using a novel web-based evaluation tool. 2023. medRxiv: 2023.2012.2022.23300458.
2. Article Report. Markets and Markets. https://www.marketsandmarkets.com/Market-Reports/natural-language- processing-nlp-825.html.
3. Mathew C, Richard F. An Engine for Growth. 2021. https://www.accenture.com/au-en/insights/health/artificial-intelligence-healthcare.

# Chapter 15

# User-Ability of AI Systems

> User ability and acceptance are paramount in AI applications. It is crucial to involve healthcare professionals in the development process to ensure AI solutions meet their needs and fit seamlessly into clinical workflows.
>
> **—John Halamka, Professor of Medicine, Harvard Medical School**

DeepMind, a subsidiary of Google's parent company, Alphabet, expanded its focus in subsequent years by exploring AI's application in various real-world domains, including healthcare, energy, and user accessibility. DeepMind's researchers and engineers worked diligently to develop innovative AI algorithms and technologies to address complex challenges. One of its breakthroughs materialized with Stephen Normandin, who turned out to be a prime example of collaboration between humans and artificial intelligence.

Normandin, a biologist, was studying the genetic basis of acute myeloid leukemia (AML) when he realized he needed more efficient tools to analyze the copious amounts of data involved. Turning to Google DeepMind, Stephen Normandin enlisted the help of their AI algorithms to analyze genomic datasets. The collaboration proved to be a notable change, as the AI could detect patterns and associations in the data that had previously eluded human scientists. With this newfound information, Normandin and his team identified potential drug targets for AML, providing hope for developing new, more effective treatments for this deadly disease.

AML is a type of blood cancer that affects thousands of people annually. Despite decades of research, AML remains one of the most challenging cancers to treat, with survival rates barely improved in the past 30 years. With

DOI: 10.4324/9781003661627-19

the help of Google DeepMind's AI algorithms, Normandin and his team could make considerable progress in understanding the disease and developing new treatments.

The key to their success was the ability of their users to analyze vast amounts of genomic data with astounding speed and precision. By analyzing millions of data points, the AI identified subtle patterns and associations that human scientists would have found impossible to discover independently. This allowed Normandin and his team to gain new insights into the genetic mutations that drive AML and the potential vulnerabilities of cancer cells.

As artificial intelligence continues to advance in healthcare, the importance of AI systems' usability grows. Developing and deploying AI systems in healthcare aims to improve patient outcomes, reduce costs, and boost efficiency. However, the success of these systems is contingent on their user-ability, which refers to the ease and effectiveness with which users can interact with and use the AI technology. Discussing the steps and formulas necessary to optimize the user-ability of AI systems in the healthcare industry is vital.

## Starting Point: Understanding the User

Babylon Health is a healthcare technology company focusing on delivering personalized and accessible healthcare services via AI and telemedicine. Their AI-powered platform enables virtual doctor consultations, access to healthcare information, and innovative health monitoring tools. Babylon Health uses AI algorithms to analyze vast amounts of healthcare data and user interactions to understand its end users better. The AI can identify patterns and gain insights into user behavior, preferences, and needs by analyzing this data.

Babylon Health uses advanced AI technology to tailor the user experience according to individual health profiles and preferences. It can make individualized recommendations for health management, suggest preventive measures based on past health data, and even identify potential health risks or conditions.

Suppose, for example, a user with symptoms interacts with Babylon Health's AI chatbot. The system can use natural language processing and machine learning techniques to comprehend and analyze the user's reported symptoms in such a situation. Based on this analysis, the AI can provide preliminary assessments, provide guidance on the next steps, and suggest whether the user should seek in-person medical assistance or continue with telemedicine.

Babylon Health's use of AI to comprehend the end user exemplifies the potential for technology to improve healthcare accessibility and remote provision of individualized care. The organization can analyze user data by utilizing AI algorithms to provide individualized recommendations and support, enhancing the individual healthcare experience.

Former CEO of IBM, Ginni Rometty, said, "AI should amplify human beings. We are the builders and the users, and the ultimate responsibility rests with us."[1] Before designing an AI system with optimal user-ability, it is necessary to comprehend the user's requirements, preferences, and constraints. This includes determining the user's level of technical expertise, the tasks they perform, and the context of the interaction with the AI system. According to a study conducted by Accenture, 82% of healthcare professionals believe that AI should involve input from end users in its design to ensure optimal user-friendliness.

## Designing for User Experience

Designing for User Experience (UX) is vital to improving the user-ability of AI systems. UX design is developing interfaces and interactions that are user-friendly, effective, and engaging. This involves designing with the user's cognitive processes in mind by reducing cognitive load and providing clear feedback.

According to a survey conducted by PwC, 73% of patients anticipate that AI will provide recommendations, while 50% expect AI will personalize their healthcare experience.

## Formulas for User-Ability in Healthcare AI Systems

We must develop user-centric AI systems to implement and adopt AI in healthcare successfully. Healthcare AI systems can provide optimal outcomes and experiences for healthcare providers and patients by prioritizing usability through design, intuitiveness, transparency, and regular updates. To remain competitive in this rapidly transforming industry, healthcare organizations must prioritize developing and implementing user-centric AI systems.

Several formulas and metrics can measure the user-ability of AI systems in healthcare to achieve this objective. These include the following:

Efficiency Formula - Efficiency = (Output/ Input) x 100%

The Efficiency Formula is a fundamental concept in artificial intelligence in healthcare. This formula measures the output-to-input ratio, expressed as a percentage, to determine the system's overall efficiency. The Efficiency Formula is essential for optimizing the use of AI technology to provide high-quality patient care while minimizing operational expenses. By measuring the outputs generated by AI systems against the inputs required to achieve them, healthcare organizations can identify areas of inefficiency and streamline their processes accordingly.

For instance, the Efficiency Formula can evaluate an AI system that analyzes medical images by measuring the number of images processed per unit of time and the computational resources required to analyze them. By optimizing this ratio, healthcare organizations can increase accuracy and speed of medical diagnoses while minimizing resource consumption. This can trigger long-term cost savings and improved patient outcomes.

In addition, the Efficiency Formula can assess the performance of AI systems in real-world scenarios. For instance, we can evaluate a chatbot powered by AI designed to interact with patients by measuring the number of successful interactions it has with patients, the level of patient satisfaction, and the resources required to maintain the system. This information can refine the chatbot's algorithms and enhance its overall performance. By measuring the ratio of output to input, healthcare providers can identify areas of inefficiency, refine their processes, and improve patient outcomes while minimizing operational costs.

## Usability Metrics—Include Measures Such as Task Completion Rate

Usability metrics are essential for measuring the efficacy of artificial intelligence solutions in the healthcare industry. A crucial metric is the task completion rate, which refers to the proportion of tasks that users can complete successfully with the AI solution. This metric helps determine the extent to which the AI solution can aid healthcare professionals in performing their duties and improving patient outcomes.

Additionally important, the determined usability metric is the learnability of the AI solution, referring to the ease with which users can learn to use the solution effectively. A highly learnable AI solution can save valuable time for healthcare professionals and reduce the risk of errors in patient care.

Other usability metrics, including task completion rate and learnability, include efficiency, satisfaction, and error rates. The efficiency of an AI solution is the rate at which users can complete tasks. Satisfaction measures the extent to which users find the solution simple to use and how beneficial it is to their duties. Error rates represent the frequency of user mistakes when using the AI solution. By evaluating task completion rate, learnability, efficiency, customer satisfaction, and error rates, healthcare organizations can identify areas for improvement and optimize their AI technology usage.

Cognitive Load Formula - Cognitive Load = Mental Effort x Time

The Cognitive Load Formula is a powerful tool to measure a user's mental effort in system interaction. The equation for cognitive load is mental effort multiplied by time usability metrics. This formula can improve the healthcare experience for both patients and providers. With the introduction of AI in healthcare, the Cognitive Load Formula becomes even more significant. With the help of AI-powered tools, complex tasks like medical diagnosis or patient management can be streamlined. However, if the cognitive load required to interact with these tools is excessive, it can lead to user frustration and subpar results.

With AI in healthcare, the Cognitive Load Formula gains even more importance. AI-powered tools can streamline complex tasks, such as medical diagnoses or patient management. If the cognitive load required to interact with these tools improves, it can lead to user satisfaction and better outcomes.

Patients and healthcare professionals can better manage complex medical information and make more informed decisions by reducing the cognitive load required to interact with healthcare systems and AI-powered tools. This can lead to more accurate diagnoses, tailored treatment plans, and better health outcomes.

At BrainX, we have recognized that industry experts have weighed in on signifying user-ability in AI systems in the healthcare industry. AI systems have the potential to transform healthcare by enabling faster and more precise diagnoses, predicting patients' health outcomes, and enhancing the overall patient experience. The successful implementation of these systems is contingent upon the ability of healthcare professionals to use them efficiently. User-ability, or the ease with which healthcare professionals can interact with AI systems, is crucial to determining their success.

Experts concur that we must create AI systems with the workflow, processes, and needs of healthcare professionals in mind. We should not view AI systems as a replacement for healthcare professionals, but rather as a tool that can supplement their work. To accomplish this, AI systems must be user-friendly and intuitive and provide healthcare professionals with actionable, precise information. They must also be adaptable to various specializations and environments.

Other formulas and metrics can be used to measure the user-ability of AI systems in healthcare. One such metric is the user satisfaction score, which can be obtained through surveys and feedback forms. This score represents how satisfied users are with the AI system's performance and user experience. Another metric is the usability score, which considers factors such as ease of use, learnability, and efficiency. This score can be obtained through user testing and observation. Using these measurements can help identify areas of improvement and ensure that the AI system is meeting the needs of its users.

In addition to these metrics, formulas can measure the effectiveness of AI systems in healthcare. One such formula is the precision-recall curve, commonly used in machine learning to evaluate the performance of classification models. The formula measures the relationship between the AI system's true positive rate (recall) and the false positive rate (precision).

Another formula that can be used is the F1-score, which measures the accuracy of the AI system in detecting and classifying data. This score considers the system's precision and recall and provides a single score reflecting its overall effectiveness.

Finally, the user error rate is another critical metric to consider when measuring the user-ability of AI systems in healthcare. This metric reflects the number and severity of user errors when interacting with the system. By identifying and addressing areas where users are making errors, we can improve the AI system to better meet its users' needs.

Industry experts agree that user-ability is crucial in healthcare AI systems. Statistics show that end-user input is vital in designing effective AI systems. As healthcare embraces AI technology, optimizing user-ability will ensure that AI systems improve patient outcomes, reduce costs, and increase efficiency. Overall, using formulas and metrics to measure the user-ability of AI systems in healthcare is essential to ensuring that these systems meet their users' needs and provide accurate and effective results. We can continually improve these systems through careful measurement and analysis to provide the best possible outcomes for patients and healthcare providers.

Two recent examples of trials related to AI in healthcare show how even high-performing algorithms might benefit from a better deployment of a user-ability strategy. Clinicians who followed the recommendations for intervention found that an algorithm developed to manage sepsis in patients at Johns Hopkins showed significant promise. However, they did not always follow the recommendations in a timely manner.

Similarly, in operating rooms, Dr. Maheshwari led a trial of a promising algorithm called Hypotension Prediction Index (HPI) that predicts the occurrence of low blood pressure during surgery. They found that following the guidance provided promising results. However, not all clinicians followed the guidance provided by HPI.[2] We wonder which factors related to user-ability could improve the adoption of the recommendations from these algorithms. More research needs to be conducted on implementing science aspects of these algorithms.

***

## Important Points

- Industry experts agree that user-ability is crucial in healthcare AI systems.
- Statistics show that end-user input is vital in designing effective AI systems.
- The Cognitive Load Formula is a potent tool for determining a user's mental effort to interact with a system. Cognitive load is equal to mental effort multiplied by time usability metrics
- Before designing an AI system with optimal user-ability, it is necessary to comprehend the user's requirements, preferences, and constraints.
- Designing for User Experience (UX) is vital to improving the user-ability of AI systems. UX design is developing interfaces and interactions that are user-friendly, effective, and engaging.

## Notes

1. Financial Times. 2024. https://www.ft.com/content/beae436b-ce83-43ab-9254-70f9f3b6b1b3.
2. Hypotension Prediction. https://pubs.asahq.org/anesthesiology/article/133/6/1214/110700/Hypotension-Prediction-Index-for-Prevention-of.

# Chapter 16

# Application Integration of AI in Healthcare

> AI is the new electricity. Just as electricity transformed numerous industries roughly 100 years ago, AI will do the same today.
>
> **—Andrew Ng, computer scientist and co-founder of Coursera**

> AI is the new electricity; we need to build the companies to harness its power for humanity.
>
> **—Dr. Piyush Mathur**

Google DeepMind and its artificial intelligence research lab have made significant strides in integrating AI in healthcare, especially in acute kidney injury and diabetic retinopathy detection. In 2014, Google DeepMind, in collaboration with the UK's National Health Service, developed an AI system that could detect diabetic retinopathy. DeepMind integrated and trained its algorithm on thousands of retinal scans to identify signs of the condition in varying patients. In a study, the algorithm achieved a 94.5% accuracy level comparable to that of human doctors, displaying the vast potential in diagnosing diabetic retinopathy more efficiently and accurately.

For further artificial intelligence integration in 2018, DeepMind partnered with the NHS to implement their diabetic retinopathy detection system across multiple UK hospitals, assisting clinicians in analyzing retinal scans and identifying patients who needed urgent treatment, leading to faster diagnosis and treatment initiation.

 DOI: 10.4324/9781003661627-20

DeepMind also collaborated with the U.S. Department of Veterans Affairs (VA) to develop an AI system that predicted acute kidney injury 48 hours earlier by analyzing patient health records and identifying patterns and factors associated with developing acute kidney injury. This achieved a 55% reduction in false-positive alerts, leading to more accurate predictions and improved patient outcomes.

DeepMind has also shown a way to explore the use of AI in radiotherapy planning. They developed a system called "ATOM," which customizes treatment plans for each cancer patient. This program incorporates expert clinical knowledge. It uses reinforcement learning to enhance the efficiency and accuracy of radiotherapy planning, reducing the burden on clinicians and potentially enhancing patient outcomes.

We must align the successful adoption and integration of AI in healthcare with people, operations, processes, and technology. Recent surveys demonstrate the importance, as they reported that 11% of American workers were employed in healthcare in 2019, and healthcare expenditures comprised over 17% of the gross domestic product (GDP). The United States spends more on healthcare per capita than other OECD nations. Knowing this, the integration of AI technologies in healthcare is vital to provide effective and efficient patient care, enhancing the lives of millions of people.

Despite the hype and potential, we at BrainX have observed a slow integration of AI and intend to continue our efforts to shed light on AI adoption patterns. From a tactical standpoint, establishing and maintaining trust, upskilling talent, having a clearly defined AI strategy, and measuring Return on Investment (ROI) are among the most significant obstacles to successful AI integration. Despite the challenges, integrating artificial intelligence will result in more precise diagnoses, effective treatment plans, and better patient outcomes. With this in focus, we must examine the details that are making integration complex, showing the necessity for the healthcare industry to keep up with the constant development of AI technology to reap the benefits of these advancements.

An enormous barrier to AI integration is the widespread concern throughout the business that AI will fall short of expectations and demand. Decision-makers are motivated by this apprehension, which has heightened mistrust. AI advancements such as ChatGPT have led to this overhype and overselling. According to a recent poll by health executives, over half are concerned about the repercussions of integrating AI into healthcare industries. The poll also revealed that 53% of respondents think that AI will be inadequately embraced or malfunction, while 49% are aware that AI has been overpriced and is unlikely to live up to expectations.

Resistance is to be expected. The best remedy for widespread pessimism over the successful integration of any innovative technology, including AI, is to promote collaboration from a variety of tactical and practical vantage points.

Opposition from employees and concerns about job security complicate AI implementation. A survey of 1,000 healthcare managers revealed that 42% believe AI will eradicate jobs, and40% believe staff lack the skills for AI adoption. Surmounting employee opposition is a critical factor in ensuring the success and widespread acceptance of AI efforts. The survey delineates the concerns and offers suggestions for cultivating an AI-prepared environment within healthcare institutions, to augment personnel acceptability and integration.

A limited skill pool and a growing need for AI adoption in the healthcare sector will necessitate an increase in the resources required by healthcare organizations to start and manage AI-based projects in the interim. BrainX has identified applications and advantages resulting from healthcare integration, including the following:

- Chronic disease management.
- Imaging and diagnostics in medicine.
- Patient monitoring and lifestyle management.
- Emergency and surgical care.
- Predictive analysis.
- Analytics of risk.
- Drug development and research.
- Sensor apparel.
- Data analysis.
- Remote assistance (Virtual).
- Mental and psychological support.

## Upskilling and Training

Upskilling is at the forefront of AI integration. Everyone at BrainX is cognizant that as AI becomes more prevalent in healthcare, most individuals will be required to gain, cultivate, and build “AI ability.” It was determined that 60% of the positions associated with AI were clinical, 34% were administrative, and 6% were primarily research-oriented.

Few health care occupations require AI knowledge. With applications in electronic medical records, computers, and the corporate internet, AI adoption is more likely to begin in large organizations and cities, although it is still in its infancy. BrainX has identified four significant barriers to the integration and deployment of artificial intelligence through its comprehensive research.

- Algorithmic limitations.
- Data access limitations.
- Regulatory barriers.
- Misaligned incentives.

## Algorithmic limitations

To avoid potential risks to patient safety and health, healthcare professionals must understand the limitations of using algorithms in healthcare. One of the first challenges is addressing bias within algorithmic programs. Bias is a significant limitation of algorithms and is only as objective as the data upon which we build them. Researchers at the University of Toronto discovered that an algorithm used to predict the likelihood of certain patients requiring additional care was biased against Black patients, making them less likely to receive the care. "We can't assume that just because an algorithm is based on data, it'll be fair or unbiased," said the lead researcher.

Another limitation of healthcare algorithms is their inability to consider individual patient needs and preferences. While algorithms can process massive amounts of data and identify patterns, they cannot fully comprehend individual patients' unique needs and preferences. "Algorithms are very good at finding commonalities, but they're not very good at finding what's unique about a patient," says Dr. Eric Topol, a cardiologist and author of *Deep Medicine: How Artificial Intelligence Can Make Healthcare Human Again*. This means that, while algorithms can make general treatment recommendations based on data, they cannot account for the nuances of each patient's situation, resulting in suboptimal outcomes.

Algorithms must contend with incomplete or inaccurate data, which can cause flaws in the programs, producing incorrect results. This issue is especially acute in healthcare, where data is frequently fragmented and incomplete, and errors can have dire consequences for patient health. "If the data is inaccurate or incomplete, the algorithm will be inaccurate or incomplete, and that can be dangerous," Dr. Topol says.

## Data Access Limitations

Data access constraints in healthcare are a critical concern that can have a negative impact on patient care. According to a recent Healthcare Information and Management Systems Society (HIMSS) survey, 55% of healthcare providers reported difficulty accessing patient data. This problem can result in delayed or incorrect treatment, which can have profound consequences for patients.

The lack of compatibility across different electronic health record (EHR) systems is one reason for data access limits. This means that healthcare personnel may not access essential patient information, such as medical histories or medication lists, if we store it in a system other than the one in which they work. Dr. Wendy Sue Swanson, Chief of Digital Innovation at Seattle Children's Hospital, stated, "The absence of interoperability is the Achilles' heel of EHRs. Accessing complete and accurate patient information is a significant barrier for healthcare practitioners."

Concerns about privacy and security are another rationale for data access limits. While protecting patient data is vital, overly stringent restrictions and standards can make it difficult for healthcare practitioners to get the information they need to provide great care. According to research by the American Medical Association, 90% of physicians had trouble obtaining patient data due to privacy and security issues.

Data access restrictions can have dire consequences, with patients receiving incorrect diagnoses or treatments because of a lack of information.

Depending on the severity of the condition, it can even result in death. Delays in accessing patient data might also result in lengthy wait times for appointments and treatments, resulting in dissatisfaction.

Healthcare providers and regulators must increase data availability and interoperability by implementing a universal EHR system that all healthcare providers, regardless of system, may access. This will allow doctors to access a patient's medical history and treatment information in one location, enhancing care quality and reducing the chance of errors.

Another option is simplifying privacy and security regulations so healthcare providers can access patient data more easily while maintaining confidentiality. We must balance protecting patient data and providing timely and effective care. This necessitates a cautious approach to privacy and security regulations to avoid unnecessary barriers to accessing patient data.

There are also efforts underway to improve interoperability between EHR systems. The Office of the National Coordinator for Health Information Technology has set a goal for all healthcare providers to exchange patient data seamlessly by 2024. This would allow providers to access complete and accurate patient information regardless of their EHR system, improving care quality and lowering the risk of errors.

## Regulatory Barriers

As artificial intelligence advances, we must consider the regulatory barriers and limitations impacting AI to reach its full potential. According to *The Medical Futurist*, "The FDA has been slow to provide guidance for AI products in healthcare, creating several regulatory uncertainties." This regulatory wall creates a barrier for companies looking to develop and market AI technologies for healthcare applications, causing uncertainty for healthcare providers and patients.

In a recent statement, the European Commission recognized the importance of clear regulations by, "Ensuring that AI systems are transparent, dependable, and respect fundamental rights." They also emphasized "Clear requirements for data collection, sharing, and use" to protect patient privacy and data security.

We must carefully implement AI with patient safety and privacy in mind.

In the United States, we must hold AI to the highest standards of transparency, accountability, and responsibility. Developing a regulatory framework is one potential solution to the challenges, where the framework would provide clear guidelines for developing, testing, and implementing artificial intelligence in healthcare applications.

The European Commission has launched the Ethics Guidelines for Trustworthy AI initiative. The guidelines emphasize the importance of ensuring fairness, accountability, and transparency in AI systems and protecting privacy and data security. Regulatory barriers and limitations pose significant challenges for healthcare organizations, and we must develop clear regulatory frameworks to guide the development and implementation of AI technology.

The regulatory approval process for a new medical technology is long and subject to substantial scrutiny. As discussed with patents, innovations can take years to receive approval. Liability concerns are a barrier, as providers are still hesitant to adopt innovative technology because healthcare regulation is more cautious than regulation in many other industries. This argues that lowering the hurdles to AI adoption will necessitate complementary regulatory innovation, allowing AI's potential benefits to be achieved without jeopardizing patient rights or treatment quality.

## Misaligned Incentives

As the use of artificial intelligence in healthcare has expanded, so has concern about skewed incentives. While artificial intelligence is revolutionizing our sector, we must address the negative implications of incentives that do not align with patient outcomes. According to the National Academy of Medicine research, "Misaligned incentives can lead to lower quality of care, higher costs, and worse health outcomes." Patients may not receive the best possible care if they do not align AI deployment incentives with patient outcomes.

Implementation and use of AI in healthcare will, however, depend on aligning incentives with patient outcomes. If the incentives driving AI deployment do not align with patient outcomes, there may be unintended consequences. For example, if the primary incentive is cost reduction, AI systems may prioritize cheaper treatments over the best possible care for patients. This could lead to suboptimal treatment decisions and compromised patient outcomes.

If companies prioritize profit or market share as incentives, there is a risk that they may develop and deploy AI technologies without sufficient validation or evidence of their effectiveness. This may cause overreliance on unproven or unreliable AI algorithms, compromising patient safety and quality of care.

To ensure that patients receive the best possible care, prioritizing patient-centered goals such as improved health outcomes, enhanced patient experiences, and reduced healthcare disparities is a necessity. To identify and mitigate any unintended negative consequences of AI systems, it will be necessary to validate AI algorithms through rigorous testing and to ensure transparency in their development, deployment, and ongoing monitoring and evaluation.

By aligning the incentives driving AI deployment with patient outcomes, we can harness AI's full potential to enhance healthcare, improve patient safety, and deliver better care to individuals in need.

## Policy Implications

While artificial intelligence has the potential to boost efficiency and reduce costs, it may also automate certain functions and lead to job displacement, raising concerns in both public and private policy. According to a PwC report, up to 20% of healthcare occupations in the United States may be automated by 2030.

One of the major policy consequences of AI in healthcare is the need for regulatory norms to assure patient safety and data protection. As artificial intelligence systems grow increasingly widespread in medical decision-making, ethical and legal frameworks to guide their development and use are crucial. With policy and implementation, we must ensure that AI does not promote bias and discrimination and that it is visible, explainable, and accountable.

AI in healthcare confronts policymakers with both opportunities and challenges. Concerns have been raised concerning patient safety, data security, and the impact on jobs. Policymakers must create stringent regulatory rules, guarantee that healthcare personnel have proper training, and address concerns about job displacement, training, and upskilling. We can revolutionize how we offer and receive healthcare by taking a proactive approach to policy. Policymakers can enable useful integration through creative policy implementation by adopting tried-and-true strategies, such as clarifying guidelines, supporting research, and creating competition, which may be the most beneficial.

## Lack of Interoperability

Although interoperability is vital for simplifying data sharing, it poses a significant integration problem. AI cannot aid the healthcare sector if it does not have access to extensive data from several sources. According to a recent Society of Actuaries study of health leaders, most leaders felt AI would deliver measurable financial benefits within the next five years. Health leaders described the most important hurdle to deploying AI programs inside their business as a lack of financing.

## Lack of Cloud Adoption

According to HIMSS Analytics research, only 22% of healthcare firms have used cloud technology. The same research also shows that 49% of healthcare firms intend to use cloud technology within the next two years. Despite these optimistic results, healthcare trails behind other industries in terms of cloud usage. Adopting cloud technology is a major challenge. Despite the potential benefits of these technologies, there has been a persistent lack of industry adoption of cloud technology and artificial intelligence.

One key reason for the sluggish adoption of cloud technology in healthcare is concerns about data security and privacy. Healthcare firms rightly dread exposing sensitive patient data to potential data breaches, so many healthcare organizations have been sluggish in adopting cloud technology despite the industry's potential benefits.

The perceived cost of implementation is another element influencing cloud adoption. Healthcare businesses may regard cloud technology adoption as an unnecessary investment in an industry where resources are tight. This, however, is short-sighted thinking because the long-term cost reductions provided by cloud technology to healthcare companies far outweigh the original expenditure.

Despite these obstacles, healthcare organizations are still pioneering cloud and AI adoption. Mayo Clinic, for example, has implemented a cloud-based data analytics platform to improve patient outcomes and lower costs. Similarly, Boston Children's Hospital used artificial intelligence to predict sepsis in pediatric patients, resulting in lower mortality rates.

The slow adoption of cloud technology and artificial intelligence in healthcare is a complex issue, with a range of factors contributing to the slow pace. Healthcare organizations must recognize the potential benefits of these technologies and work to overcome the challenges they face. With the right investments and partnerships, the healthcare industry can fully realize the potential of cloud technology and AI to improve patient outcomes and reduce costs. It is time for the healthcare industry to embrace these technologies and advance into a brighter future.

***

To balance the slow and steady integration rate, we must acknowledge the broad vision for AI today. It is crucial to bear in mind that we should consistently err on the side of overestimating the magnitude of change that will unfold in the following two years, while simultaneously underestimating the scale of change that will transpire in the subsequent ten years. This is a bold vision for a sound plan for AI integration across the country's healthcare sectors. We cannot emphasize the importance of AI application integration.

According to an Accenture analysis, healthcare organizations that invest in AI technology might save $150 billion per year by 2026. Technology can only generate the best outcomes when there is seamless connectivity, interoperability, and data exchange between apps. Interoperability is critical. The integration aspect has emerged as a transformative force with the recent resurgence of artificial intelligence. But with great power also comes great responsibility, and given the need for careful attention to privacy protection, ethical considerations, and fairness in algorithmic decision-making, it is impossible to overstate the significance of ethical AI integration in healthcare.

We must also prioritize the comprehensibility and interpretability of AI algorithms when integrating AI responsibly. Healthcare professionals must comprehend how AI generates its conclusions or recommendations. AI can help build trust and confidence in its findings by producing results that are easy to understand, empowering healthcare professionals to make wise, ethical, and unbiased decisions. Growing evidence suggests that if we do not carefully observe and address biases, AI systems may perpetuate them.

Research shows that they have biased some AI algorithms against certain racial and gender groups, which results in differences in diagnosis and treatment outcomes. To reduce algorithmic bias, responsible AI integration requires creating transparent frameworks and using a variety of training datasets.

We must be responsible and advocate for strong legislation and an expanded joint effort toward responsible implementation solutions that prioritize ethical considerations, privacy protection, and equity in algorithmic decision-making. Healthcare organizations can unleash AI's transformative potential while upholding patient trust by protecting patient privacy and data security, addressing algorithmic bias, and aiming for transparency and interpretability.

By conducting ongoing research, collaborating, and sharing best practices, we can enhance patient care and achieve better outcomes in healthcare. Healthcare benefits from AI's full potential by embracing responsible integration, catapulting the sector into a new era of Precision Medicine and personalized healthcare.

***

## Important Points

- We must align the successful adoption of AI with people, operations, processes, and technology.
- By conducting ongoing research, collaborating, and sharing best practices, we can enhance patient care and achieve better outcomes within the healthcare community.
- Using AI integration in healthcare necessitates responsible implementation strategies that put ethical considerations, privacy protection, and equity into algorithmic decision-making at the top of the list.
- We must give fairness and equity top priority when incorporating AI algorithms.
- Concerns about data security and privacy are one of the primary reasons for the slow adoption of cloud technology in healthcare.

# 5

# THE WHEN (OF AI IN HEALTHCARE)

# Chapter 17

# Ethical Implications and Governance of Artificial Intelligence

The rapid progress of AI in recent years has raised important moral concerns and the need for robust legal frameworks. The worrying possibility of AI control is summed up perfectly in this comment by famous physicist Stephen Hawking. It emphasizes the hazards of unrestrained artificial intelligence development. Stephen Hawking's statements serve as a sobering reminder of the significance of responsible and ethical governance in developing and deploying artificial intelligence systems worldwide.

There have not been sufficient efforts to start AI governance and design failsafe control mechanisms to safeguard AI's potential for humanity and limit its societal damage. According to Dafoe, the emerging discipline of AI governance investigates how humanity can best navigate the transition to advanced AI systems.[1] At BrainX, we expect that such governance will be challenging because of the technology's strategic significance, its diverse implementations, and the unpredictability of its future development.

To help bridge this knowledge gap in the development of AI control, this essay examines portentous AI ethics and governance, probing the urgent challenges and arguments presented by AI's uncontrolled development and the unknown potential for responsible versus destructive deployment. This contemporary topic is important and rife with contentious issues in which people hold strong opinions. This leads to the persuasive argument of

DOI: 10.4324/9781003661627-22

whether there should be an immediate debate on the significance of ethical considerations and effective governance in artificial intelligence.

What is the current governance and ethical framework required to address artificial intelligence's potential risks and repercussions and ensure its responsible and beneficial integration into society? Who is answerable for developing and utilizing AI systems that cause harm? We address many of these questions in our award-winning 2023 Kaggle competition essay, "Ethical AI Is All We Need!!," in which we analyzed over 400,000 publications from the last two decades of artificial intelligence publications for the adoption of ethical standards as proposed by the European Commission guidelines on Trustworthy AI. We applied innovative transformer-based language models, the AI model itself, to gain temporal insight addressing the four key aspects:[2]

- Contextual Topics Learning.
- Development Maturity Learning.
- Gender Representation Learning.
- Sentiments Learning.

Within the pages of these AI papers, through contextual subject analysis, we dive into the critical concerns of Diversity & Fairness and Societal-Environmental well-being. "Development maturity learning" aims to evaluate the maturity of research articles. Researchers determine this level by considering the likelihood of the research having significant real-world applications, using high-quality data, replicability, and providing clear descriptions of AI systems that can be implemented in an accountable manner.

Learning about development maturity pushes us deeper into the ethical aspects of transparency, societal and environmental well-being, robustness, safety, and accountability. The goal of gender representation learning is to promote justice and diversity. The goal of sentiment analysis in previous research publications is to gain insight into the emotions portrayed by AI models (Figure 17.1). This approach helps us understand the behavior and attitude driving technology development and the ethical implications. Our data-driven analytical findings address critical ethical problems, such as gender prejudice, heterogeneity in publishing maturity, and sentiment proportions, with larger implications for fairness, inclusivity, and responsible AI activities.

AI systems have become an indispensable aspect of our lives, yet we face complicated questions regarding their accountability. How should

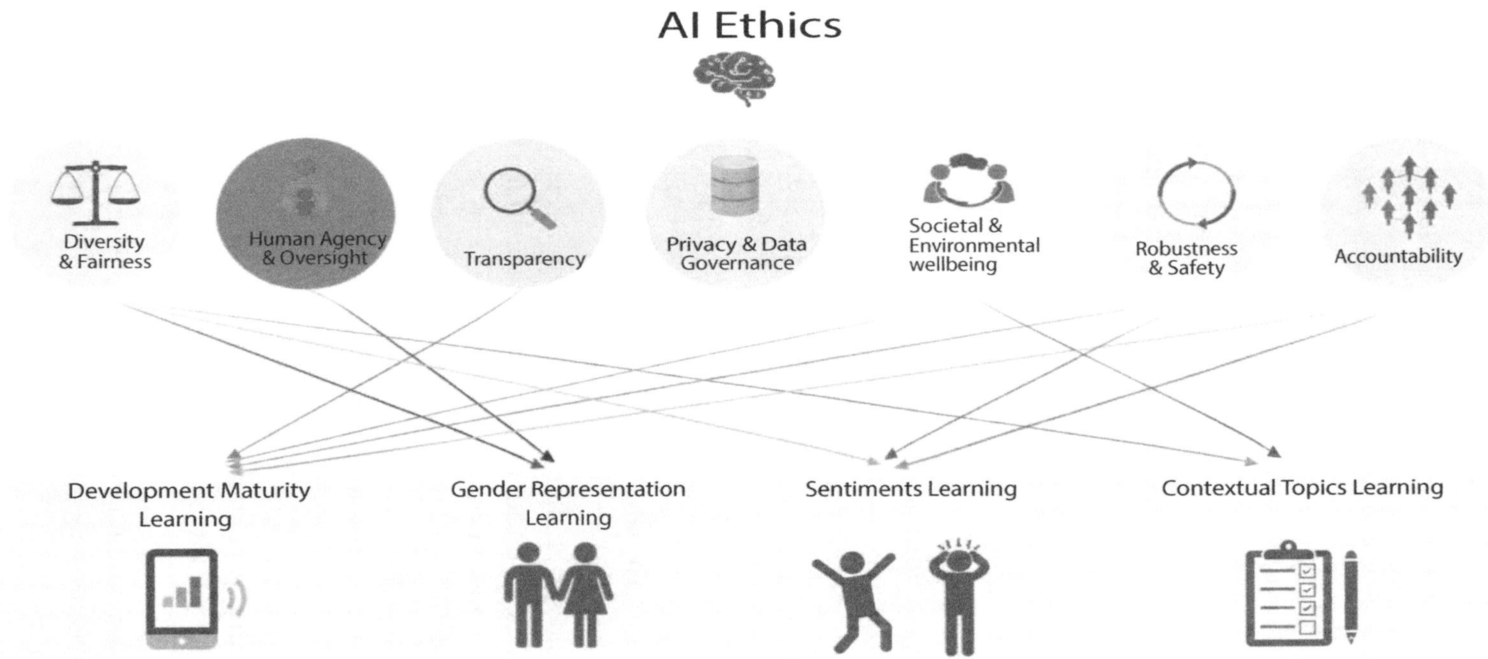


**Figure 17.1 Key principles and ethical application of artificial intelligence**

***Source*: Ethical Artificial Intelligence (https://www.kaggle.com/code/shreyamishra610/ethical-ai-is-all-we-need)**

society ensure that we hold AI systems accountable for the automated decisions and actions they take? While some argue that traceable accountability is necessary to ensure ethical behavior, others stress signifying early human oversight and technology constraints.

To maximize AI's potential and avoid potential harm, it is critical to find a balance between human rights and AI system responsibility and set constraints on AI growth. Who will create and enforce these AI constraints? It is worth considering whether the ethical principles advocated by AI developers will genuinely influence the creation of safe and beneficial AI, or if they will merely serve as a deceptive tactic to avoid public scrutiny from industries, governments, or malicious individuals.

Often, unsupervised AI systems decide with far-reaching consequences and without human interaction. Accountability for AI systems, creators, and users adheres to human ethical values. Accountability ensures that we act when an AI system causes harm, including rectifying the issue, preventing additional damage, and compensating affected parties. Responsible AI usage will be rewarded through accountability, fostering trust between AI systems, developers, and society, while discouraging harmful AI utilization.

The difficulty in identifying the accountable agent in AI systems is because of the complexity of AI development and the lack of understanding of the underlying AI mechanisms for most users. The complexity of algorithms involved in machine learning and relevant AI systems represents a "black box" of unknown, unexplainable algorithms and software coding processes to the public (Adadi and Berrada).[3]

This "black box" effect makes it challenging to trace the decision-making process of AI systems. This lack of understanding and traceability raises concerns about the potential for unjust or inaccurate accountability and a lack of trust in the accuracy and undiscoverable incentives behind various AI system developments (Mora-Cantallops et al.).[4]

AI algorithms should be transparent and understandable. Developers must aim to design algorithms that explain their decisions clearly and understandably. This allows AI users to understand how the algorithms arrived at their results and makes detecting potential biases easier. Individuals can use explainable AI to question and hold AI systems accountable for unjust or biased decisions.

While making AI systems accountable is critical, complete responsibility may require more realistic measures. To ensure justice and accuracy in holding AI systems and their authors accountable, we should seek to understand the constraints, identify the authors and creative source of AI algorithms, and find approaches to improve interpretability. Simply put, AI systems are human creations, and the AI human developers should face a major portion of the blame for their activities. Rather than relying only on holding AI systems accountable after misuse or harm, external and internal, we should create human oversight early in the AI development, deployment, and operations process.

Designers must understand their responsibility and accountability to the public. Understandable design practices, ongoing testing, and transparent design decision-making throughout AI development can reduce potential risks and ensure that AI systems align with societal values (Barredo Arrieta et al.).[5]

Rather than absolute accountability for all parties involved in the exploitation and harm of AI systems, a more selective or proportional approach may be required. We should evaluate AI systems based on their decisions and behaviors within the context of their intended use and capabilities, while identifying both developers and users. We should closely monitor the level of automation in AI judgments and always consider the possibility of immediate human intervention in AI development (Antoniadi et al.).[6]

This approach recognizes the delicate relationship between AI and human involvement, finding a balance between AI systems' benefits and limits. AI users need access to clear descriptions of AI decision-making processes to scrutinize and challenge potential biases or errors before they happen. Transparent AI systems create trust, enable improved decision-making, and assure accountability for AI algorithm outputs. Human monitoring is always required during the creation and implementation of AI. Individual accountability for the outcomes and repercussions of AI systems will help ensure that humans control all areas of AI. Clear lines of duty and accountability will prevent AI systems from working autonomously, ensuring that AI is always coordinated with human values and society.

We should also prioritize personal privacy and data protection in AI governance. Informed consent, transparency in data collection, usage, and storage policies, as well as safeguards and regulations to avoid unauthorized access and breaches, should all be part of AI safeguards. Respecting privacy rights and guaranteeing safe personal data management should be a core universal factor in AI governance (Mazurek and Maagocka).[7]

AI developers are responsible for developing AI systems with safety and security as top priorities. This comprises stringent testing, verification, and validation procedures for identifying and mitigating potential risks and vulnerabilities (Schwartz et al.). By following recommended guidelines, such as implementing secure coding standards and protocols, we can ensure the protection of AI systems from outside threats and maintain the integrity and functionality of data. Developers should create explicit criteria and regulations for the use of AI technology, especially in sensitive sectors like healthcare, banking, and law.

AI developers and organizations should continuously monitor AI systems once they have been deployed to discover and address potential hazards. They should issue regular updates to monitor and resolve security threats and keep AI systems up to date with new standards. To keep AI systems safe and secure, timely responses to such vulnerabilities are required. To collectively improve the safety and security of AI systems, AI developers should actively interact and share expertise within the AI community. Sharing innovative practices, research findings, and threat intelligence aids in developing a culture of responsibility and accountability. Collaboration can also entail working with legislators and the public to solve problems and incorporate different points of view.

Developers should also provide transparent documentation and reports on AI systems' development, training, and operation. Documenting data sources, algorithms, and decision-making processes is one example. Transparency assists external monitoring, such as regulatory organizations and auditors, in assessing AI systems' safety and security measures.

We must design and manage AI systems to maintain justice and eliminate discrimination. Accountability and transparency measures should prevent biases and unequal outcomes, particularly for underrepresented groups. To prevent continuing discriminatory AI practices, it is vital to monitor and audit data inputs, model training, and evaluation processes (Nazer et al.).[8] Developing trust and preventing the exacerbation of existing discriminations and prejudices across countries and cultures ensures everyone is treated equally. Concerns regarding potential biases have surfaced as AI algorithms gain significance in decision-making processes across many businesses.

Addressing biases in AI algorithms begins with the data used for training. AI developers must prioritize varied and representative data sources. This entails adding data from multiple demographic groups, cultures, and backgrounds into training datasets. We can reduce biases by including a diverse set of impartial data, resulting in more equitable automated decision-making outputs from AI systems. Developers should also employ internal testing methodologies to discover and reduce biases in AI algorithms before deploying them. This requires undertaking extensive audits and evaluations of the algorithms in use.

Fairness indicators and other metrics can help reveal discrimination in AI findings. Once developers identify biases, they can implement corrective measures, such as adding broad representative, more diverse data, retraining the algorithm, or changing the decision-making process to mitigate biases. BrainX members collaborated with worldwide teams to identify areas where bias could sneak into AI algorithm development and implementation. We also advised ways to prevent additional biases from affecting these algorithms, such as right problem framing, managing biases in data pretreatment, reducing biases during modeling and validation, and fair model implementation.

Explainable AI systems can also reduce public apprehension of AI applications. Developers must aim to design algorithms that explain their decisions in a clear and understandable manner. This allows AI users to understand how the algorithms arrived at their results and makes detecting potential biases easier. Explainable AI allows affected individuals and the public to challenge and hold AI systems responsible for unjust or biased outcomes.

Developers should review algorithms regularly to measure their efficacy across various demographic groupings and scenarios. These evaluations should incorporate real-world use cases and simulated situations to detect decision-making biases (Hickok).[9] Prioritizing fairness allows us to leverage the potential of AI technology while protecting against bias propagation, achieving a more equitable society.

Establishing ethical guidelines and regulatory frameworks is crucial in addressing biases in AI algorithms. Collaboration between governments, industry organizations, and research institutions is necessary to develop and enforce standards that promote fairness and equal treatment. We must not produce "proxy discrimination" hidden behind the use of AI systems and misguided development (Prince and Schwarcz).[10] Preventive guidelines should outline the ethical responsibilities of AI developers and organizations in preventing discriminatory proxy practices, emphasizing the importance of addressing biases and ensuring fairness in decision-making processes.

BrainX members actively contribute to developing frameworks through international consensus groups, such as DECIDE-AI and TEHAI. These groups provide guidance for evaluating algorithms and publications that use AI in healthcare. Organizations can adopt these evaluation frameworks, including structured checklists, to assess the purpose, accuracy, and ethical use of AI in healthcare.

Data collection, storage, and use in AI systems create substantial ethical and privacy problems, particularly in sensitive fields such as healthcare, banking, and law. Establishing privacy legislation is critical for data protection and the use of AI technology (Manheim and Kaplan).[11] Ethical principles should emphasize the importance of gaining informed consent from persons whose data is being gathered. We must thoroughly inform individuals about how AI systems will use their data, as well as the potential consequences. Transparency about data collection techniques, aims, and potential hazards should enable people to make educated decisions about sharing their data.

Ethical principles should also encourage the use of the least amount of data possible (data minimization). We should only collect the data needed for specific AI operations, decreasing the danger of misuse. The principles should encourage gathering and using data only for the intended purposes, with no unlawful secondary use without specific authorization.

Privacy legislation should include de-identification measures, such as those used in healthcare personal data storage, to safeguard individual privacy (Murdock).[12] Personally identifiable information should be properly erased or encrypted to ensure that data cannot be linked back to individuals. This enables the use of data in AI systems while reducing the danger of re-identification and unwanted access. Guidelines should require security procedures to secure data throughout its lifecycle. Guidelines should mandate establishing adequate measures such as encryption, access controls, and frequent security audits to secure data throughout its lifecycle to avoid unauthorized access, data breaches, or malicious actions.

Transparent reporting procedures should be in place to notify individuals about how their data is being used and to enable routes for complaints and compensation in the event of data mistreatment. In addition, guidelines should expressly prohibit the use of sensitive data for discriminatory or unethical objectives. Fairness principles should ensure that artificial intelligence systems in healthcare, finance, and law do not use criteria such as race, gender, or socioeconomic background to influence decisions and outcomes.

The rapid growth of artificial intelligence has also generated worries about the potential ethical consequences of employment displacement (Agrawal et al.).[13] Individuals and communities may confront considerable issues, as AI-driven automation replaces certain occupational roles.

What are firms' and governments' measures for mitigating the negative social and economic implications for affected persons and communities? Job displacement caused by AI has the potential to cause economic and social turmoil.

Loss of employment can cause financial insecurity, income inequality, and decreased social mobility. Individuals and communities may require a stronger sense of purpose and identity, exacerbating current social challenges.

To address these disruptions, local and federal governments need to take measures to protect individuals whose jobs AI systems have displaced (as stated in the *PREPARING for the FUTURE of ARTIFICIAL INTELLIGENCE* report by the National Science and Technology Council, Executive Office of the President).[14]

Additional accountability measures should assess the broader socioeconomic impact of the consequences of AI systems. We should develop and govern AI to maximize benefits while minimizing socioeconomic harm to individuals and communities. Therefore, ethical considerations should include evaluating potential economic disparities, job displacement, and systemic biases.

One strategy to lessen the impact of AI job displacement is for corporations and governments to accept responsibility for investing in lifelong learning and reskilling initiatives that empower affected workers and families. Businesses and governments will need to take proactive measures because of job displacement caused by artificial intelligence. Affected persons can learn new skills that fit growing career prospects by accessing inexpensive and relevant education and training, such as working closely with AI systems, such as robotics (Vrontis et al.).[15]

Governments can reward businesses to engage in such programs while also cultivating a culture of continual learning and adaptability. Governments can also provide complete assistance to those transitioning into new jobs. During the transition period, this includes career counseling, job placement support, and financial assistance. Support networks, mentoring programs, and access to job retraining options can help affected individuals cope and make the move easier.

Given the long-term issues connected with AI-driven job displacement, governments should implement a remedy, such as a universal basic income or other safety net initiatives. These contentious safety net policies guarantee a minimum income level for all persons, regardless of employment status. Such programs can aid in mitigating the negative effects of AI job displacement, providing financial stability, and promoting social and economic well-being (Furman and Seamans).[16]

Businesses and governments should also collaborate on workforce planning to predict future job market changes and synchronize skill development activities. Businesses may proactively detect upcoming job trends by developing collaborations between industry, educational institutions, and politicians. They should educate individuals with the skills needed to flourish in the growing labor market that AI will significantly alter. Before they completely adopt AI in enterprises, governments should address the problems associated with AI-driven job displacement while building a more inclusive and fair society by prioritizing the well-being and empowerment of affected individuals and communities.

AI has become a global phenomenon, surpassing national boundaries in its development and application. Multinational collaborations and agreements are critical to ensure AI's responsible and ethical use, producing uniform ethical principles and governance structures (Steels and Ramon).[17] Ethical concerns have global ramifications as AI technologies and applications grow more interconnected. International cooperation is required to collectively manage these difficulties and promote consistent standards.

International collaborations allow diverse stakeholders to combine their resources, knowledge, and expertise (West and Allen).[18] Governments, business leaders, academic institutions, and civil society organizations can work together to create universal ethical norms and governance frameworks that consider diverse cultural viewpoints and experiences. Shared accountability promotes a sense of community ownership, which leads to more comprehensive and practical solutions.

Internationally agreed-upon ethical norms aid in creating fair competition for AI development and deployment worldwide. They can establish a set of ideas and regulations that promote responsible and ethical behavior across boundaries (Jobin et al.). An international agreement on ethical norms eliminates the potential for jurisdictional differences and prohibits unethical actions from occurring in places with lax legislation. International collaborations and agreements for governance frameworks foster trust and confidence in AI systems.

When AI systems adhere to global standards, users, customers, and stakeholders can have greater confidence in their dependability, fairness, and accountability. Organizations such as the United Nations, the European Union, and multinational companies have made considerable progress in formulating ethical AI principles (Hogenhout).[19] Global cooperation can hasten the creation of uniform ethical frameworks and avoid duplicative efforts by leveraging these projects.

Multilateral treaties can lay the groundwork for multinational collaborations in AI ethics. They can serve as a forum for participating countries to negotiate, share knowledge, and coordinate, establishing consensus on rules and governance structures. By working together internationally, we can share and learn from the best approaches and lessons in AI ethics. Countries can improve their ethical standards and governance frameworks by learning from one another's achievements and failures. The international community can work together to promote AI's responsible and ethical use across borders by recognizing shared responsibility, equalizing ethical standards, building trust, leveraging existing initiatives, establishing multilateral agreements, sharing best practices, providing capacity building, and ensuring continuous review.

As we continue to create AI systems and use one of humanity's greatest and ultimate achievements, we must remain diligent watchmen while also pressing for the urgent ethical imperatives of managing AI for the welfare of all. Fallible humans construct AI systems that operate autonomously, deciding and carrying out actions that have far-reaching consequences for individuals and societies worldwide. AI systems have no emotions or remorse as of now, and they continue to learn and respond based on their programmable brain.

## Notes


1. Dafoe A. Opportunity. https://www.allandafoe.com/opportunity.
2. Ethical Artificial Intelligence. https://www.kaggle.com/code/shreyamishra610/ethical-ai-is-all-we-need.
3. Adadi A, Berrada M. Peeking inside the Black Box: A survey on Explainable Artificial Intelligence (XAI). *IEEE Access* 2018;6:52138–52160. https://doi.org/10.1109/access.2018.2870052.
4. Mora-Cantallops M, et al. Traceability for trustworthy AI: A review of models and tools. *Big Data and Cognitive Computing* 2021;5(2):20. https://doi.org/10.3390/bdcc5020020.
5. Arrieta AB, et al. Explainable Artificial Intelligence (XAI): Concepts, taxonomies, opportunities and challenges toward responsible AI. *Information Fusion* June 2020;58(1):82–1152.
6. Antoniadi AM, et al. Current challenges and future opportunities for XAI in machine learning-based clinical decision support systems: A systematic review. *Applied Sciences* 31 May 2021;11(11):5088.
7. Mazurek G, Małagocka K. Perception of privacy and data protection in the development of Artificial Intelligence. *Journal of Management Analytics* 2 Oct 2019;6(4):344–364.

8. Nazer L, et al. Bias in Artificial Intelligence algorithms and recommendations for mitigation. *PLOS Digit Health* 22 June 2023;2(6):e0000278–e0000278. Accessed 1 July 2023.
9. Hickok M. Lessons learned from AI ethics principles for future actions. *AI and Ethics* 6 Oct 2020;1:41–47.
10. Schwarcz D, Prince AER. Proxy discrimination in the age of Artificial Intelligence and big data. *Iowa L. Rev* 2019;105:1257.
11. Manheim K, Kaplan L. Artificial Intelligence: Risks to privacy and democracy. *Yale Journal of Law and Technology* 2019;21:106.
12. Murdoch B. Privacy and Artificial Intelligence: Challenges for protecting health information in a new era. *BMC Medical Ethics* 2021;22(1):122.
13. Agrawal A, et al. Economic policy for Artificial Intelligence. *Innovation Policy and the Economy* Jan 2019;19:139–159.
14. National Science and Technology Council. *Preparing for the future of artificial intelligence.* Washington (DC): Executive Office of the President; 2016 Oct. https://obamawhitehouse.archives.gov/sites/default/files/whitehouse_files/microsites/ostp/NSTC/preparing_for_the_future_of_ai.pdf.
15. Vrontis D, et al. Artificial Intelligence, robotics, advanced technologies and human resource management: A systematic review. *The International Journal of Human Resource Management* 12 Feb 2021;33(6):1–30.
16. Furman J, Seamans R. AI and the economy. *Innovation Policy and the Economy* Jan 2019;19(1):161–191.
17. Steels L, Lopez de Mantaras R. The Barcelona declaration for the proper development and usage of Artificial Intelligence in Europe. *AI Communications* 21 Dec 2018;31(6):485–494. Accessed 21 Sept 2019.
18. West DM, Allen JR. How Artificial Intelligence is transforming the world. Brookings, 24 Apr 2018. Work Cited.
19. Hogenhout L. A framework for ethical AI at the United Nations. ArXiv:2104.12547 [Cs], 9 Apr 2021. arxiv.org/abs/2104.12547.

# Chapter 18

# The Debate on the Governance of Artificial Intelligence

> The development of full artificial intelligence could spell the end of the human race.
>
> **—Stephen Hawking**

The quote by renowned physicist Stephen Hawking encapsulates the chilling implications of artificial intelligence governance (Naib).[1] It highlights the potential risk to humanity associated with the uncontrolled advancement of AI technology. Hawking's quote is a fearful reminder of the need for responsible and ethical governance to ensure the safe development and deployment of AI systems worldwide.

One significant opposing viewpoint is whether worldwide open AI governance is harmful to AI development or even viable. Many people view this advanced technology as gaining an edge in the global competition. According to Vladimir Putin's paper, *Weapons of the Weak: Russia and AI-Driven Asymmetric Warfare*, "Artificial intelligence is the future, not just for Russia, but for humanity. It brings with it enormous potential and unpredictable threats. Whoever becomes the leader in this sphere will become the world's ruler." Vladimir Putin's comment relays his argument against AI governance, as he emphasizes the potential and threats it brings for not only Russia but also humanity. It emphasizes the view that AI has enormous potential and that the race to lead in this sector is a worldwide race for

DOI: 10.4324/9781003661627-23

dominance. Putin argues that rigid governance may impede a country's ability to become a dominant force in the AI environment by emphasizing the prospects and risks involved with AI.

Preventing the advancement of artificial intelligence may cause a power imbalance in the world, potentially subjugating people who lack such intellect. According to this viewpoint, pursuing unconstrained AI development and deployment is required to guarantee a position of balanced influence and power in the future (Daugherty and Jay).[2] However, it is important to emphasize that this phrase does not constitute a full case against governance but a covert virtual fight for AI dominance.

The intensification of worldwide rivalry for AI domination necessitates establishing international AI governance to regulate its potential for societal benefit while minimizing its harm. "The growing discipline of 'AI governance'... explores how humankind may best oversee the transition to powerful AI systems," writes Dafoe. "Given the technology's strategic importance, its various applications, and the uncertainty associated with its development trajectory, we expect that such governance will be difficult" (Dafoe and Affairs, 121).[3]

This essay addresses AI governance, analyzing the urgent difficulties and arguments posed by its uncontrolled development and potential versus harmful deployment to help bridge the knowledge gap in creating AI management. This topic has become extremely relevant, involving contentious matters on which people have strongly differing opinions.

While some claim that accountability is necessary to ensure ethical behavior, others contend that the technical limits of AI development traceability make it difficult to trace backward and identify the individual accountable for a specific action producing AI harm in use (Koulu).[4] The complexity of AI systems makes it hard to determine who is accountable. AI algorithms are a mysterious "black box" of unknowns, inexplicable algorithms, and coding procedures (Adadi and Berrada).[5]

Determining accountability for AI systems developed using open-source coding presents a complex problem in tracing the coders and developers involved. AI systems' lack of knowledge and transparency raises worries about potentially unfair or inaccurate responsibility (Mora-Cantallops et al.).[6] AI algorithms should be transparent and understandable. Explainable AI allows individuals to question and hold AI systems accountable for unjust or biased decisions.

Supporters of unregulated AI underline the necessity of encouraging innovation and technological advancement. They contend that rules can hinder advancing AI by introducing unnecessary limits and bureaucratic impediments. Researchers and developers can freely explore innovative ideas and experiments with unrestricted AI, resulting in groundbreaking discoveries and breakthroughs in various fields. Supporters of unregulated AI argue that government involvement may stifle economic growth (Naib).[7] Artificial intelligence technology can potentially disrupt businesses and generate new work possibilities. Proponents claim that allowing the market to govern AI development and deployment would benefit society from the positive economic impact AI may offer.

Another criticism is that comprehensive artificial intelligence governance produces a hierarchical hierarchy of authority, undermining the democratic capitalist approach to controlling society and industry.[8] There is also the question of whether the ethical principles advocated by AI developers will genuinely impact creating safe and beneficial AI or if they are putting on a show to avoid public criticism (Seger).[9]

Because AI systems are human creations, the AI human developers should face a major share of the accountability for their acts, if intended. Rather than relying only on holding AI systems accountable after misuse or harm, external and internal, we should create human oversight early in the AI development, deployment, and operations process. The designers should be held accountable.

Understandable design practices, continual testing, and transparent design decision-making throughout AI development can help to mitigate potential dangers and guarantee that AI systems are consistent with society's values (Barredo Arrieta et al.).[10]

A more selective approach may be required rather than ultimate accountability for all parties involved in the exploitation and harm of AI systems. Should we evaluate AI systems based on their decisions and behaviors within the context of their intended use and capabilities? We should closely monitor the level of automation in AI judgments and always consider the possibility of immediate human intervention (Antoniadi et al.).[11] This approach recognizes the delicate relationship between AI and human involvement, finding a balance between AI systems' benefits and limits. Human monitoring is always required throughout open AI creation and transparent implementation. Ensuring individual accountability for the outcomes and repercussions of AI systems allows humans to maintain control over all aspects of AI, guaranteeing alignment with human values.

AI governance should prioritize protecting human privacy and data.

Informed consent in data collection, usage, storage methods, and precautions to prevent unauthorized access should be part of the AI protective measures.

Respecting privacy rights and guaranteeing safe personal data management should be a core universal factor in AI governance (Mazurek and Maagocka).[12]

To ensure justice and non-discrimination, we must design and manage AI systems to prevent continuing discriminatory AI practices. It is vital to monitor and audit data inputs, model training, and evaluation processes (Nazer et al.).[13] AI biases can potentially perpetuate unfairness and unequal treatment, with far-reaching societal effects. Addressing biases in AI algorithms begins with the training data. AI developers must prioritize data sources that are diverse and representative. We can reduce biases using diverse impartial facts, resulting in more equitable decision-making outcomes. Before using AI algorithms, developers should employ internal testing methodologies to uncover and minimize biases.

Once developers find biases, they can take remedial steps such as adding vast amounts of representative data, retraining algorithms, or changing the decision-making process to eliminate biases and enhance fairness. To uncover biases affecting decision-making, AI bias evaluations should comprise real-world use cases and simulated situations (Hickok).[14]

It is critical to avoid producing "proxy prejudice" camouflaged behind the usage of AI systems and incorrect development (Prince and Schwarcz).[15] Preventive recommendations should define AI developers' and organizations' ethical obligations in preventing discriminatory proxy practices, emphasizing correcting biases and ensuring fairness early in decision-making processes.

Proponents of ungoverned artificial intelligence systems argue that government and industrial regulators may also be biased in how they govern (Margetts and Dorobantu).[16] Governance and ethical guidelines are subject to interpretation, which introduces the risk of subjective biases influencing decision-making. Individuals and organizations may have varying interpretations of ethical behavior and responsible development. This subjectivity can lead to inconsistencies and disputes, potentially impeding progress and hindering the adoption of emerging technologies.

The rapid growth of artificial intelligence has also generated worries about the potential ethical consequences of employment displacement (Agrawal et al.).[17] As AI-driven automation replaces certain occupational roles, individuals and communities may confront considerable issues. Loss of employment can result in financial insecurity, income inequality, and decreased social mobility. Ethical issues should also involve assessing potential economic imbalances, employment displacement, and institutional prejudices. By addressing these social effects, AI governance may ensure that AI serves the greater good and benefits society on several levels.

Businesses and governments should share the burden of investing in lifelong learning and reskilling initiatives to empower people displaced by AI. Affected persons can learn new skills that fit growing career prospects by accessing inexpensive and relevant education and training, such as working closely with AI systems like robotics (Vrontis et al.).[18] Governments can reward businesses to engage in such programs while cultivating a culture of continual learning and adaptability.

Governments can also provide complete assistance to those transferring into new jobs. This includes career counseling, job placement support, and financial assistance during the transition period. Support networks, mentoring programs, and access to job retraining options can help affected persons cope and make the move easier.

On the other hand, company executives see AI as a driver for work transformation rather than a danger to employment. AI is no exception to the rule that technical improvements frequently generate new opportunities for businesses. Workers will focus on more complicated and creative efforts as AI systems take over repetitive and tedious duties. Businesses may increase efficiency, improve customer experiences, and create new employment roles centered on AI development by embracing AI technology. AI can transform and reinvent the future of work, enabling a more efficient and rewarding workforce rather than displacing jobs.

AI is a worldwide phenomenon, with national borders separating its development and application. International cooperation is required to handle these difficulties collectively and promote consistent standards. Through international collaborations, diverse stakeholders can combine their resources, knowledge, and expertise (West and Allen). [19]

Governments, business leaders, academic institutions, and civil society organizations can work together to create universal ethical norms and governance frameworks that consider diverse cultural viewpoints and experiences. Shared accountability generates a sense of joint ownership, which results in more thorough and practical solutions.

Internationally agreed-upon ethical norms help create a level playing field for AI development and deployment worldwide (Jobin et al.).[20] An international agreement on ethical norms eliminates the possibility of disparities and prohibits unethical actions from taking place in regions with relaxed legislation.

International collaborations allow for the exchange of best practices and lessons learned. Countries can improve their ethical standards and governance frameworks by learning from one another's achievements and failures. The international community can work together to promote AI's responsible and ethical use across borders by recognizing shared responsibility, harmonizing ethical standards, building trust, leveraging existing initiatives, establishing multilateral agreements, sharing best practices, providing capacity building, and ensuring continuous review.

As we continue to discuss how to manage AI systems, let us remember that AI is one of humanity's greatest creations. We must remain attentive and demand imperatives to govern AI for the welfare of humanity while not limiting its growing potential. AI systems built by humans today have no emotions or remorse and continue to learn and behave based on their programmable brain. As a result, the danger of AI systems arises from competing countries, organizations, or individuals who have either uninformed naivety or knowing malintent.

Unfortunately, being naïve is not a punishable offense, and we often conceal malintent from scrutiny. Because of these unknowns, we must continue to analyze each AI system to see if future harm to global civilization is possible while balancing the growth of such a powerful technology.

In the June 30, 2023, *Times News*, Nick Bostrom, a futurist and philosophy professor at Oxford University, reflected on the need for increased awareness and scrutiny of AI system development, saying,

> We are moving towards transformative AI capabilities that will potentially shape the future of our species and our life on this planet. AI poses grave concerns, but it can also aid in resolving many problems. It would be a mistake to respond with indifference or complacency.

## Notes

1. Alakbarov N. Artificial intelligence and the end of capitalist system. In: Bozkuş Kahyaoğlu S, editor. *The impact of artificial intelligence on governance, economics and finance, volume I. Accounting, Finance, Sustainability, Governance & Fraud: Theory and Application.* Singapore: Springer; 2021. pp. 125–140. https://doi.org/10.1007/978-981-33-6811-8_9.

2. Dougherty J, Jay M. Russia tries to get smart about Artificial Intelligence. *The Wilson Quarterly* 22 Mar. 2018;42(2). Accessed 15 July 2023.
3. Dafoe A, Journal of International Affairs. Global politics and the governance of Artificial Intelligence. *Journal of International Affairs* 2018;72(1):121–126. www.jstor.org/stable/26588347.
4. Koulu R. Proceduralizing control and discretion: Human oversight in Artificial Intelligence policy. *Maastricht Journal of European and Comparative Law* 2020;27(6):720–735. https://doi.org/10.1177/1023263x20978649.
5. Adadi A, Berrada M. Peeking inside the Black-Box: A survey on Explainable Artificial Intelligence (XAI). *IEEE Access* 2018;6:52138–52160. https://doi.org/10.1109/access.2018.2870052.
6. Mora-Cantallops M, et al. Traceability for trustworthy AI: A review of models and tools. *Big Data and Cognitive Computing* 2021;5(2):20. https://doi.org/10.3390/bdcc5020020.
7. Alakbarov N. Artificial Intelligence and the end of capitalist system. 1 Jan. 2021, pp. 165–178. https://doi.org/10.1007/978-981-33-6811-8_9. Accessed 21 June 2023. Nations, United.
8. Alakbarov N. Artificial Intelligence and the end of capitalist system. 1 Jan. 2021, pp. 165–178. https://doi.org/10.1007/978-981-33-6811-8_9. Accessed 21 June 2023. Nations, United.
9. Seger E. In defence of principlism in AI ethics and governance. *Philosophy & Technology* 2022;35(2). https://doi.org/10.1007/s13347-022-00538-y.
10. Barredo Arrieta A, et al. Explainable Artificial Intelligence (XAI): Concepts, taxonomies, opportunities and challenges toward responsible AI. *Information Fusion* 2020;58(1):82–115. arxiv.org/pdf/1910.10045.pdf. https://doi.org/10.1016/j.inffus.2019.12.012.
11. Antoniadi AM, et al. Current challenges and future opportunities for XAI in machine learning-based clinical decision support systems: A systematic review. *Applied Sciences* 2021;11(11):5088. https://doi.org/10.3390/app11115088.
12. Mazurek G, Małagocka K. Perception of privacy and data protection in the development of Artificial Intelligence. *Journal of Management Analytics* 2019;6(4):344–364. https://doi.org/10.1080/23270012.2019.1671243.
13. Nazer L, et al. Bias in Artificial Intelligence algorithms and recommendations for mitigation. *PLOS Digit Health* 2023;2(6):e0000278–e0000278. https://doi.org/10.1371/journal.pdig.0000278. Accessed 1 July 2023.
14. Hickok M. Lessons learned from AI ethics principles for future actions. *AI and Ethics* 2020;1. https://doi.org/10.1007/s43681-020-00008-1.
15. Prince AER, Schwarcz D. Proxy discrimination in the age of Artificial Intelligence and big data. *Iowa Law Review* 2019;105:1257. heinonline.org/HOL/LandingPage?handle=hein.journals/ilr105&div=35&id=&page=.
16. Margetts H, Dorobantu C. Rethink government with AI. *Nature* 2019;568(7751):163–165. https://doi.org/10.1038/d41586-019-01099-5.
17. Agrawal A, et al. Economic policy for Artificial Intelligence. *Innovation Policy and the Economy* 2019;19:139–159. https://doi.org/10.1086/699935.

18. Vrontis D, et al. Artificial Intelligence, robotics, advanced technologies and human resource management: A systematic review. *The International Journal of Human Resource Management* 2021;33(6):1–30.
19. West DM, Allen JR. How Artificial Intelligence is transforming the world. Brookings, 24 Apr. 2018, Work Cited.
20. Jobin A, et al. The global landscape of AI ethics guidelines. *Nature Machine Intelligence* 2019;1(9):389–399.

# Chapter 19

# Quantum Computing Strategies for Healthcare

Quantum computing has reached a pivotal moment in its evolution. No longer confined to theoretical speculation or laboratory curiosities, it now stands at the threshold of broader scientific and industrial engagement. Yet technology is still very much in its adolescence. The present generation of devices, known as noisy intermediate-scale quantum (NISQ) machines, operate with tens to a few hundred qubits, but these qubits are fragile, error-prone, and difficult to scale. Their circuits cannot yet sustain the depth required for solving truly intractable problems, and so their outputs are often statistical approximations rather than reliable solutions. Despite these limitations, NISQ devices have opened an era of experimentation in which the boundaries between quantum theory and practical application are being actively tested.

Several hardware modalities coexist in this landscape: superconducting circuits, trapped ions, neutral atoms, photonic processors, and semiconductor spin qubits, each with distinct trade-offs in fidelity, coherence, connectivity, and manufacturability. Superconducting qubits, exemplified by IBM's and Google's devices, have achieved some of the highest gate fidelities, but face scaling challenges due to crosstalk and cryogenic infrastructure demands. Ion-trap systems excel in coherence and all-to-all connectivity but are harder to miniaturize. Neutral atoms and photonic systems promise scalability through modular architectures, while silicon spin qubits draw upon the vast legacy of semiconductor fabrication. No single approach has yet emerged

DOI: 10.4324/9781003661627-24

as the definitive path, suggesting that the future will likely involve either a convergence of platforms or a heterogeneous architecture.

Because physical qubits are inherently noisy, progress toward useful quantum computing depends on error management. In the near term, error mitigation techniques—such as zero-noise extrapolation and randomized compiling—offer partial relief, allowing researchers to extract approximate results from shallow circuits. In the longer term, the ambition is fault-tolerant quantum computing: logical qubits encoded across many physical qubits to correct errors dynamically. The resource overhead is daunting—estimates suggest thousands of physical qubits may be required to stabilize a single logical qubit—but recent advances in error-correcting codes and decoding algorithms offer cautious optimism. IBM, for example, has outlined a roadmap toward logical qubits by the end of the decade, combining surface-code style architectures with improved decoders to reduce overhead.[1]

Meanwhile, the software ecosystem has matured rapidly. Frameworks such as Qiskit, Cirq, and PennyLane enable researchers to design algorithms agnostic of the underlying hardware, while compiler optimizations and noise-aware scheduling help adapt circuits to specific device topologies. Hybrid quantum–classical algorithms dominate this NISQ period, with variational methods like the VQE and the Quantum Approximate Optimization Algorithm serving as templates for exploring quantum advantage in chemistry, optimization, and machine learning. Yet, most demonstrations remain proof-of-concept, with quantum results compared against small classical benchmarks rather than against the full weight of classical high-performance computing.

The trajectory of the field points toward gradual but steady progress. The consensus is that the next decade will be defined by three interwoven movements. First is the transition from NISQ devices to modular, error-corrected architectures, where multiple smaller processors are linked through quantum interconnects to form larger, scalable systems. Second is the refinement of hybrid workflows, in which quantum subroutines complement powerful classical solvers for "right-sized" problems and tasks small enough to run on near-term quantum devices but hard enough to challenge conventional approaches, such as fragment-level molecular simulations or discrete optimization subproblems. Third is the co-evolution of adjacent quantum technologies, particularly quantum sensing and quantum communication, which may reach practical deployment sooner and feed novel signal types into future quantum computing pipelines.

The risks and bottlenecks are equally clear. Error rates remain stubbornly high, and without dramatic improvements in qubit quality, scaling alone will not deliver an advantage. Calibration, control, and crosstalk grow exponentially more difficult as qubit arrays expand. Classical computing continues to advance, raising the threshold against which quantum machines must compete. The shortage of quantum-trained professionals further complicates adoption, with many enterprises lacking a coherent roadmap despite growing investment.[2]

Even so, investment and momentum continue to build. Governments and corporations alike are pouring resources into the field, treating quantum as a strategic technology with implications for security, industry, and scientific discovery. Reports from institutions such as MIT, McKinsey, and Deloitte all reflect cautious optimism: progress is uneven, but the direction is unmistakable. The next few years will likely not deliver general-purpose quantum supremacy, but rather incremental demonstrations of "quantum utility" or cases where a quantum device provides tangible benefits over classical computation in a narrowly defined but meaningful domain.[3]

The outlook, then, is one of careful anticipation. Quantum computing today is neither hype nor panacea. It is a field in transition, moving steadily from concept toward reality, from experimental toys to specialized tools. Its future depends on pragmatic strategies: hybrid adoption, ruthless benchmarking against classical baselines, and sustained advances in both hardware and software. If these paths are pursued with rigor, the coming decade may see the long-awaited emergence of fault-tolerant machines—and with them, the possibility of a new computational paradigm.

Quantum computing (QC) is increasingly viewed as a transformative force in medicine, capable of solving problems that overwhelm even the most powerful classical systems. Although today's machines remain in the noisy intermediate-scale quantum (NISQ) era, strategies are emerging that allow quantum tools to be meaningfully integrated into medical discovery, diagnosis, and delivery of care. The key is not to imagine quantum computing as a distant panacea, but as a practical partner to classical computing—an accelerator that, when applied to the right problems, can deliver measurable value to healthcare systems.

One of the most promising areas for QC lies in drug discovery and molecular simulation. Many of the bottlenecks in pharmaceutical design are quantum-mechanical at their core: electronic structures, binding energies, and reaction pathways. Classical computers can only approximate these interactions, often with significant errors. Algorithms such as the Variational

Quantum Eigensolver (VQE) and the Quantum Approximate Optimization Algorithm (QAOA) have been developed to address these challenges. By capturing electron correlations more precisely, they hold the potential to improve docking accuracy, predict binding affinities, and reduce costly false positives in the drug pipeline. Hybrid strategies that apply QC to chemically significant fragments and then integrate the results into classical QM/MM pipelines are emerging as the most realistic pathway for near-term adoption. In this way, pharmaceutical teams can test quantum-accelerated subroutines today, rather than waiting for fully fault-tolerant machines to appear.[4]

Another domain where quantum methods are showing promise is oncology, particularly in radiotherapy planning. Treatment planning for intensity-modulated radiotherapy (IMRT) requires optimizing beam angles and distributions across tumor tissue and organs at risk, an optimization problem of enormous complexity. Classical solvers can take hours to identify suitable solutions, often relying on heuristics. Recent work has demonstrated that quantum annealing and quantum-inspired optimization techniques can generate plans more efficiently while maintaining or improving quality.[5,6] These methods emulate tunneling dynamics to escape local minima and have been mapped to subroutines in beam-angle selection. Though many approaches remain "quantum-inspired" rather than fully quantum, they nonetheless reveal a path forward: radiotherapy centers could integrate hybrid optimization routines, first as parallel validation tools, and eventually as core planning components once hardware improves.

Beyond therapy, quantum machine learning (QML) has become a rapidly growing field with implications for healthcare data. Genomics, medical imaging, and electronic health records (EHRs) generate massive, high-dimensional datasets that challenge even state-of-the-art deep learning models. By encoding data into high-dimensional Hilbert spaces, QML models may capture subtle correlations that classical models overlook. A 2025 systematic review highlights a surge of proof-of-concept studies in areas such as EHR-based disease prediction and imaging classification.[7] Yet the review also notes that consistent superiority over classical models has not been demonstrated, with most studies constrained by small sample sizes, shallow circuits, and the difficulty of encoding clinical data. The most strategic path is benchmarking-first culture: QML should be treated as one candidate among many, evaluated against robust classical baselines using transparent metrics that include calibration, computational cost, and interpretability.

The field of genomics and systems biology offers another compelling test case. Variant calling, haplotype phasing, and multi-omics integration all involve combinatorial optimization at massive scales. As the layers of genomic, proteomic, and metabolic data expand, even the most powerful classical methods struggle with computational load. Quantum optimization could provide acceleration here, particularly in repetitive or structurally complex genomic regions.[8] Rather than attempting wholesale replacement, researchers are beginning to envision modular hybrid workflows: quantum subroutines embedded selectively within established genomic pipelines. Such incremental adoption reduces risk while providing practical test beds for quantum advantage.

A parallel but distinct frontier lies not in computation but in quantum sensing and bioimaging. Nitrogen-vacancy (NV) centers in diamond, functioning as nanoscale magnetometers, have demonstrated unprecedented sensitivity in detecting magnetic signals at room temperature. Recent work has achieved widefield optical readout of local nuclear magnetic resonance (NMR) signals.[9] This opens the possibility of diagnostic imaging modalities with molecular-scale resolution, potentially useful in oncology, pathology, and neuroscience. Unlike quantum computing applications, which may take years to achieve clinical superiority, quantum sensing technologies could be among the first quantum innovations to reach patient care directly, creating new types of biomedical signals that future quantum computers may help analyze.

Taken together, these developments point to a pragmatic roadmap. The most effective strategies begin with hybrid pipelines, where quantum routines are integrated into validated classical workflows. Every new algorithm must be benchmarked against strong baselines using gold-standard, open datasets. Institutions should target "right-sized" problems—areas where Hilbert-space advantages are plausible, such as modeling molecular fragments, solving discrete subsets in radiotherapy planning, or analyzing genomic regions where classical methods falter. Alongside computation, advances in quantum sensing should be monitored closely, as they may open entirely new avenues of biomedical diagnostics. Above all, healthcare organizations must foster a culture of benchmarking, methodological rigor, and partnership with hardware and software vendors, ensuring that adoption is both evidence-based and strategically scalable.

In March 2023, the Cleveland Clinic, in partnership with IBM, unveiled the world's first quantum computer dedicated exclusively to healthcare research. Housed within the Lerner Research Institute on the Clinic's main campus, the IBM Quantum System One is encased in a sleek, climate-controlled chamber designed to maintain the extreme conditions necessary for stable quantum operations (Figure 19.1). Its installation marked a historic milestone: a major medical institution hosting its own quantum computer not as an abstract experiment, but as a practical engine for biomedical discovery.

The system represents the leading edge of what is possible in the noisy intermediate-scale quantum (NISQ) era. Although its exact specifications, qubit number, gate fidelity, and error rates remain proprietary, IBM's current devices typically operate with over 100 superconducting qubits and have demonstrated gate fidelities surpassing 99%. While not yet capable of fault-tolerant operation, the machine allows researchers to run hybrid quantum–classical workflows, combining conventional supercomputing with quantum acceleration on carefully selected subproblems. In this way, the Clinic's quantum computer is less a singular powerhouse and more a collaborative partner in computation, opening new possibilities for medicine while acknowledging the limits of today's hardware.

The early applications of this system are ambitious and wide-ranging. Teams at the Clinic have focused on quantum-accelerated drug discovery, using quantum algorithms to model molecular fragments with higher accuracy than traditional force-field approximations. These simulations promise to shorten timelines in lead identification and reduce the costly attrition rates

**Figure 19.1 Cleveland Clinic, in partnership with IBM, unveiled the world's first quantum computer dedicated exclusively to healthcare research**

that plague pharmaceutical research. In one notable collaboration, Cleveland Clinic and IBM researchers applied a hybrid quantum–classical framework to protein structure prediction and reported that their models outperformed both conventional physics-based simulations and even AlphaFold2 on certain benchmark proteins. Such work underscores how quantum computing may complement, rather than compete with, the breakthroughs of artificial intelligence.

Beyond molecular simulation, the Clinic is exploring quantum optimization in clinical research design. Selecting trial sites, balancing patient demographics, and simulating virtual cohorts are problems of combinatorial complexity, where quantum annealing and optimization algorithms could provide efficiencies. In the realm of data analysis, the Clinic has begun testing quantum machine learning (QML) for noisy, high-dimensional datasets such as electronic health records, aiming to identify early biomarkers of disease or predict post-surgical outcomes. Parallel efforts in genomics and T-cell receptor modeling seek to leverage quantum methods for deciphering patterns in immunology and personalized medicine.

The quantum computer has also become a platform for innovation beyond the Clinic's walls. Through its Discovery Accelerator initiative, Cleveland Clinic launched the Quantum Innovation Catalyzer Program, offering startups and external researchers immersive year-long residencies with dedicated access to the system. These projects pair quantum algorithms with artificial intelligence and biomedical datasets, encouraging entrepreneurship and expanding the network of collaborators who might one day translate quantum-enabled discoveries into clinical practice.

Taken together, the Cleveland Clinic's quantum computer is not yet a fault-tolerant engine capable of revolutionizing healthcare overnight. Rather, it is a living laboratory, where quantum capabilities are being tested against the urgent questions of medicine. By embedding this machine within a leading medical institution, the Clinic has signaled that quantum computing's future will not be confined to physics labs or tech giants—it will be judged by its ability to accelerate the fight against disease.

The outlook is one of cautious optimism. Across the medical sciences, credible proofs-of-concept exist, but there are still few head-to-head demonstrations of quantum methods outperforming best-in-class classical approaches. That makes the present moment, mid-2020, the right time to build fluency, establish benchmarking standards, and launch hybrid pilot projects with clear evaluation metrics. The next decade of quantum computing is expected to progress from noisy intermediate-scale quantum (NISQ)

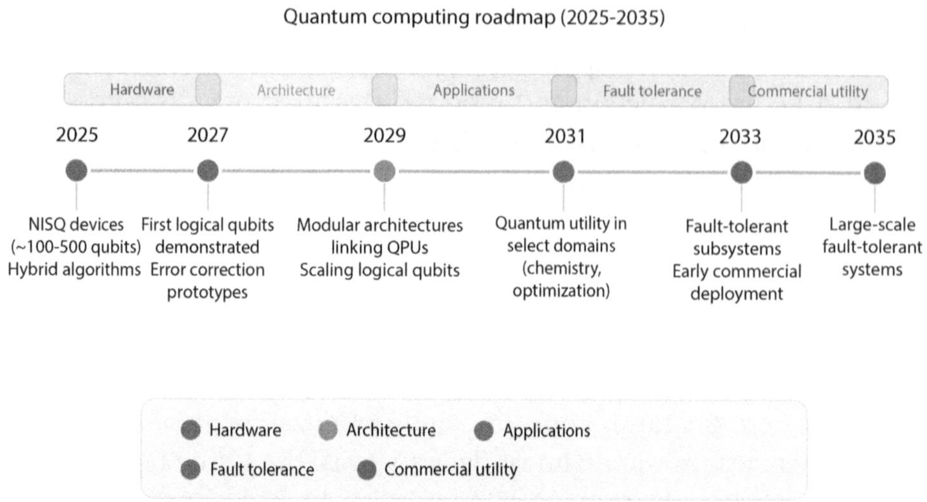


**Figure 19.2 Quantum computing roadmap (2025–2035)**

devices with hybrid algorithms (2025) to the first demonstrations of logical qubits and error correction (2027), followed by modular architectures linking processors (2029). Around 2031, practical "quantum utility" may emerge in domains such as chemistry and optimization. By 2033, fault-tolerant subsystems could enable early commercial deployment, with large-scale fault-tolerant systems envisioned by 2035 (Figure 19.2). Organizations that invest now in careful, targeted experimentation will be best positioned to capitalize as quantum hardware matures and as quantum sensing, simulation, and optimization converge into practical, validated tools at the bedside.

Quantum computing will not revolutionize healthcare overnight. Yet, by anchoring efforts in rigorous validation and targeted use cases, it offers a pathway to accelerate drug discovery, refine cancer treatments, enhance genomic analysis, and even introduce new imaging modalities. If pursued with discipline, quantum computing may not only transform the pace of biomedical discovery but also redefine the standard of precision in modern medicine.

## Notes

1. IBM Quantum. The roadmap to scale: Building large-scale Fault-Tolerant Quantum computers. IBM Blog, 2025.
2. ISACA. Organizations lack a quantum computing roadmap, ISACA finds. ISACA Press Release, January 2025.

3. MIT Sloan School of Management. New MIT report captures the state of quantum computing. MIT Sloan, 2025; McKinsey & Company. The year of quantum: From concept to reality in 2025. McKinsey Digital Insights, 2025; Deloitte. Quantum computing futures: Preparing for the next decade. Deloitte Insights, 2025.
4. Niazi, SK. Quantum mechanics in drug design: Progress, challenges, and future frontiers. Communicative & Integrative Biology 2026;19(1):2603140. https://doi.org/10.1080/19420889.2025.2603140.
5. Pakela JM, et al. Quantum-inspired algorithm for radiotherapy planning optimization. *Medical Physics* 2020;47(1):5–18. https://doi.org/10.1002/mp.13840.
6. Shinde N, et al. Quantum approaches to beam-angle optimization in radiotherapy. arXiv preprint. 2025.
7. Gupta RS, et al. A systematic review of quantum machine learning for digital health. *npj Digital Medicine* 2025;8(1):237. https://doi.org/10.1038/s41746-025-01597-z.
8. Durant TJS, et al. A primer for quantum computing and its applications to healthcare and biomedical research. Journal of the American Medical Informatics Association 2024;31(8):1774–1784. https://doi.org/10.1093/jamia/ocae149.
9. Briegel KD, et al. Optical widefield nuclear magnetic resonance microscopy. Nature Communications 2025;16:1281. https://doi.org/10.1038/s41467-024-55003-5.

# Chapter 20

# Future of AI in Healthcare

> It is difficult to think of a major industry that AI will not transform. This includes healthcare, education, transportation, retail, communications, and agriculture.
>
> There are clear paths for AI to make a big difference in these industries.
>
> **—Andrew Ng, Computer Scientist and Global Leader in AI[1]**

Back in 2020, during the height of the COVID-19 pandemic, two AI luminaries, Fei-Fei Li and Andrew Ng, convened on YouTube to discuss the current state of AI in healthcare. COVID-19 established healthcare as a top priority for governments, businesses, and investors worldwide and accelerated efforts to apply artificial intelligence to improve our health, including drug discovery, more efficient hospital operations, and better diagnostics. In the first quarter of 2021, AI-focused healthcare startups raised a record $2.5 billion. As successful implementations of AI-based healthcare products and services may not be imminent, this may be comparable to the excitement surrounding and investment in autonomous vehicle technologies a few years ago.

As we live in the 21st century, artificial intelligence is transforming the healthcare industry, and its impact is already being felt by analyzing vast amounts of medical data to identify trends, make predictions, and inform clinical decision-making. This is revolutionizing healthcare delivery, improving patient outcomes, and reducing costs. As we look into the future, the application of AI is creating predictive models helping doctors diagnose diseases more accurately and earlier. This is important in cancer care, diabetes,

 DOI: 10.4324/9781003661627-25

and diabetic retinopathy studies, where early diagnosis can be a matter of life and death.

Researchers at Stanford University have developed an AI system that identifies skin cancer with a level of accuracy that rivals that of human dermatologists. They trained the system on a database of over 130,000 images of skin lesions, and it can now diagnose melanoma with an accuracy of 91%. This is a significant improvement over the current average accuracy rate of 86.5% for human dermatologists. The system can diagnose in less than 30 seconds, whereas a human dermatologist might take up to three weeks to provide the same diagnosis. The future of AI in this arena looks bright, revolutionizing the way we diagnose skin cancer, reducing the time to receive a diagnosis, and improving patient outcomes.

The detection of heart disease with AI is making strides. Researchers at the University of California, San Francisco, have developed an AI algorithm that can use electrocardiogram (ECG) readings to predict the likelihood of a patient having a heart attack or other cardiac event within the next year. They trained the algorithm on data from over 400,000 patients, and it could accurately predict the risk of a cardiac event in 90% of cases. This technology has the potential to improve patient outcomes significantly by allowing doctors to intervene earlier and prevent heart attacks from occurring.

Following in the hopeful footsteps of heart disease, AI is improving the accuracy of medical imaging as radiologists can now use AI algorithms to analyze MRI scans and detect tumors that human radiologists have missed. The algorithms make use of tens of thousands of images identifying patterns used to diagnose and treat conditions such as brain tumors, prostate cancer, and breast cancer. One study found that AI algorithms could identify breast cancer with an accuracy of up to 94%, significantly higher than the average accuracy rate of 85% for human radiologists.

Besides improving the accuracy of diagnoses, AI is also used to improve the efficiency of healthcare delivery. Chatbots, for example, are developed to help patients self-diagnose and manage their conditions. These chatbots can use natural language processing to understand patients' symptoms and advise on how to manage them. This can help to reduce the burden on healthcare professionals and improve access to care for patients.

As AI continues to advance, its potential to revolutionize healthcare is clear. However, we must also address the challenges that arise. These challenges can arise from various development, deployment, and maintenance aspects of AI solutions in healthcare. One of the biggest challenges involves ensuring the ethical use of AI and protecting patient privacy. Another challenge is ensuring that we implement AI technologies that are accessible to all patients, regardless of their income or access to healthcare. Despite these challenges, the future of AI in healthcare is bright. With continued research and development, AI has the potential to transform healthcare, and as AI technologies become more sophisticated, they will analyze increasingly larger and more complex datasets, leading to increasingly accurate diagnoses and personalized treatment plans. AI will also play a critical role in developing new drugs and therapies, accelerating the pace of medical innovation.

The potential of AI in healthcare is enormous. From improving the accuracy of diagnoses to developing personalized treatment plans, AI is already transforming the way we deliver healthcare. While there are challenges that must be addressed, AI in healthcare will undoubtedly offer benefits that outweigh the risks. As researchers continue to develop new applications for AI, we can expect to see even more transformative innovations in the years to come. It is an exciting time for healthcare, and AI is at the forefront of this revolution.

Most large healthcare companies employ artificial intelligence, but they are still learning to use it effectively and efficiently. One of the key uses of machine learning and AI is predicting everything from emergency department volumes to personnel management and triage times. The tremendous promise of AI in healthcare lies in transforming clinical workflows by automating or augmenting clinicians' and staff's work. AI will fully automate repetitive duties, and we can also use it to enhance the performance of healthcare professionals and improve patient outcomes. To create a truly intelligent health system, healthcare organizations must rethink and reimagine their workflows and processes using machine learning and artificial intelligence.

Automation shows us that intelligent machines will perform repetitive tasks soon, but the augmentation of modern healthcare is of the utmost importance (Figure 20.1). Yet, the concept of augmentation poses the question: how can humans integrate AI to enhance their performance? We at BrainX agree and recognize that senior leaders in the healthcare industry do not need to comprehend how AI works. However, they must embrace understanding AI's power and how it can help them provide individuals with more efficient and compassionate care.

A human-centered approach is essential to advancing state-of-the-art AI in healthcare. Despite the large volume of data sets and potential biases, its implementation requires the AI healthcare industry to focus on the human

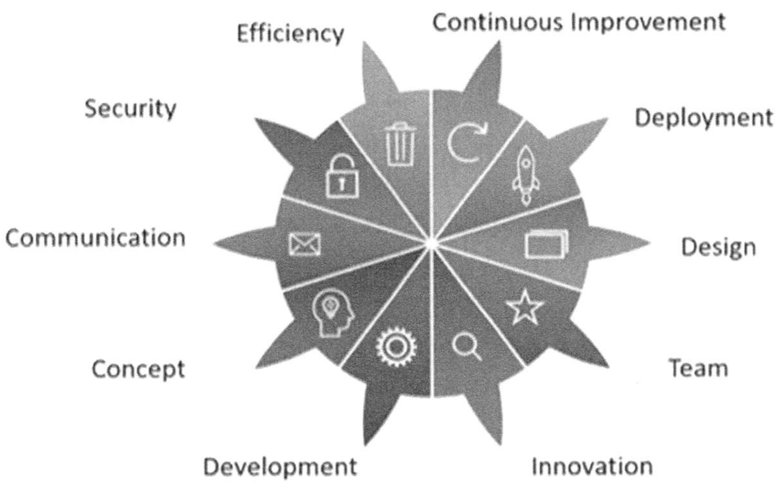


**Figure 20.1 Aspects of development and deployment of AI in healthcare**

aspect to better understand patients and the people providing care. This is the key to the effective adoption of AI-based solutions. Yet, this presents a distinct challenge for the healthcare industry, highlighting the non-digitalized aspect as AI development shifts from model-centric to data-centric, as well as developing tools and processes to make data the center of developers' work to continue improving the quality of data used to train AI programs.

As the world advances in technology, so does the healthcare industry. AI and Precision Medicine, two innovative technologies, are increasingly being integrated into patient care. Precision Medicine involves tailoring medical treatment to an individual's specific characteristics, including genetic makeup, lifestyle, and environment. Equally, AI uses algorithms to analyze substantial amounts of data and make predictions or diagnoses. Together, these technologies could revolutionize healthcare and improve patient outcomes.

Grand View Research predicts that AI in the healthcare market will reach $17.8 billion by 2025, expanding at a compound annual growth rate of 41.5% from 2019 to 2025.[2] The AI in healthcare market is projected to reach $17.8 billion by 2025, with a compound annual growth rate of 41.5% from 2019 to 2025. Adopting these technologies is driven by the need for more personalized and efficient healthcare delivery.

Regarding Precision Medicine, we are shifting away from a universal approach to medicine and embracing a personalized and customized approach. The focus extends beyond the development of new medications, encompassing a profound understanding of each patient and customizing treatment accordingly.

AI and Precision Medicine face challenges, including data privacy and security, which are significant issues. With the amount of personal health data collected and processed, there is a risk of data breaches and privacy violations. Healthcare practitioners must undergo training in the use of these technologies to ensure proper installation and data analysis. Another issue is the need for interoperability among various healthcare systems and technologies. With the massive amounts of data created by these technologies, it is important that they can communicate and share data in real-time to provide the best possible patient outcomes.

Despite the challenges, the potential benefits of AI and Precision Medicine in healthcare are too significant to ignore. Continuous research and development are essential for the successful implementation of healthcare. We have entered a new era in the field of medicine, which calls for extensive research, development, collaboration, and funding. Further investigation, including the development of novel algorithms and tools for the analysis and interpretation of patient data, along with collaboration, comprehension, and integration of these technologies into current healthcare systems, will be necessary to realize their capabilities fully.

## Precision Medicine

The confluence of AI with Precision Medicine may enable the discovery of phenotypes linked with patients who have less common therapeutic responses or unique healthcare demands. AI delivers insights through sophisticated computing and inference, allowing the system to think and learn while also empowering clinician decision-making with augmented intelligence. Translational research into this convergence, according to recent literature, will aid in resolving the most difficult challenges confronting Precision Medicine, particularly those in which non-genomic and genomic determinants, combined with information from patient symptoms, clinical history, and lifestyles, will facilitate personalized diagnosis and prognosis.

As we delve deeper, one thing to examine is whether we can employ artificial intelligence to construct a DNA report card for newborns in the future. Given the technology, we would conduct a risk rate asset appraisal and make projections about the baby's likelihood of getting cancer, diabetes, or other addictions to substances such as tobacco, opiates, or alcohol. Would a life map that allows us to personalize health and medical services to the individual level impact healthcare? There are challenges, but a predictive medicine approach considering everyone's genes, environment, and lifestyle when treating and preventing disease can be an illustrious aspect to consider.

With Precision Medicine, doctors and researchers will forecast treatment and prevention techniques more precisely in groups of different people using this approach. It contrasts with a past one-size-fits-all strategy that produced disease treatment and prevention measures for the typical person without addressing individual variances. AI will be able to tailor health and medical services down to the level of each patient and consumer, identifying appropriate therapies for a specific patient and individualizing all elements of healthcare, illness risk, and prognosis prediction, based on Precision Medicine. In the future, this will lead to improved illness identification and prevention.

Soon, AI will support the practice of Precision Medicine in health organizations by analyzing big medical data sets, drawing conclusions, and finding new correlations based on patterns found in the data specific to an individual patient. This will support a doctor's ability to develop and decide on care pathways for each patient. Before recommending personalized treatment pathways to high-risk, high-cost patient populations, clinicians will also use AI algorithms to consider the latest academic research evidence and regulatory guidelines.

AI will speed up the clinical trial eligibility screening process and produce plans for medications based on evidence. AI's forecasting powers are never 100% accurate. How can we use predictive AI markers to determine who would develop Alzheimer's disease or opioid addiction? This falls under the category of unethical and biased research because what if someone with a low cancer risk postpones screening only to develop cancer anyway? As we integrate AI into the future of healthcare, we must analyze and consider these eventualities. For these reasons, those pushing for precision and predictive medicine to become mainstream are warning the world to proceed with caution. The potential utilization of Precision Medicine for beneficial and detrimental purposes renders it both captivating and disconcerting.

## Quantum Leaping into the Future

In recent years, quantum computing has received much attention. While supercomputers operating at speeds unheard of in everyday computing have been discussed for quite some time, they are close to becoming a reality.

But to fully comprehend the impact quantum computing could have on the world of healthcare, let us first examine how quantum computing works at its core. We may wonder how quantum computers differ from those we are familiar with and rely on. It turns out that the distinction between the two is fundamental. Regular computers work with certainty; everything is black or white, and we represent data in bits, in a sequence of 0's and 1's. Bits in modern computers can only have two states: 0 or 1. This is referred to as a binary system.

With quantum computers, the story is different. Quantum computers, which rely on process uncertainty and probability, are the opposite of classical computers. Instead of bits, quantum computers employ qubits, which can be in multiple states at the same time. Qubits, rather than having a definite place, can be 0, 1, or both—a phenomenon known as "superposition." How will this affect healthcare, and how does it directly apply to solutions?

When quantum computing becomes more practical, one application will use the computers' abilities to lead processes and undertake analysis and solutions at breakneck speed. Slow and expensive trial methods have a negative impact on the healthcare and pharmaceutical industries, causing drug development and implementation delays. While AI, machine learning, and other innovative technologies have been used to hasten these processes, quantum computing opens alternative paths for them to advance and save months, if not years, of study and experimentation.

A quantum computer can evaluate any known molecule type at extraordinary rates and test medication formulations on every human cell in record time. Quantum computing will be a crucial tool in the search for cures for diseases such as Parkinson's, Alzheimer's, cancer, diabetes, and other ailments that claim so many lives every day.

While testing on living animals and cells is one technique for expanding the pharmaceutical and healthcare industries, quantum computing has the potential to enable new types of research and testing that are currently unachievable because of technological constraints. They carried out these silico clinical trials in a completely simulated environment. According to the *Medical Futurist*, quantum computing can help specialists construct virtual settings in which they can study factors such as body fluids, circulation, electrolytes, hormones, and metabolism on digital reproductions of humans.

The complex area of genetics and genomics has made significant advances in recent decades. What started out as a mission to decode human DNA has turned into a rich exploration zone where people can uncover health concerns and trace their history back to their roots.

Quantum computing will speed up progress by enabling much faster analysis and precise predictions of genetic disorders. This will help us take initiative measures to prevent disorders and gain a better understanding of our genetic composition in the shortest time possible.

The processing capacity promised by quantum computing opens the door to the healthcare and pharmaceutical industries' long-awaited goal. Instead of being reactive and delayed, the idea is to be predictive and preventive. While most advanced technologies today enable treating a wide range of ailments, we envisage that quantum computing and its enormous capacity will enable the prediction and successful eradication of such diseases in advance. The amount of data generated every day—as well as the amount of unique patient data already available—will provide a fertile field for quantum machines to perform their work and produce valuable and in-depth analysis that will aid not just in curing but also in preventing certain diseases.

## Artificial Emotional Intelligence

Consider a world in which our personal devices know more about our emotions and mental health than our family or friends. Today, AI components are increasing, allowing robots to identify and predict how humans feel. This has resulted in what is currently known as artificial emotional intelligence, which identifies emotions through many channels, such as speech, facial recognition, email, and text.

Many forward-thinking businesses use AI-enabled technologies to assess customers' feelings and emotions. Changes in facial expressions, tone and pitch of voice, body language, and even neurophysiological activity expressed by biometric markers can provide useful insights into emotional states regarding healthcare and feedback. These insights may be utilized in the future to adjust in-store displays to reflect the mood of the people in front of them. Customers can also self-monitor and manage their own physical and emotional well-being.

## Intelligence Evaluation

Intelligent testing, which combines machine learning and genetic data to improve the diagnostic skills of general testing, is ongoing in the medical field. Adaptive biotechnologies, which attempt to decode the human immune system, are an early example of this. It focuses on how immune system data can be utilized for diagnosing and curing diseases, and it has discovered a means to sequence T-cells and B-cell receptors genetically. The bodies of the adaptive immune system are the key participants. The genome of these receptors is challenging to sequence because it is unlike the rest of the human genome.

These genes reorganize throughout time as machine learning and artificial intelligence break the code of the human immune system. Adaptive AI is developing a diagnostic tool that, in the future, could let doctors spot diseases early with a simple blood test. We would eventually incorporate these intelligence tests into a routine immune screen to detect diseases and improve treatment suggestions based on the specific nature of comprehending an individual patient's situation. Premature birth affects one out of every ten babies, but what if a simple blood test could identify whether a pregnant woman is at risk of having a premature baby based on trace amounts of cell-free genetic information in her blood?

Such research is already underway, and it is now easier to detect and sequence the negligible amounts of cell-free genetic material in the blood, and then use artificial intelligence's developing prediction powers to identify women who are likely to deliver prematurely. Once performed, this gives physicians advance notice and allows them to lessen the possibility of premature delivery, increasing the likelihood of survival and the delivery of a healthy baby. This is a notable example of the impact of AI and testing.

## Biohacking

While many sci-fi-like ideas are circling the internet with biohacking, future options for health and medicine range from simple diagnostics to deep neural implants. For example, biochips can detect or predict diseases from cancer to smallpox before the patient develops symptoms. They would make such chips from intelligent molecular sensors that analyze biological elements and chemicals. We have already seen early examples of biohacking in mainstream medicine. For instance, the Food and Drug Administration (FDA) approved using the world's first artificial pancreas, which continuously monitors and measures glucose levels in patients with type 1 diabetes and then administers the correct insulin dose.

This is significant because over 283 million people must manage type 1 diabetes today. This intelligent closed-loop system will give people with diabetes more freedom to live without manually measuring glucose levels and administering insulin. As another example, recently, there was a recipient of the world's first in-heart microcomputer, designed to improve the care of those with heart failure. The wireless device allows clinicians to track patients in real time and predict when a patient is approaching a situation that requires medical attention or intervention.

In the United States, heart failure is the leading cause of hospitalization. Researchers believe that in the not-too-distant future, such technology will improve patients' health, reduce hospital admissions by forty percent, and save the healthcare industry billions of dollars annually. Although biohacking raises legal, ethical, and societal concerns, technological advances and artificial intelligence will rapidly propel it to the forefront of medicine. However, the future of AI in healthcare depends on our overall mindset, as we recognize adoption barriers as welcomed and advanced opportunities.

## Multimodal Solutions

We have seen evidence of single data types and single model-based AI solutions in research and deployment. Over the next few years, especially with the energy and excitement surrounding generative AI, we are likely to see multimodal AI solutions. These solutions will not only utilize distinct types of data at the same time, such as clinical notes, X-ray images, and auscultation sounds, but also use multiple models to generate a singular output. While these are more likely to perform in how clinicians process patient information, they are likely to see utilization with human in-loop design. Goals of patient safety, operational efficiency, and delivery of high-quality and cost-effective care are more likely to be achieved through these advances in AI models.

The potential for the emerging technology revolution to amplify human abilities and create a new world is clear. And as health leaders pioneer intelligent health systems as part of a much larger revolution in science, education, government social services, and business, it will forever change how we live, work, learn, discover, and communicate.

The new AI technology revolution can potentially create a world where we amplify human abilities. However, as we look into the future, we need to ask how we can harness this power and its transformative effect to help humans make the world a better place.

With the recent technology revolution, the authentic story of AI is just beginning. President Abraham Lincoln once said, "The best thing about the future is that it comes one day at a time." He was right. The progress we see every day, and what we will witness in the future, are the starting points that healthcare is ready to use to alter the world.

## Notes

1. Ng Andrew. Medium. https://medium.com/@alive-ai/a-letter-from-our-ceo-e08d317a903c.
2. Grand View Research Report. PDF. https://www.grandviewresearch.com/press-release/global-artificial-intelligence-healthcare-market.

# Chapter 21

# Agentic AI in Healthcare

## *The Next Frontier*

The rapid evolution of large language models (LLMs) and foundation models has not necessarily translated into their widespread implementation, especially in healthcare. While many barriers to implementation are non-technical, the lack of frameworks enabling autonomous adaptation of LLMs has limited widespread deployment. Agentic AI represents a framework solution for goal-driven, autonomous, and adaptive implementation of these models. Hence, there has been increasing research and development of these Agentic AI frameworks and tools in recent times.

In a recent review of literature, the researchers have found seven publications related to Agentic AI frameworks in diverse healthcare specialties such as radiology, oncology, emergency medicine, and rehabilitation.[1] The use cases in these specialties were diverse, including diagnosis, treatment planning, coaching, alert generation, and workflow optimizations. Although many of these are initial attempts at adaptation of Agentic AI frameworks in healthcare, they appear promising and are supported by extensive work being done in the computational science world, likely to mature and become more robust.

## Core Architecture of Agentic AI Systems in Healthcare

AI agents are computational entities that can leverage foundation models to execute tasks with minimal human intervention. Agentic AI is an

DOI: 10.4324/9781003661627-27

orchestrated framework for the deployment of specialized task-oriented agents that collaborate together toward the execution of defined goals. Agents within an Agentic AI framework can work together in differing roles such as for the collection of data, data preprocessing, reasoning, action, and orchestration.

There are many parts of an AI agent and Agentic AI frameworks that allow supported but autonomous decision-making. Agentic AI frameworks have key components which facilitate the autonomous and orchestrated decision-making to meet their goals. An agent registry allows for cataloging of various agents.[2] A task graph represents how the tasks flow through agents, while a controller orchestrates the working and coordination of various agents. A ranking engine monitors the performance of the agents, and an audit layer tracks agents' decision-making process for compliance and traceability. Tools are provided to the agents, such as web search, calculators to perform mathematical tasks, and LLM access for summarization. Agents within the framework take user input and utilize these tools to autonomously deliver on a given task or towards the fulfillment of a goal.

In a recently published study, Wang et al. demonstrated the use of an Agentic AI framework for the generation and optimization of radiotherapy treatment plans through the use of specialized agents such as Dosimetrist, Physicist, TPS_proxy, and a Human_proxy.[3] In this multi-agent framework, the agents used GPT for advanced reasoning to create autonomous radiotherapy plans for lung and cervical cancer patients. Although limited to 17 patients in their experimentation, initial results seem promising, and sometimes the planned therapies surpass those created by expert human planners.

Hence, AI agents are fundamentally different in architecture from conventional AI research and were developed over many years prior to the expansive use of LLMs. The conventional models extensively researched in healthcare for prediction tasks, such as those for the prediction of early deterioration among patients in the hospital, lack autonomous capabilities. Conventional models require significant training on pre-collected data and are very narrow task oriented. They have limited ability to autonomously adapt to deliver a reasoned response and need humans to structure pre-mapped flows. Agentic AI frameworks allow for context-driven real-time adaptation, self-initiation, and autonomous flow of orchestrated responses to user queries or goals.

## Multi-agent Orchestration: Collaboration, Coordination, and Task Decomposition

Specialized agents in a multi-agent framework allow communication, task decomposition, autonomous reasoning, and coordination to achieve set goals. These agents are adaptable, leveraging various tools provided to them, and can ask for real-time guidance from the user. Agentic AI systems therefore move beyond decision support to decision execution, enabling dynamic decision-making during patient care, real-time adaptation based on changing context, and delivery of reasoned interventions.

Kumar N. et al. described a case example in which AI agents, along with state-of-the-art 6G network technology, can enable the performance of remote robotic surgery. In this multi-agent scenario, each AI agent takes the role of various team members working in the operating theater.[4] The Surgical Perception Agent has been described to provide real-time data, including intra-operative camera feeds and images. The Haptic Feedback Agent enables the surgeon to remotely preserve the tactile feedback during the surgery. The Trajectory Planning Agent guides the robotic arms. An Anomaly Detection Agent monitors the patient and provides real-time alerts for any unexpected events. A Network Optimization Agent ensures smooth transmission of real-time data to the remote treatment team, including the surgeon. The Support Agent provides contextual clinical decision support to the operating surgeon. For continuous improvement, Learning and Adaptation Agents provide inputs into refinements for the Agentic system. Collectively, the researchers demonstrated constant communication with clinical decision support among both the agents and clinicians to enable real-time remote surgery.

## Agentic AI for Healthcare Operations and Systems Optimization

One of the biggest opportunities to leverage Agentic AI in healthcare resides in its use for hospital operations and administration. Application opportunities include workflow optimization, revenue cycle management, workforce planning, research, and optimizing communications. Dana-Farber Cancer Institute has described the deployment of a GPT-based agent for healthcare operations.[5] This agent supports research, clinical documentation, and administrative workflows across cancer care. Appointment scheduling and customer support using voice agents is another key example of AI agents being leveraged for efficiency and effectiveness in the delivery of healthcare outside of the clinical workspace.

## Trust, Safety, and Governance in Autonomous Clinical Systems

Agentic AI systems with newer, autonomous architecture pose new challenges for already challenged AI governance. In addition to the amplification of existing issues with biases, safety, privacy, and failure modes, there are unforeseen complications that might arise from their implementation. Despite increasing research to measure the accuracy and safety of Generative AI in healthcare over the last few years, there is a lack of a robust framework for the assessment of Agentic AI performance.[6] In a complex and autonomous archetype, the development and deployment of performance and safety guardrails can be even more challenging. Due to a lack of deep understanding of these rapidly developed autonomous systems, regulation will also need to evolve to prevent harm to both the patients and healthcare delivery systems.

## Implementation Science and the Path to Scalable Adoption

Similar to the challenges with the measurement of quality and safety of Agentic AI, the implementation of these systems in the healthcare environment is also very complex. First of all, it requires trained human resources for research, development, and implementation of Agentic AI. The whole science is evolving very rapidly, and health systems are not geared to have an adequately trained workforce to manage this rapid transformation. Another major challenge that requires addressing is the need for computational resources. Lastly, the availability of safe information technology infrastructure is another headwind where resource prioritization will have to be considered to achieve meaningful and scalable deployment. Industry partnership is one key solution to successfully deploy Agentic AI systems across healthcare.

Agentic AI represents a transformational opportunity for the application of frontier AI models in healthcare. The opportunity spans clinical applications, healthcare operations, research, and patient engagement. Agentic AI frameworks offer scalable approaches to improve healthcare access for patients and delivery of high-quality care. To leverage and enable the successful deployment of Agentic AI in healthcare, BrainX is leading research and development of applied solutions. With emerging collaborations with platforms for the delivery of Generative AI in healthcare, such as Genserve (https://genserve.ai/) and Prompt Opinion (https://www.promptopinion.ai/), we are looking to deploy solutions that are robust, scalable, trustworthy, and bring value to healthcare.

## Notes

1. Collaco BG, Haider SA, Prabha S, et al. The role of agentic artificial intelligence in healthcare: A scoping review. *npj Digital Medicine.* 2026;9:345. https://doi.org/10.1038/s41746-026-02517-5.
2. Srinivasu PN, Aruna Kumari GL, Ahmed S, Alhumam A. Exploring agentic AI in healthcare: A study on its working mechanism. *Frontiers in Medicine.* 2026;12:1753443. https://doi.org/10.3389/fmed.2025.1753443.
3. Wang Q, et al. A feasibility study of automating radiotherapy planning with large language model agents. *Physics in Medicine & Biology.* 2025;70(7).
4. Kumar N, Ali R. A smart contract-based robotic surgery authentication system for healthcare using 6G-tactile internet. *Computer Networks.* 2024;238:110133. https://doi.org/10.1016/j.comnet.2023.110133.
5. GPT-4 in a Cancer Center — Institute-Wide Deployment Challenges and Lessons Learned. *NEJM AI.* Accessed Mar 12, 2025.
6. Awasthi R, Bhattad A, Ramachandran SP, et al. Human evaluation of large language models in healthcare: Gaps, challenges, and the need for standardization. *npj Health Systems.* 2025;2:40. https://doi.org/10.1038/s44401-025-00043-2.

# ABOUT BRAINX

# 6

# Our Story

BrainX (https://www.brainxai.com/) was co-founded by Drs. Piyush Mathur and Francis A. Papay in 2017. Dr. Mathur is an anesthesiologist and intensivist at the Cleveland Clinic. Dr. Papay is a plastic surgeon and the former Chairman of the Dermatology and Plastic Surgery Institute at the Cleveland Clinic. They seek an organization that would collaborate, engage, develop, and produce innovative technologies, promote new research, and create platforms for artificial intelligence in healthcare. Soon after, Drs. Ashish Khanna, Kamal Maheshwari, Jacek Cywinski, MD, Avneesh Khare, MBBS, MBA, ABAIM, and Chintan Dave, MD, Raghav Awasthi, PhD, Shreya Mishra, PhD, and Dwarikanath Mahapatra, PhD, all of whom are clinician-scientists with an established national and international reputation in their respective fields, joined BrainX as founding partners.

BrainX offers expertise and knowledge for handling large datasets, research, and applications for artificial intelligence, driven by the expertise and passion of five physician-scientists with a niche area of expertise of their own. An early collaboration that exemplified this vision was with researchers at Carnegie Mellon University, where the group developed a multimodal machine learning model to predict ICD-10 diagnostic codes. Over the last few years, BrainX has aligned with the vision of delivering education using innovation and technology much like Project ECHO. BrainX Community serves as a unified platform to foster education and collaboration for AI applications in healthcare, being one of the world's largest such communities. With a current membership of over 4,000 members around the world, this platform is growing at an exponential rate. In addition, the BrainX Community hosts monthly educational sessions which are subsequently posted on its YouTube channel and website. The mission of education, research, development, innovation, and collaboration is now extending out to other parts of the world as well, including a European and Middle East chapter. In addition, other similar organizations like AIMed, Indian Institute of Technology (IIT), Delhi, Indraprastha Institute of Information Technology (IIIT), Delhi, Innovator MD, Indian Society of Critical Care Medicine, and Unofin have formed engagements with BrainX and have jointly hosted meetings and symposia. To stay up to date with the latest and greatest research in AI, BrainX Community publishes an annual year-in-review as a collection of subject specialty-specific sets of literature published in the last calendar year. The BrainX team itself has stayed heavily involved in the advancement of science, and each of its core members has published extensively alone or as collaborators.

# Suggested Readings

AI Business School by Microsoft. https://www.microsoft.com/en-us/ai/ai-business-school.

Anand Rao. *A Strategist's Guide to Artificial Intelligence*. PWC Strategy+Business, 2017.

Andrew Ng. *AI Transformation Playbook*. Landing AI, 2019. https://landing.ai/ai-transformation-playbook/.

Arrieta AB. Explainable Artificial Intelligence (XAI): Concepts, Taxonomies, Opportunities and Challenges toward Responsible AI. *Information Fusion* 2020;58(1):82–115. arxiv. org/pdf/1910.10045.pdf, https://doi.org/10.1016/j.inffus.2019.12.012.

Bern Elliott. A Framework for Applying AI in the Enterprise (webinar presentation). Gartner.com, 2018.

Jacques Bughin. Wait-and-See Could Be a Costly AI Strategy. MIT Sloan Review, 2018.

Jacques Bughin and Eric Hazan. Five Management Strategies for Getting the Most from AI. McKinsey.com and MIT Sloan Management Review, 2017.

Mihnea Moldoveanu. Why AI Underperforms and What Companies Can Do About It. HBR, 2019.

Richard Rumelt. *Good Strategy, Bad Strategy*. Crown Publishing, 2011.

Thomas Davenport. *The AI Advantage: How to Put the Artificial Intelligence Revolution to Work*. MIT Press, 2018.

Towards an Ethics of Artificial Intelligence | United Nations. www.un.org, Dec. 2018.

Weapons of the Weak: Russia and AI-Driven Asymmetric Warfare. Brookings. www.brookings.edu/articles/weapons-of-the-weak-russia-and-ai-driven-asymmetric-warfare/. Accessed 14 July 2023.

Whit Andrews, Editor. Build the AI Case. A CIO's guide to building the strategy and case to implement AI in the enterprise. Gartner.com, 2018.

# Index

For Product Safety Concerns and Information please contact our EU representative GPSR@taylorandfrancis.com Taylor & Francis Verlag GmbH, Kaufingerstraße 24, 80331 München, Germany

**Batch number: 10732714**

Printed by Printforce, the Netherlands